WINNING COMBINATIONS

THE COMING WAVE OF ENTREPRENEURIAL PARTNERSHIPS BETWEEN LARGE AND SMALL COMPANIES

James W. Botkin
Jana B. Matthews

JOHN WILEY & SONS, INC.

New York • Chichester • Brisbane • Toronto • Singapore

Recognizing the importance of preserving what has been written, it is a policy of John Wiley & Sons, Inc. to have books of enduring value published in the United States printed on acid-free paper, and we exert our best efforts to that end.

Library of Congress Cataloging-in-Publication Data

Botkin, James W., 19??–
Winning combinations : the new wave of entrepreneurial partnerships between large and small companies / by James W. Botkin and Jana B. Matthews.
p.   cm.
Includes index.

ISBN 0-471-53658-X

Printed and bound by Courier Companies, Inc.

10 9 8 7 6 5 4 3 2 1

ACKNOWLEDGMENTS

This book could not have been written without the assistance and support of hundreds of people. We owe special thanks to the Ruben Rausings Fund of Lund, Sweden. Its founder, Hans Rausing, and director, Bengt-Arne Vedin, provided the initial impetus for the book by funding a study to compare entrepreneurship and innovation in Sweden with other countries. On the American side, special thanks are due to the IC² Institute of The University of Texas at Austin, which also provided financial support. In addition, George Kozmetsky, the Director of IC², and Raymond Smilor, its executive director, contributed considerable intellectual and moral support during the years we spent writing this book.

We also want to acknowledge the invaluable contributions of Holly Arrow, our editor. She helped us develop the framework for the book, sort through a data base that contains two or three times the amount of information and case studies actually presented, and identify the themes and organizing principles of the book. Without her help this book might never have been completed.

We are indebted to the many executives, entrepreneurs, and academicians who provided information and insights and shared their experiences with us as we undertook the research required for this book. Since 1984, we have interviewed executives in more than 100 companies in North America, Asia, and Europe, and have consulted with many more. Seminars on innovation and entrepreneurship held in several locales enabled us to test many of the ideas and themes we have developed in this book. Those who were especially generous with their time and provided information that we incorporated in the book are listed below.

Acknowledgments

Sweden. Peter Tovman, Karl-Erik Sahlberg, Sten Nordberg, Kaj Thorén, Rutger Friberg, Sten Gustaffson, Kaj Savon, Jan-Erik Gustavsson, Olle Larm, Pål Krüger, Torbjorn Ek, Torkel Wallmark, Douglas McQueen, Thomas Liljemark, Sam Nilsson.

United Kingdom. Nick Segal, Roger Quince, Hermann Hauser, Gerald Avison, David Connell, Caroline and John Daniels.

Japan. Keiko Satoh, Gene Gregory, Shintaro Sakakibara, Koji Kobayashi, Michiyuki Uenohara, Tadahisa Tamura.

Eastern Europe and USSR. Daniel Bardossy, Ruslan Grinberg, Stanislav Simanovsky, Andrea Szalay, Zsuzsanna Ránki.

United States. Charles Halbower, Tom Washing, Ed Payne, Earl McLaughlin, Bob Calcaterra, Bob Ecklin, Paul O'Connor, James Riesbeck, Richard Sphon, Robert Tuite, Roger Cole, Tom Dykstra, Julianne Prager, Allen Heininger, Ken Robinson, William Payne, Gary Marple, Michele Obermeier, and Jon Saxe. In addition, special thanks go to Michael Snell, our agent, and to John Mahaney, our senior editor at John Wiley & Sons, with whom it has been a joy to work.

We also want to acknowledge the assistance of Mimi Chase-Trujillo and Jill Goldwater, who produced countless drafts and redrafts of various chapters of the book and maintained their sense of humor throughout the process.

Finally, we want to thank our respective families, who supported us in many ways throughout the researching and writing of this book. They kept assuring us that this book was worth all the time and effort we were spending. We hope the reader agrees.

CONTENTS

Contents

FOREWORD

Partnership as a way of doing business has been a dynamic element in the development of firms and markets. Alliances and collaborations have often been formed to accomplish specific goals that were too demanding for any one party to achieve alone. With the ever accelerating pace of technological change that we are experiencing today, it has become increasingly difficult for emerging entrepreneurial firms, acting alone, to accomplish in a timely manner what is needed to be successful. Add the factor of globalization to technical complexity and the managerial problems are exacerbated. In these conditions, partnering between large and small companies—done correctly—can be an especially creative and innovative strategy.

Entrepreneurship is the pursuit of opportunities and the willingness to start something new. The launching of new ideas, innovative products, and novel services is a fundamental need of every economy. Indeed, many would argue—and I would agree—that motivated and brilliant entrepreneurs have been the instrumental force in the success of modern market economies. Nowhere has the importance of entrepreneurship been better demonstrated than in the United States. It has generated new jobs, new goods, and innovative services that many view as the mainstay of our economy.

In joining these two concepts of partnering and entrepreneurship, Botkin and Matthews have articulated an important and effective strategy for success. Entrepreneurial partnerships between large and small companies address one of the puzzles of our time: how to link the innovation that entrepreneurs have historically been able to generate with the new markets and global demands at which big companies are adept at meeting. Suggesting that the Fortune 500 join forces with the Inc. 500 holds a great deal of promise as a strategy for the future.

However, combining two hitherto separate forces will meet resistance from many who still operate under traditional ways of thinking about competitiveness and cooperation. Some large company executives still believe that they can do everything within their own firms. They are encumbered by a "not-invented-here" syndrome that can limit their capacity to innovate. Likewise, some entrepreneurs resist association with large companies. To overcome these barriers will take a revolutionary effort on the part of leadership of both large and small companies.

For some time, the IC² Institute of The University of Texas at Austin has explored ways of fostering creative and innovative management. We agree with the two coauthors of *Winning Combinations* that the implementation of entrepreneurial partnerships is a creative way of thinking. Collaborating to compete is an example of innovative management in action.

Botkin and Matthews have made an important start in identifying the main principles that make alliances between large and small firms work. They have also enumerated some of the pitfalls that can be avoided by leaders in large and small firms. The real contribution of this book is the development of the concept of entrepreneurial partnering, and the principles required to be successful. Each industry has its own way of doing business; creative and innovative managers will validate and modify these types of partnerships in order to make them more appropriate for their companies.

Business for the 21st century demands a new type of managerial strategy; the rules for success are changing fast. We expect to see many large-to-small partnerships forming, dissolving, and reconnecting anew as we move through the 1990s. Some will succeed, and some will fail. Those executives and entrepreneurs who have read this book will have a much better chance to form winning combinations.

George Kozmetsky
Director, IC² Institute
The University of Texas at Austin

"WINNING COMBINATIONS is more than just a guide through the large-small company relationship minefield for businessmen, lawyers and venture capitalists. It should be mandatory reading for Fortune 500 Executives as well as entrepreneurs."

—Thomas G. Washing
General Partner
Hill, Carman, Kirby & Washing

"WINNING COMBINATIONS is an excellent view of strategic alliances and the future of entrepreneurship. Must-reading for forward-thinking executives and entrepreneurs."

—Tom Trezise
General Manager, AT&T

"Botkin and Matthews know their territory well, world-wide, and they have written a valuable book for both entrepreneurs and executives. This is an artful practitioner's manual about how to succeed in alliances between Inc. 500 and Fortune 500 companies."

—Stanley M. Davis
Author of *2020 Vision* and *Future Perfect*

"Botkin and Matthews have surveyed the joint venture field with a fresh perspective and have synthesized new prescriptive practices that will increase the probability for the success of any joint venture. WINNING COMBINATIONS is a must study for any entrepreneur or executive in these times of global competition and change."

—Dr. Louis Stokes, Ph.D.
President
Knowledge Engineering
DVS Communications, Toronto

"In the shifting patterns of global competition Botkin and Matthews offer pragmatic advice on how to make partnerships fulfill their promise. It makes thought provoking reading."

—S. Allen Heininger
Former Corporate Vice President
Resource Planning
Monsanto

"In WINNING COMBINATIONS, Botkin and Matthews have made a valuable contribution to our understanding of how winning companies succeed in our global economy."

—Jeff Bingaman
United States Senator

"Well written and concrete, this book makes an important contribution to an understanding of the strategies with which American business can compete in the new world economy."

—David E. Skaggs
United States House of Representatives

"As America is striving to stay ahead in a worldwide economy, entrepreneurial partnerships will no doubt play a major role in keeping America competitive. James Botkin and Jana Matthews' WINNING COMBINATIONS will provide a winning strategy for achieving this in the changing business climate."

—Robert L. Ecklin
Senior Vice President and General Manager
Corning, Industrial Products Division

"By going right to the core of the motivations that drive large companies, WINNING COMBINATIONS should allow many entrepreneurs to become more effective in their initial contacts as well as their critical negotiations in creating entrepreneurial partnerships."

—Duane D. Pearsall
General Partner
The Columbine Venture Fund

"Botkin and Matthews have not only given us a scheme for thinking about and evaluating the many components required for successful partnerships, but have set out the processes for how to seek out and negotiate with prospective partners."

—Gary A. Marple
President
Commonwealth Strategies, Inc.

PART ONE

The Innovation Imperative

CHAPTER ONE

Business at the Brink

THE GREAT AMERICAN TURNOFF

In 1985, Juan Rodriguez left Storage Technology and started Exabyte, a company that manufactures high-capacity 8-millimeter computer tape drives that back up and store huge amounts of data, unattended. Soon after starting the company, Rodriguez realized he needed a corporate partner to help drive his ideas into the big leagues. He went to several American firms he thought would be interested in his product. Kodak had announced publicly that it was committed to the 8-millimeter tape drive, so Kodak was one of the companies Rodriguez contacted. Kodak sent some R&D staff to Exabyte to investigate the possibilities. A team from Exabyte then went to Kodak for further discussions. The Kodak staff was enthusiastic about the product. The senior scientist, however, told Rodriguez and his colleagues, in front of 20 or so corporate engineers, "What you are proposing to do is not very interesting. I could put together a small team here and develop that product in a matter of weeks." So ended

3

the meeting and Exabyte's hopes for establishing a strategic alliance with Kodak.[1]

The fact is, not one of the large corporations Rodriguez contacted pulled together a small team, and none developed the product in a matter of weeks. But Exabyte did. It grew from no sales in 1986 to $170 million in 1990. Within four years, Exabyte went from a $2 million loss to a $28 million net profit. By 1990, Exabyte's 8-millimeter technology had become the de facto standard in workstation, minicomputer, and file server environments. And Kodak has become one of Exabyte's customers.

Unable to strike deals with American companies, Exabyte had turned to two Japanese firms instead. Sony now provides the 8-millimeter mechanical disks for Exabyte's drives. Kubota manufactures 60 percent of the products and distributes Exabyte's tape drives in the Far East. Within nine months after going public, Exabyte's stock price rose to $24 a share, up from its initial offering price of $10. Meanwhile, in exchange for its capital infusion, Kubota has learned new manufacturing techniques and has regional manufacturing and marketing rights to a very hot product. Sony has locked in a new market for its equipment and has negotiated a second strategic agreement with Exabyte. All partners have benefitted, and Exabyte's innovation has upstaged the Fortune 500 firms that never quite made it to market.

Is this an isolated case of short-sightedness on the part of a large U.S. firm? Not from what we've learned. Unfortunately, the Kodak senior scientist's response typifies how many American firms react to entrepreneurs who approach them about partnerships. Consider the story of Ed Payne, an ex–Air Force fighter pilot and Vietnam veteran who launched Gateway Technologies in 1990 to commercialize a stunning new discovery—microencapsulated phase change materials, otherwise known as microPCMs. When microPCMs are added to the inside of man-made fiber and then made into clothing or other fabrics, they automatically adjust to temperature changes: the wearer is kept cool in hot sunshine and warm in cold winter air. Sports clothing, upholstery, sleeping bags, even wallpaper could be revolutionized by this technology.

Wanting to get this technology quickly to market, Ed sought to partner Gateway with several Fortune 500 firms. He has had conversations with dozens of American "household name" corporations who were sure to be interested in this technology, and who had market access, production facilities, and capital. Then started the Great American Turnoff.

The vice president for business development of a large chemical corporation indicated great interest in the technology, but he wasn't sure he wanted to negotiate with a start-up and began dragging his feet. A vice president of a fiber manufacturer had difficulty getting his legal department to sign off on Gateway's confidentiality agreement. The vice president of a sporting clothes manufacturer was interested but had so many other projects on his plate that Gateway's proposal fell between the cracks. And so it went. Ed's initial euphoria began to wear thin. His first preference had been to partner with an American company, but U.S. corporate executives were not taking him seriously. "I kept getting pushed down in these organizations, to people with less and less decision-making authority. After six months of contacts with over 75 firms, I decided to offer this technology to some Japanese companies and explore a joint venture with them."

The response was immediate. Ed Payne reports:

> Within days of completing our confidentiality agreement, I was visited by Japanese managers who wanted to know all about the product, the patent, and my plans for a partnership. Rather than being pushed down, I kept getting pushed up to higher levels. They called in vice presidents and even the CEO. The response was completely different from the one I experienced with American companies.

Ed now faces a dilemma: Should he continue to try to contact and interest U.S. firms in his technology, or should he begin serious negotiations with Japanese firms?

Rodriguez and Payne, who represent a breed of entrepreneurs celebrated for innovation and fast-track growth, understand the value of the small-to-large alliances we call entrepreneurial partnerships. The American corporations they approached apparently do not. Entrepreneurs need to partner with firms that appreciate what they have to offer and are willing to enter a relationship based on mutual respect. Many entrepreneurs like Rodriguez and Payne originally hoped to partner with American companies. All too often that's not a viable option.

THE INC. 500 AND THE FORTUNE 500: HOW CAN THEY BAT 1,000?

Every year, entrepreneurs across America celebrate their achievements at a meeting of the Inc. 500, which is to small business what the Fortune 500 is to large business. New start-up firms are rated on their growth rates, their acceleration in sales, and the innovativeness of their products. Steve Jobs's Apple Computer was feted in this way. So was Compaq, whose business plan, scrawled on the back of a napkin, took it from zero to $100 million sales in one year.

Americans concerned about competitiveness in a global economy consider both 500 groups to be important. The Inc. 500 demonstrate American prowess in business creativity and entrepreneurship, just as the Fortune 500 represent our current economic power and global reach. The industrial and postindustrial ages in America and elsewhere have been driven by a can-do attitude that takes an idea and transforms it into a concrete product or service the market wants. This can-do attitude has been the engine of success in both the Inc. 500 and the Fortune 500 companies.

Yet neither the entrepreneurship and innovation exhibited by the Inc. 500 firms nor the deep pockets and power of the Fortune 500 corporations will be sufficient in the future to enable American business to be consistently successful in the global market-place. There is no shortage of creative ideas in America. Nevertheless, both large and small companies operating on their own are having trouble commercializing and marketing salable innovations before their international competitors dominate the markets and fill the niches. Large companies can't seem to deliver innovations fast enough; small firms often lack the capital and marketing muscle to reach international customers while the window of opportunity is still open.

Giants like IBM, General Motors, AT&T, Kodak, and Du Pont have huge war chests to finance R&D and to establish world-wide production and marketing systems. Yet they and many other Fortune 500 companies with similar strengths still have difficulty moving the innovations of R&D swiftly to market. While their corporate scientists may boast of what they can accomplish "in a matter of weeks," the time span is typically years—and in some cases, much too late.

Inc. 500 companies, in contrast, excel at commercializing innovations, and their leaner structures give them the speed and flexibility to outmaneuver the giants. Increasing globalization, however, makes it difficult for small entrepreneurial companies to act alone effectively. Their marketing and distribution channels are frequently inadequate for getting their innovative products and services to an international marketplace. The continual need of small companies for capital also limits their maneuverability. The time and attention of their entrepreneurial management is often diverted to finding and negotiating financing instead of developing markets and distribution systems.

Members of both 500 camps who take a lone-ranger approach are increasingly frustrated in their quest for speedy innovation and sustained growth. Most large corporations are relying on strategies such as intrapreneuring or merger and acquisition to respond to the innovation imperative. Yet a growing number of small and large firms have found a more creative way to compete globally: teaming up to use their complementary strengths as a competitive advantage. Their stories illustrate the coming wave of strategic alliances that constitute entrepreneurial partnerships. When the Fortune 500 and Inc. 500 team up, they can hit the ball out of the park.

DAVID AND GOLIATH JOIN FORCES

In 1986, Fran Tarkenton, former football great and savvy entrepreneur, founded Atlanta-based KnowledgeWare, Inc. The company has developed automated products that enable businesses to develop their own software. When KnowledgeWare went public, IBM bought a nine percent share. The two companies became partners in the quest to develop industry standards for computer-assisted software engineering.

With the backing of its large partner, KnowledgeWare's growth has been spectacular. It grew 100 percent in 1990 and ranked second on the *Business Week* "Hot Growth List." IBM has benefitted, too. Profits from KnowledgeWare were nearly $10 million in recessionary times, because its products help customers cut costs rather than incur expenses. To foster more innovation, IBM Chairman Akers' bold plan is to create dozens of internal semi-independent operations. These will complement hundreds of external relationships with small firms, thus making a strategy of internal and external entrepreneurial partnerships a key to IBM's future earnings growth. Whether and how well IBM succeeds in making this strategy pay off is still open to question. Success or failure will depend on implementing a set of practices and overcoming a series of potential pitfalls, which we describe in chapters five and six.

ENTREPRENEURIAL PARTNERSHIPS: TAKING THE BEST FROM BOTH WORLDS

The recent experience of KnowledgeWare, Exabyte, Gateway, and scores of other young entrepreneurial companies suggest that, in the future, their fortunes will increasingly be tied to Big Business—*and vice versa*. The worlds of the Inc. 500 and the Fortune 500 are becoming increasingly dependent on one another. Once totally separate, and often even antagonistic, entrepreneurs and corporate executives now need each other more than ever. Their needs and their strengths are often opposite and complementary. Both large corporations and small companies can brighten their global prospects by forming collaborative partnerships that capitalize on their complementary strengths while respecting the independence of each party.

The purpose of this book is to spell out the pros and cons of large-to-small alliances and to elucidate the principles and practices of successful entrepreneurial partnerships. We do this both for entrepreneurs who need the deep pockets and the global reach large companies can supply, and for corporate executives who need the innovations for which entrepreneurs are famous. Before moving on to the nuts and bolts, however, it's important to get a clearer picture of the problems we believe these partnerships can solve, to review the more traditional strategies that large and small companies are now using, and to set this new wave of entrepreneurship in historical context.

21ST CENTURY CHALLENGES: SPEED AND INNOVATION IN THE GLOBAL VILLAGE

As the new millennium approaches, the pace of change in business continues to accelerate. As businesses of all sizes in every industry struggle to develop and utilize new techniques and knowledge, the introduction of new products and services quickens. Meanwhile, competition is increasingly global, not regional or even national.[3] It is no longer enough to be more productive than other American companies in any given industry. Businesses must now compete with firms around the world.

9

Large companies have discovered that to be effective in these turbulent times, a company must be among the first—preferably the very first—to get new products and services to a global marketplace. This means that the corporation must do two things:

1. Respond promptly to emerging technologies and market changes by rapidly developing and producing innovative new products and services; and
2. Take advantage, as quickly as possible, of international marketing capabilities and distribution channels for new products and services.

Businesses of every kind must dramatically speed up the entrepreneurial process of inventing, developing, commercially producing, marketing, and distributing innovative products and services. How well a business fares in the global competition will be determined largely by the speed and effectiveness of the company's entrepreneurial capabilities.

MAJOR CORPORATIONS: THE GIANTS AT A WATERSHED

One frustrated executive at a major American automotive company recently remarked, "It seems every company is at some kind of watershed." If we look at most major U.S. corporations, it seems he is right.

During the 1980s, American companies responded to intense global competition with a renewed emphasis on quality and customer satisfaction. Great progress has been made in both arenas. Ford and Motorola have made great strides in the quality of their products. In 1990, IBM, General Motors Cadillac division, and Federal Express won Baldrige awards. Despite, or perhaps because of, the breakup of AT&T, the United States has the highest quality and most customer-responsive telephone system in the world. Americans are rightfully proud of these and other achievements.

Yet all is not well with the Fortune 500. IBM's profits have plummeted, and DEC suffered its first layoffs in a 37-year history in 1990/91. In December, 1991, GM announced it would close 21 plants and lay off 74,000 workers. Sears Roebuck may face the greatest watershed of all. Long a symbol of American success, the company may have to sell Sears Tower, the tallest building in the world. The company's troubles will affect many people: one-third of all Americans have either worked for, shopped at, or used a credit card from Sears.

Large corporations outside the United States are also feeling the pressure and are responding with an array of new initiatives. Many old-line Japanese corporations, among them 100-year-old Kubota (which manufactures small tractors), are hedging their bets by getting involved with small companies like Exabyte in electronics, biotechnology, and new materials. Kao Corporation, a cosmetics manufacturer in Tokyo, has adopted new goals of "absolute equality, noncommanding style, elimination of authoritarianism, and pooling of creativity" to spawn a totally new corporate culture.

Large corporations are looking not simply for new ideas, which are plentiful, but rather for novel commercializable ideas, which are scarce. To find them, they need more entrepreneurs who understand how to develop commercially successful innovations.

CORPORATE STRATEGIES
TO SPEED INNOVATION

We see major corporations using a range of different strategies as they attempt to become more innovative and entrepreneurial. All rely on entrepreneurs, who can be found either inside or outside the corporation.

Internal Strategies: Grow Your Own vs. Bankroll an Intrapreneur. The major internal strategy for large corporations has been to stimulate innovations from within the company by investing in research and development. Gifford Pinchot's book *Intrapreneuring*[4] took this strategy one step further in the mid-1980s. *Intrapreneuring* attempts to instill the garage-shop spirit within a large corporation. The idea is that employee intrapreneurs, when appropriately supported and buffered from corporate hassles, will develop innovations that can be transformed into fast-growth new business lines within the existing corporation. When the goal is for intrapreneurs to create distinct new units or firms under the umbrella of the parent company, that strategy is typically called *internal venturing*.

3M, Kodak, Volvo, Fuji Xerox, and Corning, among others, are trying to stimulate innovation internally. 3M has a reputation for nurturing innovation and intrapreneurship among its own employees. Fuji Xerox has a carefully targeted program to encourage internal venturing, as did Kodak. In most corporations, the new products that result from intrapreneuring and internal venturing tend to be incremental improvements or add-ons, not breakthrough innovations.

An internal strategy that aims for larger jumps is a *skunk works*, a high-cost approach that assigns internal entrepreneurial types to a special, isolated unit targeted at achieving specific breakthroughs. An elite group of entrepreneurial IBM employees developed the first IBM PC in a skunk works in Florida, far from corporate headquarters.

External Strategies: Buy, Spin Off, or Partner with an Entrepreneur. If you were to ask a group of businesspeople where most inventions come from, the majority would probably say the garage rather than corporate R&D labs. To gain access to such innovations, large corporations have developed a growing interest in new sources of entrepreneurs. AT&T is in the process of merging its recent acquisition, NCR, to position itself strategically in the computer industry. In July 1991, Digital announced the merger and acquisition (M&A) of Philips's computer division in an attempt to gain market share. Hoffman–La Roche just made a friendly acquisition of the U.S. biotech firm Genentech, which gave up going it alone for a $2 billion cash infusion in 1990.

This Genentech–La Roche deal appears to be a positive move, freely chosen by both parties and likely to benefit both. The same cannot be said, however, of a whole wave of mergers and acquisitions during the 1970s and 1980s that ranged from unwelcome to downright hostile. The trauma suffered by the acquired firm as it is forcefully restructured and merged into a larger bureaucracy often suppresses the entrepreneurial spirit and cuts off the flow of new products the corporation hoped to secure. M&A may also saddle the buyer with a crushing debt burden. AT&T's takeover of NCR required a level of debt significant even for a company with AT&T's resources.

On the low-cost end, corporations such as Corning, Kodak, and NEC (one of Japan's leading electronics firms) have helped selected employees launch spin-off firms to commercialize *shelf technology* outside of the parent company. Shelf technology consists of technology applications that have been developed internally but are not currently being used by the corporation.

Increasingly, companies are also relying on external business relationships with existing companies or entrepreneurs. The small-large alliances we recommend fall into this category. Sony, for example, has links not only with Exabyte, but with Panavision, Alphatronix, Pinnacle Micro, and several other small U.S. firms.[5] However, most collaborative partnerships to date have not been small-to-large. In all but a few industries, for example, biotechnology, large-large alliances are far more common. The Scandinavian Airline System (SAS), for example, is transforming itself from a Northern European air carrier to a global travel service by establishing partnerships with Texas Air, International Hotels, and All Nippon Airways. Sweden's two automakers, concerned about their ability to compete and survive, have teamed up with larger players: Volvo has linked up with Renault, and Saab has an alliance with General Motors.[6] In July 1991, IBM and Apple decided they could each become more competitive if they collaborated.

Another twist is when two (or more) large corporations join forces to form new companies that benefit both parents. In the mid-1980s, for example, Corning and Mitsubishi formed Cormetech, a new company designed to serve an emerging environmental control market for ceramic catalytic cleansers. Such external alliances are a mainstay of Corning's corporate strategy. Whatever the configuration, these large-large relationships have prepared many corporations for branching off into entrepreneurial partnerships with promising, innovative, but cash-poor smaller businesses or individual entrepreneurs.

SMALL ENTREPRENEURIAL COMPANIES: PAST SUCCESS, FUTURE TESTS

While large corporations are scrambling to restructure, many small companies are flourishing. Inc. 500 companies have been generating jobs while Fortune 500 companies generated layoffs. Research at MIT and elsewhere[7] indicates that small companies with 100 or fewer employees have accounted for virtually *all* the net job creation in the United States in the last decade. Small companies are able to respond to the changing demands of the market more quickly than most large corporations. The key factors in the relative success of these smaller entrepreneurial firms seem to be their ability to move quickly and their high level of innovation compared to the more slow-moving and often bureaucratic large corporations.

From superficial observation, it's easy to conclude that small business is healthy in America. Yet start-up companies continue to have a high failure rate: up to 85 percent don't make it to their fifth anniversary. This 85 percent includes companies with innovative products that have trouble getting adequate financing, need marketing assistance, or lack access to effective distribution channels. An entrepreneur may excel at researching and developing a new product, only to stumble when trying to get it manufactured, sold, or distributed, with severe consequences for the company's viability and rate of growth.

How will small, fast-growth companies adapt to globalization, which means selling in 40 to 100 countries in the world; tapping into capital markets in London, Tokyo, and New York; and distributing products and services on three or four continents? On their own, small entrepreneurial companies will have more and more difficulty getting their innovative products and services to increasing numbers of potential customers. Though their innovations may be exactly what the marketplace needs and wants, they are likely to be handicapped in reaching it. Consumers they do reach may be reluctant to buy an unknown product or service from an unknown company. Exabyte, for example, faced initial objections from buyers that ranged from "this is a new technology, developed by a start-up company" to "this is a sole-source vendor with a single plant manufacturing capability. What will I do if I can't get enough product or if something happens to the plant?" Buyers often prefer to purchase new products from large corporations with established brand names, which are seen as guarantees of product quality, adequate service, and delivery of a sufficient stream of products to meet market demand.

TYPICAL ENTREPRENEURIAL STRATEGIES TO ACCESS RESOURCES FOR GROWTH

Though small companies have less difficulty than large corporations in being innovative, they usually lack money, marketing, and management capabilities. First and foremost, they are strapped for capital. Second, they need access to marketing and distribution channels, particularly where these are international in scope. Third, their management expertise and resources are usually stretched thin.

Small entrepreneurial companies typically use three main strategies to raise money: sell products, seek outside capital, or sell the company.

Sell Product or Seek Capital.   The dilemma of most entrepreneurs is how to use their time most effectively: Do I spend my time selling enough products to keep us financially afloat, or should I concentrate on raising capital to enable my firm to move to a higher level of operation? Do I focus on existing marketing channels, or is my time better spent developing new marketing approaches?

One entrepreneur we know runs a custom software company. He needs to generate $50,000 per month in new contracts just to keep his software team together, pay the office rent, and maintain the computers and data lines. He works 100 percent of his time to generate enough contracts to cover the $50,000. He knows that he must raise additional capital to expand. He'd like to hire two people to do full-time marketing, but he can't afford it right now. Nor can he seem to find the time to search for new sources of capital.

This is a classic long-term versus short-term entrepreneurial dilemma. The founder concentrates on the short-term "sell more product" in order to get breathing room to address the long-term needs to raise more capital and improve marketing. Yet the long-term needs are often eclipsed by short-term pressures.

Sell Out and Cash In.   When faced with the challenges of growth, many entrepreneurs put their small companies up for sale. One management consulting firm in the Boston area plateaued at about $10 million in annual sales. The two owners tried for several years to break this barrier. Each year they set goals and targets to reach gross revenue of $20 million. But each year when they tallied the books, revenues seemed stuck around $10 million.

When one of the large auditing firms knocked on the door with an offer to acquire the firm, the owners were receptive. The suitor had international marketing channels, plenty of capital, and a management team that numbered in the thousands. The offer was too tempting to refuse. Both founders got employment contracts for five years, so they felt they did not have to give up their company altogether. However, they became increasingly unhappy as their creation was gradually absorbed by its corporate buyer. Five years after the acquisition, the small company's identity had virtually disappeared.

For decades, merger and acquisition has dominated the landscape of relationships between large and small firms. Many of these buyouts follow the "big fish eats little fish" model, swallowing and then dismembering small companies until there is nothing left of their former identities. Some bought-out entrepreneurs go on to develop new innovations and found new companies, but others swim into oblivion. Fortunately for small entrepreneurial businesses that want to get off the capitalization treadmill without losing control of their companies, a fourth alternative is emerging: the entrepreneurial partnership.

THE COMING WAVE: SMALL-TO-LARGE STRATEGIC ALLIANCES

According to start-up specialist Bill Payne, who has fathered six new companies since selling his first one to Du Pont, "The most successful high-growth start-ups of the 1990s will thrive through strategic linkages with larger, enlightened corporations." These start-ups are the ones we expect to see riding along the new wave of partnerships.

Over the past decades, we have seen two major surges of entrepreneurial activity. The first was "garage shop" entrepreneurship, widely practiced throughout history and popularized by the example of Hewlett and Packard, who started their company in a garage on the campus of Stanford University. This is the type of entrepreneurship celebrated by the Inc. 500, and the coveted target of acquisition by many larger firms.

A second wave was intrapreneuring—an attempt by the Fortune 500 companies to nurture the entrepreneurial spirit within large corporations, to "home-grow" innovators in the midst of an institutional environment. Both waves relied on the virtues of distinct business groups and environments: the inspiration and unstoppable determination of a garage-shop inventor versus the top-notch equipment and backing available to the creative employee of a large, well-heeled corporation.

Now, as the economy becomes more complex and global, we see a new wave forming in response to the critical questions for companies operating in the 1990s. For the large corporation, the question is: *How can our company shorten the time required to produce innovative products or services the market will buy?* For the small entrepreneurial company, the familiar question *How can we survive and grow?* has a new twist: *How can we continue to invent new products and sell them in the global marketplace?* Entrepreneurial partnership is one answer to both questions, a new strategy for accelerating innovation and growth that draws on the resources of both Inc. and Fortune 500 firms.

These partnerships are already proving mutually beneficial for both the small companies and the larger firms to whom they provide fast innovation and from whom they receive speedy and effective market access. When handled successfully, these are win-win alliances. Big business needs new ideas, and entrepreneurs have them. Small firms need global markets and strong financing, which large companies can provide. This synergy benefits both parties.

Of course, established small firms aren't the only sources of entrepreneurial talents for large corporations seeking partners. Entrepreneurs, inventors, and budding innovators may be found on college campuses, in national research labs, and in small-business communities or incubators. Amoco has begun to "harvest" technology by seeking out faculty and graduate students at selected universities who are working on the next generation of technologies of interest to the company. Perstorp (specialty chemicals) in Sweden is looking for owners or officers of small companies in incubators and research parks. The Japanese have proven themselves particularly adept at scouting for new ideas, then investing in them; they are way ahead of most U.S. corporations in supporting novel research. These firms recognize that good entrepreneurial resources are worth their weight in gold.

OVERCOMING THE BARRIERS TO PARTNERSHIP

Despite their promise as a strategy, however, entrepreneurial partnerships are still rare, and the main reason is that forming these relationships and making them work requires a fundamentally new way of thinking by both entrepreneurs and corporate executives. At its core is a basic new principle—cooperating to compete. In this country, at least, it seems that the smaller companies are much more open to this idea than their Fortune 500 counterparts. While Rodriguez at Exabyte and Payne at Gateway Technologies are "catching the wave," the U.S. executives they contacted are still standing around on the beach.

Why have U.S. executives missed out on these opportunities? It seems they have not yet recognized how entrepreneurial partnerships can benefit them. Instead, they apparently view the stream of prospective entrepreneurs knocking on the new business development door as cash-hungry supplicants who have precious little to offer in return. In many cases, they are right; in a few costly cases they have been dead wrong. It's clear that large corporations need better systems for distinguishing between gold diggers and gold mines.

Within the corporation, most senior executives, whether VPs of new business development, R&D, technology, or strategic planning, have not yet internalized the principle of collaborating to compete. Even those who realize the value of partnerships often look only to other large corporations. They see "small fry" as something to swallow or ignore. This book is intended to help executives appreciate the value of partnering with carefully selected small companies.

On the other hand, many small businesspeople are suspicious of large corporations. Given the "big fish eats little fish" history of large-to-small encounters, founders of small companies may understandably be leery of forming partnerships that they fear will destroy their company's autonomy and identity. But this need not be the case.

We suggest that any partnership offer be examined critically and carefully. Entrepreneurs must learn to discriminate between corporate sharks with a bite and swallow mentality and those suitors who have a mutually beneficial arrangement in mind. It's natural to be suspicious. However, many founders of small businesses write off strategic alliances altogether, closing off what might be an increasingly important avenue to rapid growth. Many English and Swedish innovators have refused even to consider partnerships that could have offered a fast track to business success.

For the United States to retain its entrepreneurial edge, the impressive rate of new business start-ups needs to be matched by a better rate of new business survival. Some businesses are properly winnowed out by a market that has no need of or interest in their products or services. Yet many small companies with innovative products fail because they lack money, marketing, and management savvy. When this happens, we all lose. We lose the talents of new start-up artists, we lose access to their innovative products or services, and the economy loses the force of new job generation and competitiveness. The trick is to find and develop a relationship with a corporate partner willing to give a small company a boost instead of a bite.

HOW THE BOOK IS ORGANIZED

To aid both parties in rethinking these relationships, this book clearly spells out the pros and cons for each party in large-to-small alliances. It is designed to give both corporate executives and small-business entrepreneurs an understanding of why and how to develop the collaborative relationships they need to compete more effectively in the global marketplace.

Once the parties are open to considering such alliances, they must redesign the policies and practices that reflect outmoded perspectives and strategies. This book elucidates some specific principles and practices of successful entrepreneurial partnerships, illustrating them with a variety of cases from the United States and abroad. We focus on technology-based companies because they are particularly dependent on constant innovation for growth and survival, yet the lessons apply to all companies that need innovation. And any company that hopes to prosper in the global marketplace through the year 2000 needs innovation.

Chapter 2 describes current programs to improve quality and competitiveness at various stages of a company's *value chain*, the series of linked stages in which value is added to a product. Entrepreneurial partnerships at any stage of the value chain—from invention through development, from design through production, and from marketing and sales through distribution—can help companies gain bigger dividends in sales and profits.

Chapter 3 explores the options for speeding an increasing number of innovations to market. The large company options briefly mentioned earlier in this chapter are explored in depth in Chapter 3, with ample examples and consideration of the merits and the drawbacks of each approach. Chapter 4 outlines four choices and strategies for small company growth and describes how collaborative partnerships can help many start-ups attain and maintain profitability.

The second part of the book describes the operational principles and practices of entrepreneurial partnerships. For every collaborative venture that works, another fails. Organizational structures and cultures often get in the way. Chapters 5 and 6 provide pointers on how to establish appropriate principles and practices and avoid the pitfalls inherent in entrepreneurial partnerships.

Chapter 5 gives concrete advice for achieving a productive collaboration. Twelve principles and practices are organized into three sections: finding a partner, negotiating the contract, and managing the partnership. Chapter 6 examines common problems that arise, in the words of one skeptical executive, "when birds mate with fish and try to figure out where to make their home together." Different perspectives create difficulties when small and large companies attempt to link up. These perspectives must be understood and reconciled if collaborations are to be mutually beneficial.

The chapters in part three show how companies in Europe and Japan have responded to the innovation imperative. Chapters 7 through 10 offer a refreshing perspective on how small and large businesses in Japan (Chapter 7), England (Chapter 8), Sweden (Chapter 9), and Hungary (Chapter 10) are working to speed innovation and encourage entrepreneurship. Because international alliances are becoming more common in today's world, our chief aim has been to compile a number of international cases from which executives in both small and large firms can learn. We believe they will find the examples instructive as their activities and responsibilities become increasingly international in scope. Opportunities abound for American executives and entrepreneurs who are looking to form partnerships; each chapter discusses the prospects for firms that may be seeking international partners in that country.

The Afterword reviews the three waves of entrepreneurship. It shows how the principles and practices of entrepreneurial partnership can benefit many companies, including dealerships, franchises, and a host of other business situations where rapid innovation can lead to big payoffs.

NOTES

1. Thomas G. Washing, "Industry Overview" (Paper delivered at the Hill Partnership meeting, February 8, 1990, Boulder, Colorado).
2. "Fran Tarkenton Scores in Software: Teaming Up with IBM," *Business Week*, 27 May 1991; Guy Halverson, "IBM Pursues New Strategies for Prosperity," *Christian Science Monitor*, 28 June 1991, p. 9. See also, "The New IBM: Is It New Enough?" *Business Week*, 16 December 1991, Cover Story; pps. 112–118.
3. Michael Porter, *The Competitive Advantage of Nations* (New York: Free Press, 1990); Ira Magaziner and Mark Patinkin, *The Silent War: Inside the Global Business Battles Shaping America's Future* (New York: Random House, 1989).
4. Gifford Pinchot, *Intrapreneuring* (New York: Harper and Row, 1985). Pinchot defined intrapreneuring as a revolutionary system for speeding up innovation within large firms by making better use of their entrepreneurial talents.
5. "Sony Adopts Strategy to Broaden Ties with Small Firms," *Wall Street Journal*, 28 February 1991.
6. Several names are used to describe large-to-large partnerships. "Intensive cooperation" is the Mitsubishi–Daimler Benz term. In announcing the Volvo–Renault partnership, Per Gyllenhammar termed it an "extensive collaborative agreement."
7. See David Birch, *Job Creation in America* (New York: Free Press, 1988), and Peter Drucker, *Innovation and Entrepreneurship* (New York: Harper & Row, 1985).

CHAPTER TWO

Completing the Value Chain: Trap or Trajectory?

WEAK LINKS

Recently, at an airport lounge, we overheard two vice presidents from Fortune 500 companies discussing their troubled corporations. They were concerned about losing business to a Japanese competitor.

"It's not that we don't have new ideas," said the first. "Our research lab is full of new technologies. But when we finally decide to develop one, it takes so long to commercialize it that the market's evaporated or a competitor has cornered the market before we even get there."

The second nodded in agreement. "Transferring the technology, then getting it out to the marketplace, has become a real problem for us, too," she said. "I find I'm getting hesitant to

25

start new projects. It takes so long to launch a new product that it kills my numbers. I'm better off squeezing the last dollars out of my old-line products, but I know we need new ones in the long run."

This conversation illustrates the concerns that are bringing America's corporations to the brink. It takes too long to go from concept to marketplace. It seems to take forever to transform new ideas into finished products and get them in the hands of consumers.

Entrepreneurs may have an even more serious problem—reaching their targeted market at all, early or late. Some years ago, a Swedish inventor developed a new method for sealing large steel pipes. Instead of welding, the technique fused the pipes by blasting: they were "imploded" together. Oil rigs were ideal customers, but they required extensive insurance guarantees. Acting alone, the entrepreneur couldn't get Lloyd's of London to insure him, so this large market was virtually inaccessible to him.

FROM CONCEPT TO MARKETPLACE: STAGES OF THE VALUE CHAIN

Why is it that for many companies, the path to a new product is fraught with traps, while for a few, the path is a trouble-free trajectory? To pinpoint the problems and answer this question, we need first to lay out a basic map of the commercialization process: the value chain.

Business analysts call the process by which a new idea gets to market the *value chain*. The value chain is a sequence of activities during which value is added to a new product or service as it makes its way from invention to final distribution. When a commercially valuable idea takes forever to get from concept to marketplace—or never arrives—the problem is often a weak or missing link.

The value chain is composed of several linked stages: research, development, design, manufacturing, marketing, sales, and distribution (see Figure 1). Although these stages are linked in various complex ways, for the sake of this analysis we have simplified this concept by grouping the stages into three macro phases.

Phase I: research, development, design
Phase II: production (manufacturing, fabrication)
Phase III: marketing, sales, and distribution

The value chain concept is a useful one in explaining why a company—even a large, powerful, established company—may have a wealth of innovative technology and no innovative products. If a link is weak or missing within Phase I, that technology will sit in the research lab and go no further. Like electricity, innovations reach consumers only when the lines of transmission are complete and intact.

FIGURE 1: The Value Chain

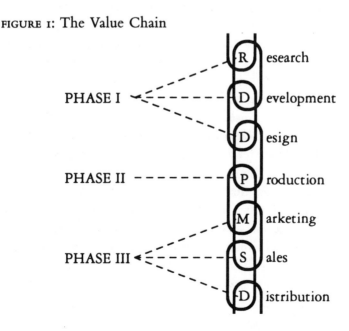

Entrepreneurs, unlike the Fortune 500 companies described above, are typically skilled at turning new ideas and technology into prototypes. Their weak link tends to be further down the chain, in Phases II or III. The inventor of the implosion method of sealing steel pipes moved successfully from research to marketing, then stalled when customers demanded a key link—insurance guarantees—that he couldn't obtain.

Few companies are competitive at every stage of the value chain *and* facile at moving a concept from stage to stage until it reaches the end consumer. One solution to this problem is suggested in the following tale.

DAVID GIVES GOLIATH A HAND (AND VICE VERSA)

In Cambridge, England, The Technology Partnership (TTP) is a small company that specializes in contract research and design—Phase I of the value chain. The company has stayed deliberately small to retain the key assets of flexibility, focus, and speed. One of its clients is Bosch, a German industrial company that found it took far too long to get a new product from idea to prototype.

Despite its muscle and size, the firm just couldn't move quickly. Bosch's R&D director lamented, "It takes me six months of politicking to assemble an internal team to create a new product." So rather than rely on internal R&D, Bosch contracted with TTP to reinvent its hand-held saber saw, an important consumer product. In less than the time required for Bosch to take aim at a market, TTP focused, fired, and hit the target, producing the successful "clic" saber system. David, with the advantage of small size and greater focus, delivered what the power of a Goliath couldn't achieve—a fast, custom-made innovation. Bosch manufactured the new saw and reaped the rewards of large sales and a dominant share in the competitive home tools market.

TTP's specialist strategy seems to be paying off, too; 1990 revenues for the company totalled £8 million.

In the case of the Swedish pipe-implosion inventor, it was a Goliath—Volvo—who came to the rescue. Acting alone, the entrepreneur couldn't complete the value chain and get his technology to its target, the oil rig market. When Volvo became his partner, the big company used its muscle to get the insurance guarantees he needed, and together they brought to fruition a business that is now a technological success story for both partners.

COMPETING IN TIME

In a world where competition is limited by monopoly or geographic barriers, a large company can take its time bringing out new innovations and still be reasonably sure of an open market window for its products. This was true for AT&T, IBM, and the U.S. auto industry in the halcyon days of the 1950s and 1960s. But as jet travel and modern telecommunications shrink space, time horizons are shrinking as well, making it imperative to innovate "just in time" to hit a market opening. As the U.S. auto industry has learned to its dismay, formerly distant competitors can now breathe down your neck with disconcerting ease and move with astounding speed.

Stan Davis, author of *Future Perfect*, describes how a Japanese consumer can order an option-packed new Toyota on a Monday and step into the car, which has been delivered to his doorstep, by Friday. American consumers are used to ordering a car from a dealer on a Monday and hoping for delivery six weeks later, assuming that the requested options weren't too unusual. "Six weekers can't compete with one-weekers," says Davis.[1]

The problem is not just the time from order to delivery. U.S. automakers are also seeking ways to cut the time from concept car to production vehicle. It commonly takes five years to move from R&D to a car the consumer can drive—two years longer than the typical Japanese cycle time.

The time element is even more critical in fields dominated by technological breakthroughs, like biotechnology and computer chips. In December 1982, Syva, one of the fastest-growing companies in the medical diagnostics field, received approval from the Food and Drug Administration (FDA) for a new test for chlamydia, a common sexually transmitted disease. The new test cut the lab processing time from six days to two, a clear advantage for patients worried that they might be infected. Was the product a commercial success? Only briefly. Hot on Syva's heels was the pharmaceutical giant Abbott, which received approval in the spring of 1983 for a test that worked in four hours or less.[2]

IBM found itself even more hard-pressed than Syva. In 1988, the company announced the development of the 16-megabyte computer chip. On the same day, NTT announced the creation of the first 64-megabyte chip. IBM's window of opportunity was narrow indeed. As product life cycles shorten, getting to market slowly may mean not getting there at all.

SPEEDY SPECIALISTS VERSUS INTEGRATED GENERALISTS

Both corporate executives and entrepreneurs are struggling to find ways to move more rapidly up and down the value chain. If they see a market opportunity, they need to find a relevant technology, then develop and distribute the products that the market is seeking. If they have a technology, they need to find a market niche and turn the invention into a commercial product before competitors fill the niche or—in the case of struggling start-ups—the business falters from lack of operating capital.

Not only do companies need a steady stream of innovations to prosper, they need to time these products to hit an open market window before it closes. Bosch had a strong distribution system and a sense of what the market needed, but found itself frustrated by the time required to develop the proper "bullet" to hit the target. By teaming up with TTP's quick-order design specialists, Bosch came out with the right product at the right time. From the reverse perspective, TTP made money designing a product it had no way to sell. A successful example such as this reveals the potential benefits when a speedy specialist and an integrated generalist pool their talents and their strengths.

Large Corporations: Power and Global Reach

Most large companies, certainly the big multinationals, are fully integrated. Mature, integrated companies cover all three phases of the value chain. They are apt to have particular strengths in marketing, distributing, and selling, as well as sources capital. Their weaknesses are apt to be in innovation and speed in getting new products to market.

Some corporations have a fully integrated value chain and are able to innovate successfully. 3M has been called the "masters of innovation," and the title is well deserved. 3M has managed to create a corporate culture in which departments work together successfully to identify market opportunities, design and produce "bullets," and hit the targets with satisfying regularity. Although 3M does engage in partnering, its chief strategy is to support and retain its in-house entrepreneurs. Internal innovation is widespread.

The key seems to be close attention to the links between stages where snags and logjams tend to develop. Every year, personnel from about half of the 3M research labs (which number over 100) review one another's work, and researchers are encouraged to visit with customers to discuss their needs and their responses to 3M products. Internal grants are available to intrapreneurs who want to focus on commercializing new ideas not supported by their division director. This emphasis on maintain-

31

ing strong links promotes extensive cross-fertilization and provides glue that helps keep the value chain intact. Corning is another fully integrated company that is successfully meeting the innovation imperative—often via joint ventures with other large companies.

Many of these large generalists, however, are not well equipped to navigate all three phases of the value chain with speed and skill. Kodak is a company that excels in invention, yet it nevertheless missed the market for instant photography. In the 1950s and 1960s when instant photography was first developing, Ed Land and Kodak had an entrepreneurial partnership. Kodak broke off the relationship in 1969, however. Soon afterwards, Polaroid became a landslide success. The outcome for Kodak was a billion-dollar loss in legal fees and court suit payments. The route to complete the value chain was ready and waiting, but Kodak created a trap in the path and fell in.

Other large generalists excel in Phase I but have trouble getting to second base. For many years before the 1984 breakup of the telephone company, Bell Labs demonstrated its prowess in research, development, and design. It created the fax machine, for example, in the late 1960s. However, its parent was slow to capitalize on the idea. By the time AT&T and other U.S. companies realized there was a market for fax machines, Japanese companies such as Canon and Ricoh had already advanced to Phase II on the value chain and were manufacturing the product. Slow and steady no longer always wins the race.

What large corporations have to offer to small partners is stability and credibility, established marketing and distribution channels, and financial resources that are almost unimaginable to strapped young companies. George Ebright, CEO of the start-up biotech firm Cytogen and former president of well-established SmithKline Beckman, comments:

> People ask me every once in a while about the differences between running a $4.5 billion pharmaceutical company and a small biotech firm. Well, up until [I joined Cytogen], my idea of raising $20

million to make an investment was to get up from my chair on the 24th floor, go down to see my treasurer on the 23rd floor, and tell him what I needed. The most demanding function of a CEO in a [small] biotech company is keeping up the funding.[3]

Small Entrepreneurs: Innovation and Speed

While large companies are typically slow in moving products along the value chain, most small companies are faster—but usually in only one of the phases. Many new high-tech firms do well in Phase I but not in Phase III. On the other hand, small entrepreneurial service companies may be strong in selling but weak in developing new concepts and product. Few entrepreneurial companies can afford to adequately develop all three phases of the value chain in their early years. The challenge these companies face is simultaneously to develop their new product or service and generate enough capital to keep the business afloat, either by selling products or accessing other sources of financing.

Gateway Technologies, discussed in Chapter 1, is licensing technology for a fabric that automatically adjusts to temperature changes. The technology has been researched, developed, tested, and proven feasible. The trouble is, as a small company Gateway lacks the resources to manufacture the fabric, and it has no expertise in marketing, selling, or distributing the myriad products that might be produced by using this technology: for example, microPCM ski gloves, socks, curtains, and wall coverings. With no Phase II or Phase III capacity, Gateway Technologies appears at first to resemble a narrow Phase I specialist, the kind of custom research company that some call a research boutique.

As a matter of fact, Gateway has no high-level research capacity either. The patent that founder Ed Payne has the rights to market is held by a small R&D lab in North Carolina that developed the sample fabric through a Small Business Innovation Research (SBIR) grant. Ed Payne is actually a "link" specialist.

His agreement with the North Carolina lab was that he would market the technology, identify companies that would conditionally manufacture prototype materials or fabrics, and get signed letters of interest from them. Having fulfilled this task, Gateway Technologies paid a lump sum for full and exclusive world-wide rights to make, use, or sell the licensed technology. So Payne has based his company on getting an innovative new technology over the hump from R&D to production—a link that is frequently weak in large integrated corporations. Clearly the only way a company like Gateway will ever see microPCM gloves on the hands of skiers is by finding corporate partners who can manufacture, market, sell, and distribute the products that the technology makes possible. This is just what Gateway wants to do.

Another entrepreneurial company, based in Boulder, Colorado, is known for its speed and innovativeness, but only in Phase II. The sole mission of RELA is to develop and manufacture products for other companies. In this case, the company provides the bridge between Phases I and III of the value chain. It works with corporations that have completed research and development, the first two activities of Phase I. RELA completes the design and manufactures the product for its corporate customer, which then puts its corporate name on the product and markets, sells, and distributes it. RELA helps its corporate clients make large jumps along the value chain by completing one whole phase of the process. In many cases, RELA has helped large corporations cut months off of product development and manufacturing processes.

Yet a third entrepreneurial company, Dell Computer, has a special strength in Phase III of the value chain. Michael Dell, who founded the company in 1984, developed innovative methods of marketing, distribution, and customer service to bridge a gap in the PC computer industry's value chain. Dell noted that traditional practice separates the consumer from the producer: One company designs and manufactures the computer while a separate retailer or dealer sells and supports it. The outcome was often customer dissatisfaction. In terms of the value chain, the customer was linked to the dealer (Phase III), but the dealer had little influence over design and was unable to correct manufacturing problems. The double layers also made PCs doubly expensive. By cutting out the retailer and establishing a direct relationship with customers, Dell cut the product price in half and smoothed the path from manufacture to marketplace. The company has also used partnerships as a strategy to improve market penetration, teaming up with Xerox in the United States and with Bell Atlantic in Europe.

We attribute Dell Computer's competitive success to two strengths: its innovative customer focus (strength in Phase III) and its skill in navigating the value chain from one end to the other. Dell Computer, for now, is meeting the "just in time" innovation imperative. Strength in one area without the second, however, could have left the company stranded—just another promising start-up that missed the tide.

Along with licensing innovative products or technology to update a large company's aging product line, small companies can offer speed and skill in negotiating trouble spots along the value chain. They are more entrepreneurial and creative in solving problems. A kayak simply has more maneuverability than a river barge, no matter how skilled the barge pilot. The freight a barge carries may be a potential blockbuster, but if the boat runs aground in the rapids, consumers downstream may never buy it. A "new" product delayed too long becomes obsolete.

ONGOING DRIVES FOR INNOVATION: TECHNOLOGY, QUALITY, AND CUSTOMER FOCUS

Partnering is by no means the only way to accelerate innovation. At least three well-known developments have had a considerable,

35

if only partial, impact on innovation along the value chain. These are:

o The drive for new technological breakthroughs via intensive R&D
o Total Quality Management (TQM) programs
o Customer focus programs

While these developments are crucial to the future health of U.S. industry, by themselves they aren't enough to drive innovation because they are each focused on only one phase of the value chain. If management loses track of the challenge—to get the innovative product or service from one end of the value chain to the other as quickly as possible—focusing on generating new technology, on total quality management, or on customer satisfaction may win the battle but not the war. Entrepreneurial partnerships, however, can help integrate all three programs and speed innovations along the value chain to the customer.

Phase I: R&D—Drive for Breakthrough Technology

The first phase in the value chain—research, development, and design—is intimately linked to new developments in technology: It is the engine that drives innovation.

Since the invention of the first semiconductor in 1950, we have seen a huge electronics and computer industry spring up where none existed before. Existing companies like Texas Instruments and IBM built huge businesses around the new technology. Industry leaders like Microsoft, Intel, and countless other start-ups were conceived as the impact of the new technology expanded like ripples on a lake. For these companies, innovation equalled innovative research, breakthrough product ideas, and products that simply didn't exist before.

More recently, the biotechnology industry has emerged in the wake of genetic engineering breakthroughs that made the commercialization of recombinant DNA and monoclonal antibodies feasible. These techniques enabled biologists to turn altered cells into tiny biological factories for manufacturing products such as hormones and vaccines.

Superconductivity is another good example of how a technology that simply didn't exist previously has created an entirely new field. In the late 1980s, the breakthrough in low-temperature superconductors was reported in rapid succession at the IBM labs in Zurich, at the University of Houston, and in Japan. Within less than a year, several new companies had formed to take advantage of the new technology. Examples include Intermagnetics General Corporation in Guilderland, New York, which makes superconducting wire and magnets, and Hypres, Inc., in Elmsford, New York, which makes superconductive electronic circuits for the military.

The genuinely high-tech companies that have sprung up like mushrooms with each surge of new technologies rely heavily on Phase I strengths to define and create their business. These are small companies, start-ups formed as the new technology formed, with R&D as their chief—and sometimes only—strength. Large, established companies typically beef up their R&D programs as a way to incorporate and profit from new technologies. Yet possessing a technology or process unique in the world cannot in itself guarantee success, for the path from invention to consumer can be filled with traps. As the following examples make clear, innovative technology doesn't necessarily lead to products the market will buy.

Trilogy, Inc., for example, was a small company that invented wafer-scale integration, a technique for putting the "brains" of an entire computer on one chip the size of a compact disk. Unfortunately, Trilogy was defeated by technical problems at the next phase: manufacturing. Eventually the company went bankrupt.

Large, integrated companies can also fall into the R&D trap when huge investments and genuine innovations lead to unsalable

37

products. Monsanto, for example, has poured money into the development of BST, a synthetic hormone that improves the productivity of dairy cows. In an interview published in *Biotech 89*, Will D. Carpenter, vice president of technology for the Monsanto Agricultural Company, confidently predicted that by 1991, BST "will have had several years of sales in the United States, and I think it will begin to be a big-ticket item."[4]

By the middle of 1991, however, BST was still awaiting final FDA approval and had already been banned in two big dairy states, Wisconsin and Minnesota, primarily for economic reasons. The R&D division did its job well: the product has been judged safe and effective by a National Institute of Health panel of experts. Yet Monsanto may have critically misjudged the market. With dairy surpluses already depressing prices, farmers don't perceive increased milk production as beneficial, hence may not be enthralled with BST.

A third new technology, superconductivity, provides yet another example. Some companies have been successful in R&D that uses superconductivity to develop powerful magnets. A primary application of such magnets is their use in a new type of train, known as the "mag-lev" train. While the Japanese and German governments have made commitments to use magnetic levitating trains, the U.S. has yet to do so. Thus American companies with skills in superconductivity will either have to compete abroad for their markets, or will have to survive a prolonged period until a domestic market for magnetic levitation emerges. Both market alternatives are beyond the capabilities of most small R&D companies.

Ed Payne of Gateway Technologies sees the obsession with Phase I as a chief reason many start-up companies fail: They don't know where or how to market their products, and they spend too much time trying to perfect the technology. In large companies, the Phase I obsession, when not matched with strong links all along the value chain, results in the dilemma described by a senior Kodak executive: "In Kodak's R&D lab, we used to say the technology was piling up at the door. You couldn't get the stuff out . . . because you couldn't convince manufacturing, marketing, and others to buy into the concept."

Phase II: Production—The Total Quality Management Push

Newscasters never tire of reporting that the United States has lost still more manufacturing jobs and that the quality of U.S. manufacturing is second-rate.[5] This has focused attention on the issue of quality. "Quality Is Job 1" is the theme of Ford Motor Company's advertising campaign. GM's version is "Putting Quality on the Road." Any number of other companies are concentrating on the same message while working to improve the quality of their products. The quality issue has been a special challenge for large, mature companies with aging manufacturing plants and processes.

Most thinking about quality is applied to manufacturing excellence, and most models are taken from manufacturing and product-oriented cases. Parts per million and defects per thousand are familiar terms applied to tangible goods. In the 1980s, quality was *the* issue for industries that had invested heavily in Phase II of the value chain. Nearly every U.S. and European manufacturing company, following the example of the Japanese, installed quality circles, total quality management, and other quality-enhancement and quality-control programs. The Deming award for quality became widespread in Japan, and the Malcolm Baldrige award for quality was adopted in the United States.

More recently, the application of quality concepts has been expanded to industries that produce a service rather than a tangible good. Federal Express, which specializes in the distribution stage of the value chain, became the first service company to win the Malcolm Baldrige award for quality in 1990. The Scandinavian Airlines System (SAS) joined up with Continental Airlines to form a Quality Services Institute (QSI) in Houston, Texas. QSI's mission is to teach quality service to airlines and other companies that depend heavily on service as a distinguishing factor in competition.

There are some countries where the quality push is still a long way off. When some Soviet business executives attending an international meeting were asked how they viewed the Western concern for quality, one replied, "Exotic. In the USSR, consumers compete to buy goods. Companies don't need quality to sell them." In most Western markets, however, quality has become a *sine qua non* of successful business and is less and less a market differentiator. While some manufacturing quality programs still have far to go to achieve their goals, no one can seriously claim that companies worldwide are not addressing the issue. While the quality revolution may not be as robust as the technology revolution, the concern for quality is no longer the weak spot it was only a decade ago.

As quality becomes less a differentiator and more a requirement, companies that have invested heavily in quality programs may find that they are still losing ground. This can happen if they forget that their task is to move a quality product through all the phases of the value chain as quickly as possible—not just to manufacture a quality product.

A company that has recently gained national attention for its concern about building high-quality products is a GM subsidiary, Saturn, in Spring Hill, Tennessee. The plant is the first fully integrated automobile manufacturing facility built in the world in the past 20 years that incorporates all the quality-enhancement ideas known to date about car building. It uses the world's most innovative technologies and manufacturing processes to provide quality improvements, such as its aluminum "lost foam casting" engines.

Here is an automaker that seems to have both Phases I and II down pat: top-of-the-line technology, plus a quality focus that permeates all aspects of manufacturing. What's more, Saturn has a strong commitment to partnering as a corporate strategy. Looks like a sure recipe for success, right? Well, maybe. The business has remarkable potential, but there are some worrisome signals.

One warning sign is that Saturn has become so obsessed with TQM that some managers are complaining it has gone too far. "It's almost impossible to get a car through the assembly line, because somewhere there's someone who stops it to make a quality check," says a high-level Saturn executive. Saturn has been way behind schedule in bringing cars to market. To fulfill the company's impressive potential, its management needs to keep in mind that there are three aspects to the quality imperative. The first is innovation. The second is to develop a quality product. The third is to speed the innovative product to market before the customer buys a car made by Saturn's competitors.

Phase III: Marketing, Sales, and Distribution— Customer Focus

When most people think of innovation, they think of high-tech products or processes per se. Yet recent innovations have been made in Phase III—marketing, sales, and distribution—as well. There has probably been as much innovation in this area as there has been in Phase I, with its new computers, biotechnologies, and other high-tech products. As products in more mature industries become commodities, the innovation involves how the products are marketed and sold.

For example, although computer technology is continually changing and developing, at this point desktop computers all perform virtually the same functions. As changes such as more powerful chips are introduced, they quickly appear in most versions of desktop computers on the market. A major difference is how the hardware is sold. IBMs, Compaqs, and Macintoshes are all sold through dealerships, whereas Dell Computer sells and services computers directly by telephone.

The technology in Dell's computers is "plain vanilla." The company's success (from zero to a half billion dollars in six years) cannot be attributed to a radical new technology, but to the company's Phase III innovative strengths in customer service and marketing. Michael Dell analyzed the value chain and found a better way to complete it than his competitors had.

As national boundaries fade in importance and products from every country are distributed worldwide, there is a proliferation of innovative niche markets. Mass customization is one way to serve those markets. Entrepreneurs have long built their businesses on niche markets, but they were seldom able to obtain economies of scale required for rapid growth. Large companies, however, are beginning to master international niche marketing as multinational corporations work to adapt and market single products for each of their myriad local markets. One executive told us:

> We recently took some television glass and tube technology and tried to transfer it to Romania, Poland, the USSR, China, and Japan. Each one was absolutely different. Same technology, but different cultures. The problem was the same: getting television in everybody's house. But the method of marketing and selling the technology was different because of the [local] culture.

Mass customization is itself an innovation.[6] World Wide Catalogues, Inc., for example, customizes its catalogues by incorporating the family name from the mailing label onto the T-shirts offered for sale in the catalogue. Each shirt is personalized yet sold to a mass market. Automakers mass customize through endless numbers of options. Personal computer companies market add-on cards that can enhance a computer with functions such as sound or graphics.

However, overemphasizing customization can lead strategists to ignore the imperative to complete the whole value chain as quickly as possible. Japanese, American, and European house builders all allow consumers to choose among options to customize the design of each house. Only the Japanese builders, however, allow home buyers to choose from among hundreds of options one week and produce a finished product shortly thereafter. American and European builders have not yet mastered fast delivery. The difference between the two groups is that each has developed a Phase III strength, but the Japanese builders are also competing in time, innovating and reaching customers much faster than U.S. companies.

ENTREPRENEURIAL PARTNERSHIPS: HOW TO INNOVATE ALL ALONG THE CHAIN

All three developments—technology breakthroughs, quality manufacturing, and customer satisfaction programs—are important. As companies plot their corporate strategies for innovation and growth they must remember, however, that success in meeting the innovation imperative depends on getting through all the phases of the value chain as quickly as possible.

A company that wants to flourish in the global marketplace and do everything single-handedly needs to use up-to-date technology, focus on quality manufacturing, and improve customer satisfaction. It needs a global distribution system, strong customer relations, and the ability to generate customized products that fit different market niches worldwide. And it has to do all this fast, generating a new product as soon as it identifies a potential market, retooling manufacturing facilities quickly if a new design requires this, and entering emerging foreign markets with dispatch. That's like scanning the horizon with binoculars in one hand while making custom bullets, loading, and firing with the other hand at markets that open up, then move, then vanish. Fewer and fewer businesses can do this alone and do it well.

On the battlefield of global competition, alliances allow partners to divide up the tasks. Entrepreneurial partnerships enable small and large companies to combine their respective talents to

43

blaze a quick, smooth path from new idea to final sale. As one corporate executive noted:

> Alliances occur between two companies at different points in the value chain. They get together because one supplies the other with some component that is missing. It can be the need to move "forward" on the chain (you have a technology and need someone to manufacture and distribute the product) or "backward" on the chain (you spot a market and look for the technology and someone to manufacture the product). So alliances are formed between companies who need technology, manufacturing, distribution, marketing, and/or financial assistance.

We see entrepreneurial partnerships as a strategy to put all the pieces together and make sure that all the stages are covered and that the links between the stages are also strong. It's important to stay focused on the *function* of these partnerships—just forming alliances won't automatically improve your business. For a large company, entrepreneurial partnerships should be part of a larger strategy to shore up the weak points in the value chain, farm out processes the company simply isn't good at, and bring in top-notch technology and ideas—whatever the source. A wonderful product idea and excellent market penetration won't generate profits by themselves. The product needs to be commercialized to generate profits. Companies having trouble getting from idea to prototype should consider partnering with a company that does this quickly and well.

For small companies, partnerships can be a way to parlay speed, innovation, and specialized talents into profits without having to develop all phases of the value chain into a fully integrated company. An entrepreneur who tries to develop every phase of the chain simultaneously—and intends for his or her company to grow by leaps and bounds—is simply out of touch with current business realities. Shortage of capital is apt to constrain growth, and partnering can solve two problems: It eliminates the need to develop some phases of the value chain in which your partner is strong, and it may open up a new source of low-cost financing. Companies whose strategy is to go it alone may still grow, but they will sacrifice rapid growth in their quest to build a completely integrated company.

The rewards of partnering for small businesses are apt to be a much higher survival rate, as suggested by the biotech industry. In this business, "the industry standard configuration has been a partnership between a biotech company and a large, established pharmaceutical/chemical/agricultural corporation."[7] Cornell researchers Barley, Freeman, and Hybels, who have tracked all biotech companies founded since the industry emerged, note that only nine percent of companies in their data base have ceased operation over the 15-year history of the field.[8] This is especially striking when one considers the long lead times for product development, the huge capital requirements, and the fickle response of the financial markets to small biotech companies. The single most persuasive factor in explaining the low mortality rate is the network of large-small partnerships that pervades the industry. Small partners get some help with R&D (for example, the interface between biology and organic chemistry), reliable financing, distribution channels for their products, and assistance with the regulatory problems peculiar to the biotech field.

In other industries, a large company's access to worldwide markets may be the single greatest attraction to small companies that want to grow quickly. Businessland and Canon were attractive partners for Steve Jobs's entrepreneurial company NeXT, which needed access to the larger companies' channels for distribution. Many other large corporations—both domestic and foreign—are proving similarly attractive to small high-tech companies.

We believe that with few exceptions, only those individuals, companies, and corporations willing to network creatively will make a big impact in the future business world. Corporations that continue to demonstrate the NIH (Not Invented Here) syndrome may find that they have developed an even more crippling disease: the Nothing Invented Here—and maybe even Nothing Produced or Sold Here—syndrome.

Entrepreneurs who rely on traditional financing sources and try to build fully integrated companies may soon find themselves on the auction block. Colleagues who have networked, collaborated, and partnered their way to financial strength may be among the bidders. There is nothing wrong with selling your company as a way to realize value. But if the goal from the start was total independence, then being acquired is hardly a rousing success. Ironically, a networking, collaborating to compete strategy can help preserve independence and shield smaller companies from hostile takeovers.

In the next two chapters, we look more closely at the options available to large and small companies, respectively. The major challenge to large companies is becoming more entrepreneurial and speeding innovation. The major challenge to small companies is surviving and developing a sustainable strategy for growth. The ultimate goal for both is completing the value chain successfully by transforming good ideas into products, sales, and profits.

NOTES

1. Stan Davis, *Future Perfect* (Reading, Mass.: Addison Wesley, 1988).
2. Robert Teitelman, *Gene Dreams* (New York: Basic Books, 1989), pp. 110, 121.
3. G. Steven Burrill and Kenneth B. Lee, Jr., *Biotech 91: A Changing Environment* (San Francisco: Ernst & Young, 1990), p. 129.
4. G. Steven Burrill, *Biotech 89: Commercialization* (New York: Mary Ann Liebert, 1988), p. 173.
5. See, for example, Michael L. Dertouzos, Richard K. Lester, and Robert M. Solow, *Made in America: Regaining the Productive Edge* (Cambridge, Mass.: MIT Press, 1989).
6. See Davis, *Future Perfect*.
7. Burrill and Lee, *Biotech 91*.
8. Stephen R. Barley, John Freeman, and Ralph C. Hybels, "Strategic Alliances in Commercial Biotechnology," in *Networks and Organizations*, ed. R. Eccles and N. Norhia (Boston: Harvard Business School Press, forthcoming).

CHAPTER THREE

Home-Grow, Bankroll, Buy, or Partner? Choices for Large Corporations

The communications of many large companies reflect a traditional go-it-alone, internally oriented mentality toward innovation. Consider this statement in the General Electric brochure *Consideration of Submitted Ideas*:

> In all honesty we must tell you that most of the ideas which are new to us and practical for our use originate within General Electric Company rather than outside of it. This is because the Company has a large scientific and technical staff which is continuously working to improve our products and methods. Besides its own original work, this staff has access to a large number of prior patents, prior publications, and other sources of information. In this circumstance, you will understand that many of the outside ideas submitted to the Company are already known or available to it. As to such ideas, which are not original or new to the Company, we do not offer compensation. It is only reasonable, we believe, that compensation should not be given for the duplication of old or previously available ideas should the Company at any time elect to practice them.

Other companies that used to personify this "fortress" mentality have radically changed their convictions. IBM, for example, signed partnership agreements with Apple and with Siemens in 1991; it also announced new alliances with Wang Laboratories and with Lotus Development Corporation. IBM's president, Jack Kuehler, commented, "Alliances allow us to share the heavy costs we might otherwise bear independently." Another IBM spokesman noted, "Today, the scale of investments that are required to stay competitive in technology . . . are huge. That's what's driving IBM's alliance strategy. It's a way of sharing costs. It's a way of spreading risks. And it's a way of bringing solutions to our customers."[1]

If you are an entrepreneur looking for a large corporate partner, it's obvious that the IBMs will be more receptive than the GEs. Learning to recognize which corporations are likely to make good partners can help you avoid at least some of the disappointments Exabyte and Gateway Technologies executives experienced in searching for an American corporate partner.

Corporate executives plotting how to get more innovation and compress the value chain need to consider whether their company's culture constrains available choices, and to understand clearly the pros and cons of different strategies. We believe small-large entrepreneurial partnerships are an excellent strategy—but we would never suggest them as appropriate strategies for every company.

Gifford Pinchot, author of *Intrapreneuring*, realizes now that the strategy he recommended created problems for corporate planners and staff in several companies. As he told *Inc.* magazine, "I've had too many of my friends get beaten up too badly for doing what I thought was right."[2] In this book, we are proposing that companies explore a strategy we think is promising—entrepreneurial partnerships—but only if these types of alliances have a fighting chance to succeed. This chapter should help corporate executives assess those chances.

FOUR STRATEGIES AND THE CULTURAL COMPONENTS

All companies have a corporate culture—the set of unwritten rules and behaviors that shape beliefs about which strategies and actions are likely to succeed and which are unthinkable or taboo. Some companies have cultures that condition them to be good partners. Others have cultures that prevent them from thinking of partnership as a serious option. In this chapter, we identify a range of corporate strategies for innovation and specify what their cultural components are likely to be. Executives of large companies need to assess whether entrepreneurial partnerships are a good fit with their culture, or whether their internal focus and emphasis on integration rule out that option. Small companies need to learn how to screen prospects to determine which corporations might make good partners.

Corporate strategies for innovation can be grouped into four categories. All categories rely on entrepreneurial resources, either from inside the company (internally oriented) or outside the company (externally oriented). Another criterion for distinguishing strategies is whether the company demands that the entrepreneurial resources be fully integrated into the corporation or whether it is willing to encourage and preserve the autonomy of entrepreneurs. Combining these two elements, we have identified four basic choices illustrated in Table 3.1:

1. Intrapreneuring (internal, integrated)
2. Internal venturing (internal, autonomous)
3. Merger and acquisition (external, integrated)
4. Entrepreneurial partnership (external, autonomous)

Although the chief focus of this book is the last category, entrepreneurial partnerships, most companies are not yet using this strategy. Thus we cannot simply advise small companies to seek out a company that already has experience in small-large partnerships. By reviewing the typical strategic choices of cor-

TABLE 3.1: Sources of Entrepreneurs

	Internal	*External*
Integrated	Intrapreneuring	Merger and Acquisition
Autonomous	Internal Venturing	Entrepreneurial Partnerships

porations and by looking at how their strategies have changed, it is possible for small-company entrepreneurs to pinpoint which corporations are ready for entrepreneurial partnership. The review should also help large-company executives determine which strategy or strategies are most appropriate for their present culture.

INTERNAL SOURCES OF ENTREPRENEURS

When attempting to accelerate innovation, some companies naturally turn to internal strategies. Chief among these are intrapreneuring and internal venturing. The difference between the two is that in intrapreneuring, the entrepreneurial resources are the regular company employees who are stimulated to be more innovative and entrepreneurial in their everyday work. There is no separation between these intrapreneurs and the other employees; hence we call this a fully integrated, company-wide strategy.[3]

In internal venturing, entrepreneurs are encouraged to form their own mini-start-ups within the company, and they usually are organizationally separated into a New Ventures unit. This strategy helps intrapreneurs to become more autonomous and to develop an identity that is distinct from the overall corporate culture.

Intrapreneuring: Nurturing Home-Grown Intrapreneurs

Intrapreneuring is a company-wide, internally oriented strategy. One executive we interviewed described intrapreneuring as a corporate attempt to promote values and behavior that are more typically found in small, entrepreneurial companies by encouraging employees to behave as if they were in a start-up company. Employees and managers throughout the company are expected to contribute to the process of innovation, which is accepted as a central value in the corporate culture.

3M represents one of the very best examples of intrapreneuring in the United States. Our interviews with corporate executives convinced us that the strategy works at 3M because the structure, policies and procedures, corporate culture, and performance objectives all support the concept that innovations will be developed from within the company.[4]

At least 25 percent of 3M's sales are expected to be from products no more than five years old. In a company that markets more than 25,000 products around the world, this expectation means that everyone is looking for and attempting to develop new products. The company has made innovation a high priority and has incorporated this expectation into all employees' and managers' performance objectives. The president has stated publicly that overhead budgets will not increase faster than sales; the corporate priority is to develop and sell new products. In support of this strategy, employees are encouraged to use company equipment, company time, and company labs to try out new ideas. Trying out a hunch on company equipment is not seen as wasting time. Management expects everyone to be an innovator, and accepts—even expects—a certain amount of failed ideas and "duds."

Intrapreneurs are rewarded when their ideas work but are not penalized when they don't work.

Employees frequently cross informally into other sections to review, critique, take, borrow, and generate ideas. Innovators who might otherwise feel stifled by the regimentation of a large organization are more apt to stay on and remain creative in a fluid environment that emulates the small-company atmosphere. In addition, the high-tech, capital-intensive materials technology for which 3M is noted is hard to develop in a low-tech home garage.

From a large company's perspective, intrapreneuring may be the right strategy for a firm that has a strong emphasis on self-sufficiency and doesn't need breakthrough innovations. Critics of 3M's emphasis on 25 percent new products every five years say this results in incremental changes in products rather than major breakthroughs. Managers at 3M would not dispute this point. They note that considerable innovation has come from the re-formulation of old processes or products in new ways. Such incremental improvements are what the Japanese call a process of *kaizen*—a concept more highly regarded in Japan than in the United States, as Chapter 7 makes clear.

Executives should also consider how flexible the company's beliefs and assumptions are about how employees should behave. Firms that have a strongly hierarchical structure and value employees primarily on the basis of consistent, measurable results may find the behavior of 3M's employees at odds with their basic organizational procedures. A rigid hierarchy is inherently incompatible with the kind of experimentation 3M encourages among its employees, and a reward system that doesn't recognize the value of creative failures will squelch an intrapreneuring program quickly.

From a small-company perspective, 3M-type corporations that emphasize step-by-step innovation and a self-sufficient, internally oriented strategy should not be high on a list of potential partners. They don't need your help, and chances are, they don't want it either. The brochure *About Your Idea. . .*, which 3M sends to people who are feeling out the prospects for partnering, says it all:

> We understand you have an idea you think may be of interest to 3M.
>
> We should say at the outset that only rarely does 3M use an idea submitted to us by a person outside of the Company. Our general practice is to rely on 3M's own technical and scientific resources for new products. However, we welcome the opportunity to consider your idea and thank you for getting in touch with 3M.

The message is clear: Thanks, but no thanks. While 3M has engaged in partnering as a secondary strategy, its central focus is internal, with full integration. As attractive as 3M might appear on the surface as a potential partner, entrepreneurs may want to look elsewhere for companies more likely to see a partner's contribution as valuable, even critical to their success.

Corning has also tried a variation of intrapreneuring. To meet its needs for constant innovation, which it defines as "converting ideas into dollars," Corning has developed a special training course that helps employees understand that innovation is a "process" with stages within it. Corning hopes the course will help employees to identify high-quality innovations before too much time and effort are spent on developing prototypes that have little chance of success. Corning breaks the innovation process into five stages: ideas, tests of feasibility, tests of practicality, potential for profitability, and requirements for commercialization. Decisions to fund each of these five stages follows rigorous guidelines. This course is one of three required activities for all Corning management (the other two are courses on quality and on diversity), which highlights the importance that Corning attaches to innovation. Is the course successful? "They line up in the halls to take it," a Corning executive told us.

Corning has also experimented with a more flexible, less hierarchical structure as a way to encourage employees to be more innovative. This approach has been used to increase speed at a particular stage on the value chain: Phase II manufacturing.

Corning's "Factory of the Future" at Blacksburg, Virginia, for example, has only two job classifications: maintenance worker and production worker. There are no bosses; instead, the emphasis is on equality and shared responsibility. The teams are self-supervised, and work is carried out 24 hours a day, 7 days a week. Staff and engineers are both on the factory floor, rather than in separate offices. Everyone dresses informally, and male visitors have to take off ties before they can go onto the factory floor. There are no special or assigned parking places in the lot. Morale is high, and employees are free to suggest and to experiment with better, more efficient, and more innovative ways of carrying out their jobs.

For Corning, a real value of the internal focus is in making the corporate culture more flexible. Restructuring to empower employees can speed the movement of ideas, processes, or products from one phase of the value chain to another by decreasing the layered, bureaucratic resistance to that movement. In contrast to 3M, however, Corning's chief strategy for innovation is more external and emphasizes autonomy, not integration. As one senior Corning executive said of intrapreneuring, "It's not enough to meet our needs."

Executives at large corporations may note that even if their main focus is not internal, some elements of intrapreneuring may be useful in loosening up the corporate culture and supplementing other strategies. For small companies seeking partners, it's important not to write off a company just because it encourages intrapreneurs—as long as the company has not chosen this as its *core* strategy. In fact, a history of employee empowerment programs may well be a good sign in a prospective partner company, for it can help to make the corporate cultures of large and small partners more compatible.

In some cases, an internal strategy of encouraging innovation meshes very smoothly with an external strategy of partnering. Saturn, for example, has a system of partnering all managers with their union counterparts. Except for the very top executives, no one has a title. These innovations in internal relations mirror a change in external relations along the same model, with a sense of equality and respect between partners replacing the hierarchical pyramid inside the company and the old adversarial win/lose model of dealing with outsiders. Externally, Saturn's approach is to make service providers partners to the process. For example, Ryder is a Saturn partner, and the driver of the Ryder truck who delivers to the Saturn plant becomes a member of an extended family. Here, the corporate value that Saturn is emphasizing is partnership, both inside and outside the company.

Internal Venturing: Bankrolling Autonomous Intrapreneurs

Internal venturing is a system of providing corporate venture capital to support new ideas developed by individual employees or work units. Unlike the company-wide approaches described above, internal venturing does not seek to integrate intrapreneurs more comfortably into the corporate fabric or to stimulate all employees to be more intrapreneurial. Instead, it helps would-be entrepreneurs within the company to develop their own autonomous projects separate from their regular jobs. Rather than have the whole company mimic the small-company atmosphere, an incubator-like environment is simulated in a special remit.

The most common internal venturing approach is to set up a separate office to handle early stage idea flow—that is, to collect innovative ideas, sort through them, then separate the feasible projects and put them into a special division until they are proven quantities. These units are generally called New Business Ventures or the Office of Innovation. Companies with shelves full of ideas and technology may find the idea of commercializing some of these technologies through a new business ventures division especially appealing. As one corporate executive noted, "We developed VCRs ten years before the Japanese introduced them, but that technology sat on the shelf." And shelf technology is more like fish than wine: it's more valuable when it's fresh than when it's aged.

In hindsight, the executive could see clearly the cost of doing nothing—a cost that is rarely obvious at first. "We'd have been better off to create a business venture, spend some money to test market the product without our name on it, then determine whether there was a market for VCRs. We had the technology, but it sat on the shelf. Now it's clear that we missed a huge market opportunity."

Kodak probably had one of the most extensive programs of internal venturing of any company until it turned its time and energy to integrating a new acquisition, Sterling Drug, into the corporation.[5] The program was created to help feed the core businesses and to develop a series of small successful companies from the ideas of Kodak employees. It was launched after Colby Chandler, chairman of the board, decided that Kodak needed a new strategy for stimulating more cost-effective innovation.

Eastman Kodak, with the eighth largest industrial research budget in the United States, spends more than a billion dollars annually on R&D. Internally, the problem was not a shortage of innovations coming out of R&D, but of getting people in the corporation to "buy into" the ideas that had been developed, then to manufacture, sell, and distribute them. In terms of the value chain, Kodak was strong in Phase I R&D, but was having trouble commercializing the ideas quickly and cost-effectively— a skill typical of small-company entrepreneurs.

Kodak chose an internal venture capital model to bridge the gap between the two ends of the value chain. The corporation established a New Opportunity Development unit to manage the innovation and new business development process, and it formed a holding company called Eastman Technologies for any new ventures that became operational. To provide a climate conducive to growing new businesses, both units were located in a separate building that was operated as an incubator, offering the new business ventures affordable space and access to on-site business planning, management assistance, and a variety of support services.

The Office of Innovation opened in 1984. Between that date and 1989, it screened over 4,000 proposals. About one-third of the ideas came from R&D, one-quarter from manufacturing, another quarter from marketing, and the rest from administration. Over 300 were judged promising enough to receive seed funding, and of those seeds, more than 100 were commercialized as separate units or adopted by existing departments. A total of 14 became new businesses and were spun out into the holding company.

One successful venture began when an engineer and a security guard proposed that Kodak manufacture and market a "Smart Card" based on a new proprietary manufacturing process. The manufacturing research organization agreed to sponsor the venture, which eventually merged with another initiative to form the Kodak Video ID system.

Ultratechnologies, a consumer battery business that is now a Kodak subsidiary, commercialized an innovation based on lithium technology originally developed for the Kodak Disc camera. Another new start-up, Sayett Technologies, was born when an engineer and a market analyst teamed up to develop what became the Kodak Datashow product. After Sayett became profitable, with $20 million in sales the first year, Kodak's Motion Picture and Audio Visual Division "acquired" the start-up as a captive supplier. Two years later, however, Kodak divested Sayett because its market niche was too small to be of long-term strategic interest.

The three-stage winnowing processes that all the new ventures had to survive included assessment criteria such as the "fit" of the new venture with established units, marketing and distribution requirements, probable viability as a stand-alone enterprise, and growth potential. The latter factor became a major concern. Even the most successful ventures were generally perceived to be too small and to take too long to mature to have a substantial impact on a corporation as large as Kodak.

Kodak's program was based on an internal venture capital model, yet neither the intrapreneurs who started the new ventures nor Kodak received financial rewards comparable to those generated by successful venture capital operations.[6] Kodak is now emphasizing business focus, divestment and downsizing, and profitability improvement rather than intrapreneuring and internal venturing. From the perspective of a Kodak executive who tried to make it work, "the bloom is off the rose" of internal venturing as a corporate strategy for innovation. Three chief reasons Kodak became discouraged may have been:

1. *Low Yields.* "Fewer than one percent of all the ideas submitted generated virtually all of the value."[7] It takes an enormous amount of time and effort to create an environment in which ideas will flourish, and still more to weed them out in a multistage process. The costs may be out of proportion to the benefits.

2. *Management Requirements.* New ventures take an inordinate amount of management time and attention. In addition to all the time spent by personnel in the New Opportunity Development unit, legal counsel and the board of directors found they spent a disproportionate amount of their time on the new ventures.

3. *Corporate Exposure.* Kodak's new ventures had instant credibility with markets and suppliers, which certainly gave these start-ups a boost. Unfortunately, this close association also exposed the parent company to liability problems and similar headaches, especially when the new companies were operating in areas with which the parent corporation was not familiar.

Kodak and 3M, as well as Du Pont, Exxon, and Monsanto, to name a few, have tried the internal venture strategy and found it wanting. So the track record to date isn't encouraging. Some would judge Kodak's program as very successful: over 100 new products or business lines were adopted. This demonstrates that entrepreneurship and innovation can be successfully extracted from the larger corporation and nurtured in a small, separate unit even if the overall culture is not designed to support entrepreneurship. What the programs have failed to demonstrate is how this extraction and nurturing can be made cost-effective for a large company. Perhaps the reason is implicit in one executive's comments: "Real entrepreneurs aren't in big company bureaucracies, and big companies are not good at giving the opportunities and rewards that real entrepreneurs want." Kodak's program obviously turned up a number of successful intrapreneurs, but perhaps the "real" entrepreneurs—those who will bet their own money and future on an idea in which they believe—are more apt to leave and start their own companies than work with a new ventures unit. As Chapters 7–10 illustrate, Japanese and European versions of internal venturing seem to be yielding more promising results.

Skunk Works. One exception to the generally gloomy prognosis for internal venturing in the United States is a special category of internal but autonomous venturing called *skunk works.* A skunk works is a unit that has a specific mission, usually within a well-defined time frame, to develop a new product or process. Several large companies have used this strategy when they needed to develop a new product in a tight time frame.

Skunk works typically operate in relative isolation from corporate management. They must have a champion inside the corporation who provides upper-level, corporate support for the skunk works operations and who buffers the special unit from the potentially adverse impact of traditional management rules and regulations. Skunk works are typically exempted from many corporate rules and regulations, such as use of purchase requisitions, time and materials budgets, time cards, and quality and performance audits.

One Monsanto executive remarked to us:

> The entrenched technology in any company makes it difficult to innovate. Our way of thinking "within the dots" makes it difficult for us to go outside the dots. We run new ideas through the old grid and innovate on the margin because we only experiment with things that we know, from our corporate experience, work.

Skunk works enable employees to get out of the corporation and away from the entrenched technology and the traditional corporate approach to problem solving. Instead of trying to encourage an entrepreneurial, small-company atmosphere within a large corporation, companies using this strategy create a temporarily separate unit that can behave like a small company and ignore traditional corporate procedures. In contrast to internal venturing, which attempts to take innovations and grow new business units around them, this strategy creates an artificially separate unit that is charged with creating a well-defined innovation that usually will be absorbed back into the parent company.

The projects developed in skunk works are almost all products which meet specified performance characteristics. The success of skunk works is usually measured by the project team's ability to meet product development milestones and deliver the desired product on schedule. Skunk works have been used for the development of products that have a "bet your firm" connotation, such as IBM's PC or Canon's first automatic camera.

The cost of operating a skunk works is high, not only in terms of real cost but also in the organizational cost of dealing with a maverick unit of people. However, in cases where skunk works were successful, cost was a secondary consideration because of the potential value of the new product in the competitive environment. Developing a personal computer was a strategic imperative for IBM after Apple had produced one.

While intrapreneuring works best for the step-by-step process of incremental innovation, a skunk works is aimed at larger steps. However, it's often difficult to achieve major breakthroughs on command and on a planned schedule. Like internal venturing, this is an expensive strategy; unlike the gathering and sifting approach of internal venturing, a skunk works focuses the time, energy, and know-how of a few hand-picked employees on a defined task that must be accomplished within a specific time frame. But as one Corning executive remarked: "Skunk works are old hat today. The competitive scene no longer allows the luxury of a few, 'big' innovations. We have to have a steady stream of innovations, not just the occasional big one."

Corporate executives should use this strategy primarily when there is a core group of intrapreneurs and a targeted, high-priority innovation that can best be developed in a skunk works project. If your company is already enmeshed in an internal venture program, Pinchot advises that "unless a new idea fits a company's overall corporate strategy, it should be spun out or licensed, or the proponents should 'grit their teeth and let it die.' "[8]

For small-company entrepreneurs, corporations that are knee-deep in internal venturing should probably be crossed off the list of "potentials." Their attention and resources are, for the time being, internally committed. The skunk works strategy, in particular, signals that even when the corporation has identified the need for a specific, highly important new product (one your company may have to offer), it is likely to want to develop it internally.

Companies that have recently emerged from an experiment in internal venturing may be ripe to try partnering with independent small companies rather than creating small companies internally. They may well have a heightened appreciation of what existing small companies can offer. Alternately, frustrated with what they perceive as the excessive autonomy of venture companies, they may attempt instead to merge and integrate outside entities. Kodak, for example, shifted its attention from internal venturing to the opposite pole—the external, integrated strategy of M&A—when it acquired Sterling Drug.

EXTERNALLY ORIENTED STRATEGIES

The possible list of externally oriented strategies is a long one. Corporations can acquire and merge large companies or small ones; they can partner with other companies large and small. They may have one-on-one or multiple relationships. They can participate in university research centers or fund incubators. We make sense of this welter of possibilities by dividing them into two sets: one set that seeks to integrate those resources into the company, and one set that respects the autonomy of the other partner and is willing to accept and even encourage the development of innovations outside the company. The first fit into our M&A category; the second into entrepreneurial partnerships.

These divisions create some odd bedfellows. Spin-offs go under the second category; so do large-large joint ventures that create a new start-up company. Some acquisitions fall under partnerships rather than under M&A. Relationships with universities and incubators fit neither category precisely, but are really long-term enabling strategies that position corporations for future partnerships. As such, they are discussed in Chapter 5, "Making Partnerships Work."

Merger and Acquisition: Buying and Integrating Other Companies

One traditional strategy for moving backward and forward on the value chain is to buy another company that has what you want and merge the company into the existing corporate structure. Traditional American managers who want to control or reduce risk as much as possible are attracted to this strategy. They are driven to own, control, and have power over the outside company that's being acquired.

Because of these cultural values, American companies have tended to integrate acquired small companies into the large company. Often they will break up an acquisition and scatter the pieces throughout the company to achieve more synergistic relationships with similar units in the large corporation. This strategy may successfully integrate the acquired company and its products into the larger corporation. More often than not, however, the merger also destroys the capacity of that small company to continue being innovative; the disaggregated and fragmented acquisition can no longer develop the stream of innovations that the large company needs. In terms of innovation strategies, M&A may be like eating your seed corn.

KMPG–Peat Marwick certainly found this to be true after extensive experience with acquiring and merging small firms during the 1980s. The world's largest accounting firm, KMPG–Peat Marwick has traditionally provided tax advice and preparation, and it oversees the books of many large corporate clients. More recently, it has moved into the consulting business, using primarily an M&A strategy. During the 1980s, small companies that had specialized consulting services were purchased outright and merged into the accounting company's corporate culture.

The M&A strategy can be judged a partial success, for it did achieve two important benefits: it developed the firm's consulting capacity and also eliminated competitors. M&A failed, however, as a strategy for innovation. The innovative nature of the small companies was generally submerged in the conservative accounting culture. One senior partner gave the following example: "We acquire a small software firm. The first thing that happens is that we take the creative genius who founded it, shave his beard, and replace his T-shirt with a three-piece suit. Pretty soon he's a well-heeled executive rather than a creative producer."

When initially confronted with the need to alter its strategies for innovation, Kodak also considered the M&A of numerous small firms. Management outlined three options:

1. Develop the company's own ideas through internal venturing, the "internal gems" strategy.

2. Buy up a number of smaller companies and create one large unit, the "string of pearls" strategy.
3. Acquire a "crown jewel," another large company.

As we have seen, Kodak settled initially on the internal gems strategy. When that proved disappointing, it shifted to option three and acquired Sterling Drug. While the merger may help Kodak diversify, it is unlikely to address the innovation imperative for a simple and obvious reason: Another large company is unlikely to deliver what a small company can provide—new ideas and quick turnaround capacity.

Strategy two, the string of pearls, would at least have targeted companies that had what Kodak needed. But the KMPG–Peat Marwick experience suggests that the entrepreneurial resources Kodak acquired would probably have dissipated quickly, even though it has a somewhat "looser" culture than a CPA firm has. Conspicuously missing from the options list is the external strategy that Kodak tried long ago with Ed Land: entrepreneurial partnerships.

The lesson for large companies is clear: although M&A certainly can be useful for consolidation and expansion, it may not be a good choice as an innovation strategy. The only exception to this rule is if the corporate culture is quite intrapreneurial, providing acquired entrepreneurs with the supportive, creative environment they need. Intrapreneuring and M&A of small companies could conceivably work together in this case. But few American companies can match the intrapreneurial culture of a 3M.

Small entrepreneurs looking for corporate partners should pay very close attention to a corporation's history of M&A, for companies committed to this strategy may very well seem interested and respond positively to initial contacts. The need for integration that drives this strategy, however, is not conducive to relationships that preserve and value the autonomy of both large and small partners. Before walking into the open jaws of an interested "partner," investigate whether those jaws have a history of snapping shut once the small company develops partnership ties.

This alligator behavior is far more common among U.S. companies than among Japanese companies that practice what they call *international M&A*. Upon closer inspection, this strategy appears misnamed: It is really the A without the M. Domestically, M&A barely exists in Japan. Companies are seldom, if ever, bought and sold. Internationally, however, the Japanese have been quietly acquiring a number of small U.S. companies in recent years. Yet they do not often move the company or change its name. Whenever possible, they leave the management team intact. They consciously develop technology linkages back to the parent company, and they provide the money that enables the start-up or small company to move through its current phase and onto the next phase of the value chain. Even though this strategy is termed international M&A, the actual style is closer to collaboration. As such, it belongs in the final category: entrepreneurial partnerships.

Entrepreneurial Partnerships: The External Partner System

In the first two chapters, we described entrepreneurial partnerships as small-to-large alliances formed for the mutual benefit of each partner. The small partner typically brings innovation, speed, and entrepreneurship; the large partner typically provides capital, market access, and possibly management assistance as well. In its simplest form, there is one large corporate partner and one small-company partner. In actuality, a whole variety of arrangements combine the basic elements of entrepreneurial partnership: some combination of large and small; external orientation; emphasis on entrepreneurial resources for innovation; autonomy; and mutual respect between partners.

Spin-offs, for example, can be the result of a small-large relationship that is formed to commercialize an innovative technology or product. Joint ventures between two large companies that create a new, small, entrepreneurial company also qualify. Large equity investments in small companies, when the purpose is to nurture and gain access to external technology rather than to swallow up and integrate the resource, also fit our guidelines.

Large-to-large collaborations are a common external strategy that maintains the autonomy of the partners and can be used to complete the value chain or access technology. They lack the large-small connection required to fit our entrepreneurial partnership category. Even so, we do discuss this strategy in a separate section at the end of the chapter because it is an important indicator of corporate readiness for entrepreneurial partnership.

Teaming with Small Entrepreneurial Companies: The Prototypical Entrepreneurial Partnership. More and more large companies have begun to team with small entrepreneurial firms. Merck, one of the leading pharmaceutical companies, was among the first to develop partnerships with small firms when some of its key patents began to expire. This encouraged others to take similar action. Seagrams, for example, has invested over $20 million in Biotechnica International to develop new methods of fermentation. Digital Equipment has an array of relationships with small companies as well as large. Asea, Brown Boveri in Europe owns or has equity investments in over a thousand small companies worldwide that provide power transmission and other electrical equipment. As we'll see in more detail in Chapter 9, the Swedish chemical company Perstorp has entrepreneurial partnerships with over 30 small firms in Europe and the United States.

Typically, large corporations form relationships with small companies for the following reasons:

1. *The small company specializes in an area that the large company wants to move into.* Hence, forming an alliance with the

small company allows the large one to jump into the technology or access the resource without having to do the basic research and development. This is one reason Perstorp and Seagrams are partnering.

2. *The risk is reduced because the small company has already developed the idea or the technology.* As a result, it's quicker and less costly to form an alliance with that small company than to develop the technology internally.

3. *If things work out between the two companies, the relationship can be expanded down the line.* Hence, the large company can position itself for low-risk, future expansion.

4. *Executives are realizing that no matter how hard they try, very few companies can excel at every stage and phase of the value chain and do it all quickly.* In many cases, it's faster, easier, and more cost-effective to supplement in-house technology and expertise with resources outside the company than to rely on internal personnel to achieve the necessary level of innovation, speed, and organizational development.

A good example of the last point is recent developments in X-ray lithography, one of two approaches to creating a breakthrough 256-megabyte DRAM chip.[9] The big players like IBM, AT&T Bell Labs, and Toshiba have invested many years and hundreds of millions of dollars to solve the problem of creating the tiny stencils needed for making the minute but powerful chips using X-rays. Now, however, it looks like a tiny upstart may upstage them: Hampshire Instruments, a small company based in Rochester, New York, has developed an innovative X-ray system that may solve the DRAM technical problems. Motorola and AT&T are currently testing Hampshire's system to see if it can be adapted to mass-production techniques.[10] Although corporate planners may wring their hands that this solution was "not invented here," they would be foolish to ignore Hampshire Instruments, as Kodak did Exabyte.

After repeated reminders like this of small-company strengths in invention and innovation, some firms that used to be internally focused have begun to look outward, dissatisfied with the results of complete self-reliance. The most notable example is probably IBM. For most of its history, IBM was known as an internally oriented company that emphasized integrated self-sufficiency. When it did business with outsiders, it acted more like a predator than a partner. Epson, for example, supplied printers to IBM in the 1970s. When IBM saw how profitable the printer business was becoming, it canceled its contract with Epson and started manufacturing printers itself, retreating from external partnering and reemphasizing integration.

Challenged by Apple and the need for a PC, IBM then developed the well-known skunk works—still an internal strategy, but with more emphasis on autonomy as a key element in innovation. Since that time, IBM has begun to embrace multiple external, autonomous relationships. The relationship with Apple made headlines in the business news, but IBM's partnership with Steve Jobs's new company, NeXT, was probably the one that signaled IBM was a major player in the partnership scene. IBM now develops partnerships with companies of all sizes, from well-established Siemens and Apple to Fran Tarkenton's tiny KnowledgeWare. By the time the Apple deal was negotiated in July 1991, IBM had already established more than 500 partnerships with small companies and had acquired more than $500 million worth of equity in these small firms.[11]

Equity investments are a common feature of entrepreneurial partnerships and can even include majority positions. This kind of friendly acquisition, which we describe as the A without the M, can serve all the purposes of entrepreneurial partnership without the destructive effects of a merger on the entrepreneurial resources. Much of the business world reacted to Hoffman–La Roche's acquisition of 60 percent of Genentech, for example, as though it were a traditional M&A event. One business writer described the arrangement by recounting how the large company "pounced" on Genentech, and went on to speculate, "Now that [Genentech] has been gobbled up, everyone is looking around to see who will be next."[12]

Investment banker Frederick Frank, who helped Genentech negotiate the deal, describes the event in very different terms:

> Because maintaining the integrity of [Genentech's] culture was considered crucial, a normal merger was ruled out. I went off to locate a match that would maintain Genentech's independence while enabling it to gain access to additional financing and an international infrastructure. People often overlook the fact that Genentech did not have an international infrastructure. . . .[13]

As an American banker most familiar with traditional M&A, Frank took pains to point out that this was not a "normal" merger. Instead, he used words like "integrity" and "independence" to make it clear he was talking about autonomy, not integration. Frank also was apparently surprised by the extent to which Roche shared the views of Genentech executives concerning the company's autonomous culture: "One of the things that was so interesting about Roche was that it was important to them that Genentech's culture be preserved. . . . They did not want to Roche-ize Genentech; they're proud of their culture, but they recognize it's different."[14]

That difference is precisely what made Genentech worth over $2 billion to Hoffman–La Roche; it would be extremely foolish to destroy that difference by merging the smaller company. Resisting the urge to merge requires a level of respect for autonomy that many large American corporations do not have. Perhaps that was why, as Frank reports, "Roche was the preferred choice from day one."[15]

Small companies looking for a partnership that includes substantial equity investment should keep in mind the Genentech story. Any list of corporate prospects should include European and Japanese firms, many of which are farther along in grasping the importance of *vive la différence.*

Spin-Offs. As a strategy for innovation, spin-offs fit best in the entrepreneurial partnership box, yet they straddle the internal/external axis. The entrepreneurial resources cross the line from internal to external in the process of forming the new company. In this sense, spin-offs seem a close cousin to internal ventures, except that they are born outside the company rather than inside it. Some internal ventures, after a lengthy hatching period inside the company incubator, are spun off into the external business world. Spin-offs are more like a live birth, and they are expected to stand on their own feet and make their way without too much coddling. Companies that encourage spin-offs are clearly looking outward; however, they see the world outside the company as the proper setting for an aspiring entrepreneur.

There are two kinds of corporate spin-offs: corporate-driven and employee-driven. In the first case, the corporation decides to spin off a company to develop an innovation without the constraints and overhead charges of the large corporation. This is a bit like cutting a skunk works or internal venture free from its complicated mooring inside the company. Alternately, a corporation may encourage a particular employee to take some shelf technology it has decided not to develop internally and build a separate company around it. Chris Whittle of Whittle Communications commented: "We have vaults of ideas. We have ideas stacked up around here in holding patterns, and I'm talking about major concepts. Our problem is finding the people to execute the concepts we have."[16] Another executive told us: "Innovations are not the problem. Turning the innovation into a quality product within a reasonable period of time is our problem." Solving this problem is something at which entrepreneurs excel.

An overabundance of partially developed ideas is an opportunity for an entrepreneurial employee who may have worked on the technology and who understands its potential better than anyone else. Spinning off the technology enables the entrepreneur to develop it in a less bureaucratic environment. The strategy may also be far more cost-effective than continuing to develop a product internally. As a Monsanto executive commented, "Large companies are not as innovative as small ones because the big companies have too much money. Entrepreneurs don't have much money, and it's amazing how that focuses the mind."

In the second type of spin-off, an employee provides the initiative, taking technology off the shelf and forming a new company to commercialize it. Rather than trying to prevent such employees from leaving the fold—an underlying objective of many internally oriented strategies—the parent company may speed them on the way with an equity investment as a blessing (and a calculated investment).

The impetus for employee-driven spin-offs can also be a lay-off or the cancellation of an employee's pet project. After working intently on a project and having a sense of its commercial potential and the market, an employee may be suddenly pulled off the project, out of a job, or both. McData was formed under just these circumstances. Jack McDonnell was lured from Silicon Valley to Boulder, Colorado, to work on a network communications product at Storage Technology. After working on the product for 22 months, the corporation had a financial downturn, and the project was canceled. Jack and the five others who had worked together formed a company and built the product. Their former employer became one of their customers. Eight years later, McData had 12 percent of the world market share for its products, and $20 million in retained earnings.

Joint Venture Spin-Offs.   A variation on this scenario is a technology with a clearly defined future market potential but no existing market niche. The parent company may want to wait for the market to catch up with the technology. Cormetech, a Corning-Mitsubishi creation that could be called a joint spin-off, is a new company that has a product designed and ready to be manufactured. It had to wait for Congress to pass the amended Clean Air Act in November, 1990, which required power companies to install catalytic pollution controls.

Corning saw a new market developing in Germany for products to remove nitrogen oxides from electricity-generating power plants powered by coal, gas, or oil. Reasoning that the United States would soon pass similar legislation, Corning approached

Mitsubishi Heavy Industries and Mitsubishi Petrochemical to establish a new company to market and manufacture ceramic-based catalysts for power plants.[17] This was the beginning of Cormetech, which is an acronym for Corning Mitsubishi Environmental Technologies.

The initial Corning investment was $3 million to cover three years. The Japanese partners have put up an equal share. The business plan calls for Cormetech to break even in three years by selling to pockets of nitrogen-oxide-regulated states. But the big payoff is predicted for 1995/1996, when Cormetech hopes for a share of a mammoth market—up to $1 billion—created by federal environmental regulations.

Despite its long experience with joint ventures, Corning did something new when it started Cormetech. Usually, Corning supplies the technology and its partners supply marketing and finance. With Cormetech, things are reversed. Corning will supply the marketing and the Japanese companies will supply much of the technology. The development of Cormetech is an example of three international corporations working in a well-defined partnership that produces a fourth company—a spin-off that has the resources of three parent companies at its disposal, and an international management team at the helm.

From a large-company perspective, spin-offs may be an ideal external strategy if the problem is an overabundance of R&D and not enough commercialization. The entrepreneurial core of the new company can be formed by former employees, outsiders, or some combination of the two. Corning, for example, has a published policy that explicitly allows employees, under certain circumstances, to form start-ups based on technologies that Corning has decided not to develop. The policy statement notes that "Advice, expertise and equipment may be provided . . . to entrepreneurs, for a fee. . . . Compensation . . . could be in the form of part ownership of the venture."

TABLE 3.2: Benefits of Strategic Alliances

O   Access to more patents and technology

O   Develop strategic customer-supplier
    relationships

O   Access to new markets

BENEFITS OF STRATEGIC ALLIANCES

Large companies have much more experience forming alliances with other large companies than with small ones. Sometimes they form partnerships that serve a long-term entrepreneurial purpose. Often, however, the alliances are more transactional in nature: a one-time, across-the-board exchange rather than a long-term developmental relationship. Regardless of the type of collaboration, they all expect to achieve specific benefits as outlined in Table 3.2.

Access to More Patents and Technology.   According to the most recent survey of biotech companies by Ernst and Young, strategic alliances are the norm in the biotech industry, and are increasing in importance. The standard configuration is a partnership between a biotech company and a large, established pharmaceutical company. Alliances are formed because "each partner has an asset (a product, technology, or research capability) or a resource (capital, manufacturing capabilities, and/or a marketing/distribution channel), that the other can leverage."[18]

Pharmaceutical companies as well as firms in the food, agricultural, chemical, and energy industries have all recognized that innovations in biotechnology are likely to affect their market shares—certainly in the long run if not the near term. Although some have established their own biotechnology laboratories, many of these diversified corporations have formed strategic alliances with small biotechnology firms to obtain access to a broad range of research. These alliances can be characterized as an exchange of knowledge for money and, later, marketing assistance. Through these alliances, the big companies avoid the risks of a start-up, and the small firms get the funds that enable them to concentrate on their research and product development.

In addition to being able to produce new products more quickly than large firms, small dedicated biotech firms, with their close ties to universities, often serve as bridges between university labs and industry. Hence, they provide access to even more patents and technology than what's contained in their company. For example, several researchers at Hawaii Biotechnology Group are also faculty members at the University of Hawaii, which has strengths in biotechnology research.

Develop Strategic Customer/Supplier Relationships. Strategic customer/supplier relationships offer obvious benefits to both partners. For example, Digital is a partner of Asea, Brown Boveri (ABB). Digital sells its computers to ABB, and ABB sells power materials back to Digital. Both partners have ready markets for their goods. AT&T has 14 similar strategic partners, which are really strategic customers. While these partnerships tend to be more transactional than developmental, they are still essential for each company to access products that enable it to be innovative and speed progress along the value chain.

Access to New Markets. American companies have formed alliances with the Japanese to be able to sell their products in Japan. Japanese automakers, on the other hand, are interested in large-company alliances with American automakers because they want to sell cars in Europe, but European countries have traditionally limited the amount of direct Japanese sales. American auto com-

74

panies do not face those limitations, so the Japanese may have to joint venture in order to get into Europe and its new market.

One-to-one large-large corporate alliances tend to focus on developing a product line or accessing a particular technology or market. Often, the relationship can be analyzed in terms of a value chain division of labor, with one company swapping Phase I proprietary technology, for example, to access a broader market (Phase III). The biotech arrangement noted above fits this model.

Large companies that are comfortable with an external focus typically form multiple partnerships, and many of these will be with other large companies. When another company clearly has what you need, whether that is patented technology or a lock on a hard-to-penetrate market, the solution is obviously to explore a partnership with that company. Corporations comfortable with these arrangements should not overlook partnerships with small companies as a further aspect of the external, autonomous orientation. It is easy to assume that the big players will be the big companies, but this is not always the case, as the Hampshire Instruments DRAM story illustrates.

Small companies looking for large corporate partners should consider a history of large-large partnerships as a positive sign. It indicates a strong external orientation and the ability to deal with "outside" cultures. The trouble may be getting corporate executives to take small companies as seriously as the larger partners. In the crush of multiple partnerships, one more deal, especially one with a small company, may get lost in the shuffle. See Chapter 9, for example, for the story of a small Swedish medical products entrepreneur whose patent, purchased by Corning, just drifted along, unattended, in and out of various subsidiaries and acquisitions.

EVOLUTION OF STRATEGIES

The process of globalization has forced many companies to change their cultural orientation from internal to external. American corporations have typically valued control, integration, and an internally oriented self-sufficiency. As the world changes around them, however, too much emphasis on internal control can lead to loss of control in the marketplace; an exaggerated castle-and-moat mentality can leave a company stranded up on a hill, far from the ferment of new ideas in the burgeoning global village. Some corporations are beginning to change and adapt, with mixed success. For some, entrepreneurial partnerships can become a cornerstone in building new strategies for global competition. Others may find they need to develop a different balance between internal and external foci, and between integration and networking with other autonomous actors.

As we have noted, IBM, in the course of a decade or so, has shifted from a strongly internal, integrated orientation to become one of the most active players in entrepreneurial partnerships. An important lesson of the IBM progression for both corporate executives and entrepreneurs is that companies can and do change their cultures and their orientations. It is important for small companies to look at the focus and the direction of change. Where is a company's main energy focused? If a company's strategy is shifting, what is the dynamic?

Some companies make good partners and others are not worth the time to approach. Corning and perhaps IBM may be good candidates. Utilities like PSCo in Colorado, NYSEG in New York, and "telephone utilities" like U S WEST and other Baby Bells may likewise be moving toward partnering. If Exabyte had looked more closely at the culture and history of the companies on its potential partner list, perhaps the firm would have found other U.S. firms with which to partner instead of Japanese ones. Then again, the winnowing process may have led Exabyte executives directly to Sony and Kubota, and saved them the time and energy of pursuing unsuitable firms.

Don't try to be too hasty to categorize a company and cross it off your list. Most Fortune 500 companies probably engage in all four strategies—from internal integrated to external autonomous—to some degree. Since different divisions within a large company, and even different executives within each division, have different needs for control and self-sufficiency, one company can practice several different strategies at the same time. Kodak, as noted above, has tried internal venturing, large-small alliances, and spin-offs.

Merger and acquisition in this context is often a harbinger of pressures to reestablish control by recentralizing and reintegrating diverse approaches. It seems that most companies go through cycles from internal orientation to a more external focus, from respect for autonomy to a reassertion of control and integration. Such cycles have no set time horizon. One cannot say that a cycle typically runs over one, two, or more decades. Corporate planners should take note of their own company's dynamic to see if a shift to small-large partnering goes with or against the tide of change in their own company.

Large companies search for innovation strategies that are both profitable and compatible with their culture; entrepreneurs struggle with some of the same issues as they map out their strategies for growth. Some entrepreneurs prize their self-sufficiency so highly and are so internally oriented that they are unsuitable for partnership. Others rely on partnering and networking as a way of life; they could make excellent partners. The next chapter describes in more detail the kinds of choices and strategies available to small firms.

NOTES

1. *Boulder Daily Camera*, 7 July 1991; *Christian Science Monitor*, 8 July 1991.
2. "Intraprewho?" *Inc.*, June 1991, p. 30.
3. Gifford Pinchot did not make a distinction between these two strategies but called them both intrapreneuring. However, the integration-autonomy distinction is an important one to make when choosing what strategies are most apt to work in individual companies.

4. Personal interview with Julianne H. Praeger, Executive Director, Corporate Technical Planning and Coordination, 3M, 9 June 1989.

5. Robert J. Tuite, "Strategies for Technology-Based New Business Development" (Paper delivered at the International Forum on Technology Management, Brussels, June 1989). The case material is drawn from this source plus an interview and subsequent discussions with Dr. Tuite.

6. Most successful venture capital firms aspire to returns on their investments of 20 to 50 times their investment. See George Jenkins, "Venture Capital Is Cautious: Who Will Seed Start-Ups?" *Harvard Business Review*, Nov.–Dec. 1989, p. 117.

7. Tuite, "Strategies," p. 8.

8. "Intraprewho?", p. 30.

9. DRAM stands for dynamic random access memory, and the chips store data inside computers.

10. Laurent Belsie, "A Computer Chip Provides a Lesson," *Christian Science Monitor*, 24 July 1991.

11. Laurence Hooper, "Big Blue Cultivates New Markets by Thinking Small," *Wall Street Journal*, 27 February 1991.

12. Margaret Sharp, "David, Goliath and the Biotechnology Business," *The OECD Observer*, June–July 1990, pp. 22–24.

13. G. Steven Burrill and Kenneth B. Lee, Jr., *Biotech 91: A Changing Environment* (San Francisco: Ernst & Young, 1990), p. 107.

14. Ibid.

15. Ibid.

16. "Gathering of the Entrepreneurs," *Inc.*, November 1989, p. 33.

17. Paul O'Connor, personal interview, summer 1989; Robert Ecklin, personal interview, February 1990.

18. Burrill and Lee, *Biotech 91*, p. 40.

CHAPTER FOUR

Beaver, Bear, Monkey, or Kangaroo: Choices for Entrepreneurs

During the 1980s, young people in universities across the country filled business classes to overflowing, preparing to market themselves to corporate recruiters. The objective: a good job with high pay, rapid advancement, and the stability of working for a top-rank corporation.

Meanwhile, executives who had what these college students wanted were leaving the Fortune 500 in droves, abandoning their corporate career paths to become presidents of brand-new companies that they hoped would join the Inc 500. Juan Rodriguez and three colleagues left IBM to start Storage Technology, and later he left to start a new company, Exabyte. Jerry Caulder, now CEO of Mycogen, an up-and-coming agricultural biotech company, joined Mycogen after failing to persuade his employer, Monsanto, to invest in promising companies like this one. George Ebright left his post as SmithKline Beckman's president in 1989 to become CEO of Cytogen, another biotech start-up. The actions of these former corporate managers and others like them demonstrate that founding and running entrepreneurial start-ups is not just a calling for mavericks and misfits. It is now very chic to be an entrepreneur.

Other aspiring entrepreneurs, like Michael Dell, are leapfrogging the steps of college and corporate life to join the Inc. 500. Voted Entrepreneur of the Year by *Inc.* magazine in 1989, Dell founded his own computer company at age 19. Six years later he had taken Dell Computer public, and his start-up had grown into an international company doing a half-billion dollars in sales. The 1980s, the decade of M&A mania and the decade of quality, could also be called the decade of the entrepreneur. People such as Steve Jobs, Bill Gates, and Michael Dell have helped change the minds of Americans about the acceptability of being an entrepreneur.

The media and press extolled the virtues of entrepreneurship, suggesting that small companies may be the saviors of our economy. Countless articles have depicted small entrepreneurial companies as Davids out-maneuvering Goliath corporations that are too muscle-bound to adapt quickly to changing conditions. Research conducted by David Birch of MIT and others reinforces that notion. Birch sparked controversy and debate with his first report in 1979, "The Job Generation Process," in which he said that small businesses created 82 percent of U.S. jobs. Although subsequent research has indicated some regional variation in the percentage of jobs created, the fact is that companies with fewer than 100 employees are generating jobs much faster than those with more than 100 employees.[1]

For every successful company like Dell Computer and Genentech, however, hundreds of new companies fail or remain permanently stuck on first base. The chief challenge they face is not the innovation imperative, but survival and growth. Start-ups don't need to access entrepreneurial resources; they *are* those resources. They do, however, need to complete the value chain quickly to realize sales and profits and to achieve the fast growth that most hope for. When plotting their strategy, these small companies can opt for an internally or externally oriented path, just as corporate executives may focus on either internal or external sources of entrepreneurs. Start-ups that choose an external strategy can use entrepreneurial partnerships to help secure their future and achieve a satisfying growth curve. Founders facing the constant need to sell products and raise capital can use partnerships to give their companies a boost.

For a small company to become a large corporation, the entrepreneur must have a vision of how to get from small to large. The choices entrepreneurs make when they start the company will help determine whether the company will stay relatively small or grow rapidly into a large corporation. Not all start-ups aim to be huge in size: some focus mainly on achieving growth in earnings while keeping the plant and staff "lean and mean." While corporate executives ponder their innovation strategies, small-company founders face a more fundamental question: What do I want my company to be when it grows up?

Corporate executives searching for small companies with whom to partner need to assess not only what those companies have to offer them, but also how the partnership will fit the small company's culture. As the CEO of Cytogen, a health products biotech company, notes: "If the arrangement is not good for both parties, it will not be good for either party for long."[2] Externally oriented small companies see partnering and networking as either their core business or their primary strategy for growth. These companies typically make excellent, highly committed partners. Internally oriented small companies may also turn to partnering as a source of cash or market access, but they will not have the same commitment to their partners and will tend to see this strategy as a temporary means to a different end, not as an ongoing way of doing business. Partnering with these companies, though obviously desirable if they have just the resource you are looking for, can be a much trickier undertaking.

FOUR STRATEGIES, FOUR CULTURES

Just as we identified four corporate strategies for innovation, we have identified four basic strategies for small-company growth, using the internal/external axis plus a small/large axis. Internally oriented small companies rely on internal resources to complete the value chain and achieve profitability. Rather than licensing out a product or arranging manufacturing or distribution deals with other companies, they aim for full integration, from idea to sale. Externally oriented start-ups use a networking strategy, relying on a range of partners to help get from one end of the value chain to the other.

The small/large axis distinguishes between those companies that hope to grow as big as possible as quickly as possible—measured by size of work force and physical plant as well as sales and earnings—and those that plan to stay relatively small, with employees numbering in the tens or hundreds rather than in the thousands. All entrepreneurs hope to make money and to have hugely profitable businesses. But profits and size don't necessarily grow in tandem, and the downsizing strategies of some of the largest corporations show that the two can be inversely related.

Tables 4.1 and 4.2 illustrate the four choices and strategies. In Table 4.1, we have characterized companies in terms of animals of different sizes with different characteristics:

o Beavers (internal, small generalists)
o Bears (internal, large generalists)

TABLE 4.1: What Animal Am I? Four Choices

	Internal	*External*
Small	Beaver	Monkey
Large	Bear	Kangaroo

TABLE 4.2: What Animal Am I? Four Strategies

	Self-Sufficient	*Networker*
Small	Beaver Growth by hard work and accretion	Monkey Growth by network and linkages
Large	Bear Growth by rapid, full-service expansion	Kangaroo Growth by leaps and bounds

o Monkeys (external, small specialists)
o Kangaroos (external, large networkers)

Some start-up companies develop the full value chain themselves; we think of these self-sufficient types as value chain generalists. Others rely on partnering with others to help them complete the chain; they are value chain specialists or networkers (see Table 4.2).

We chose beavers to represent small generalists because of their relatively small size and their strategy of building their lodges and dams by diligent hard work. Bears, the largest terrestrial omnivores, seemed a good symbol for the large generalists. Monkeys are small, clever animals who move quickly and rely on an elaborate social system for survival—reminding us of entrepreneurs who rely as much on their wits and networking ability as they do on sustained hard work. Kangaroos are large animals that cover lots of ground in great leaps and bounds. An infant kangaroo travels with great speed, too, secure in its mother's pouch. Unlike bears, who establish and defend a large but well-defined territory, kangaroos are more migratory, traveling long distances to wherever the forage is best.

INTERNAL GROWTH OPTIONS: THE VALUE CHAIN GENERALISTS

The traditional model for companies that came of age in the 1950s, 1960s, and 1970s was internal. Just as large companies tended to rely on internal strategies, small companies grew by completing the whole value chain themselves. When the two joined forces, the model was typically merger, not partnership. Relationships with large companies were either directly competitive or looked more like "master-slave," with small firms becoming captive suppliers, for example, of large ones. Those companies that did beat the odds and grew into large corporations typically did so using internal strategies.

The two types of companies that employ primarily internal growth strategies are beavers and bears. Of the thousands of companies throughout the United States, beavers are the most common. These are the small stores and cottage industries throughout our communities, plus service businesses like small accounting firms, hairdressers, and law firms with a handful of lawyers and administrative staff.

But bears are the companies we hear about the most. These are the fast-growth, full-service companies that develop capabilities in all phases of the value chain. Like bears, who are born tiny and quickly put on weight to become the largest terrestrial omnivores, these companies grow fast and end up with large territories. What the two models share is an emphasis on self-sufficiency and integration from one end of the value chain to the other.

Beavers: Growth by Hard Work and Accretion

Not all companies need to grow into large corporations for the entrepreneur and/or the company to be considered a success. Some people who strike out on their own are content to earn as much as they made in a previous corporate job. Others want to be their own boss, and they don't want to supervise a whole hierarchy of employees; that's what they left a large corporation to escape. Those who want to start a company and remain relatively small, exploit a niche market or territory, and who are not afraid to work hard to keep their business profitable remind us of beavers, whose mission in life is to build a den and keep it provisioned.

Beaver-type companies are typically integrated generalists that manage a product or service through all phases of the value chain. An entrepreneur can do this on a small scale if he or she deliberately wants to remain small or if fast growth is not an issue. An entrepreneur we know in New Mexico selectively breeds and raises her own sheep; shears, cards, and spins the wool; experiments with different ways of dyeing the yarn; weaves clothes; and sells them in a storefront room of her home. Her company is an example of a value-chain generalist that is involved in research, design, development, manufacturing, sales, and distribution on a very small scale. As business flourishes, she may provide employment to other family members and neighbors. However, capturing huge market shares, developing a cadre of salesmen and women, and opening branches in other states are simply not issues for this entrepreneur. The culture in this and similar companies is appropriate to a small, self-contained enterprise.

Entrepreneurial beavers typically develop a full-service company but sell their products or services only to customers in a prescribed area. They are very internally oriented, looking outward not for partners but for customers. Such companies may be quite profitable early in their lives. They tend to grow slowly, as their founders add new products to maintain sales and gradually add new customers. New growth and expansion come through expanding the product line and the local customer base, and through marginal expansion of the territory, often to include adjoining regions or states. Like beavers who create their own environment and invest heavily in the dam and lodges they build, the growth of these companies is incremental and gradual. Their territories are clearly defined.

Beaver companies often lack professional management and operate not according to a business plan and explicit policies but idiosyncratically, adhering to unwritten norms that reflect the personality of the founding father or mother. Their way of doing business often checks their growth beyond a certain size. The founder, for example, may resist attempts by subordinates to standardize procedures, develop clearer job definitions, and, in general, to rationalize operations. If the company has a board of directors, it may be made up largely of the founder's family members and subordinates, who may be reluctant to cross swords with the founder.

Many founders of beaver-model companies seek a corporate suitor only when they feel the time has come to cash in their investment by selling the company. Start-ups that follow the generalist, full-value-chain model are more apt to think of a bank than a corporate partner as a source of operating capital. Although the greatest challenge may be starting and growing the company to adolescence, if the plan is eventually to sell a controlling interest in a company in order to realize profits, the founder might want to start identifying possible corporate buyers sooner rather than later. As one successful entrepreneur noted, "We identified Du Pont, then spent the next three years making sure key people in Du Pont became aware of our product, saw what a competitive advantage we could provide them, and began to think that they couldn't live without us."

Early access to financing via corporate equity investments could also be combined with a strategy to sell off the company at a later date to one or more partners. The founder shifts away from the sell product strategy as a way of generating income to the sell out strategy as a way of cashing in the equity he or she has built up in the company.

Large companies that value integration may find beavers good prospects for M&A if these companies have an inherently attractive product line, customer base, or technology that fits well with the buyer's core business. Although the entrepreneurial resources are apt to evaporate with the acquisition when the founder and other top personnel retire, the product, customer base, or technology will remain.

Some beaver companies become bears when they switch from one growth strategy to another. The beaver may switch from the small internal model to the large internal model, transforming itself to a bear.

Mrs. Fields Cookies is an example of a full-service company that started as a beaver and has shifted to a bear-model pattern of growth. What started as a small company that sold cookies through manufacturing (baking) and retail sales outlets is now a corporation that encompasses all aspects of the value chain. Mrs. Fields started out in her own kitchen—the food industry version of Hewlett and Packard's garage. Now Mrs. Fields Cookies is a sizable corporation, fully computerized, with facilities throughout the nation. When she started her company, Mrs. Fields did not necessarily envision this future. The momentum of her success and the ability of the firm to develop economies of scale transformed Mrs. Fields Cookies from a modest baking venture to a substantial corporation.

Bears: Growth by Rapid, Full-Service Expansion

Bears follow the fully integrated growth pattern that was typical of companies that grew up in the 1960s and 1970s: they develop products, hire sales staff, and conquer new territory. Like solitary bears, they single-handedly define and defend a territory and have as their mission in life eating as much as possible, expanding and protecting their huge territories, and growing bigger and bigger. IBM matches the bear model: It grew quickly, added products and extended its territory, and now has a global reach.

Often these entrepreneurs intended for their companies to become large corporations as quickly as possible: From the beginning, the company was a "baby" large corporation. IBM, for instance, was once a small company, but Tom Watson always envisioned that it would become a major corporation. From the beginning, he developed policies, procedures, and operating principles that were suitable for a large corporation rather than a small company. Although he didn't use our terminology, Watson knew his company was a baby bear and mapped out his growth strategy accordingly.

Dell Computer is a more recent example of the birth and rapid growth of a bear. The kind of explosive growth Dell Computer has achieved is usually the result of a radically new technology. But Dell's innovations have been primarily in marketing and customer service, and the emphasis on direct customer contact extends from one end of the value chain to the other.

At Phase I (research, design, and development), Dell Computer involves end users directly through customer-contract R&D. At Phase II (manufacturing), the company works closely with customers to custom build machines to client specifications. Phase III (marketing and distribution) is handled primarily by direct telephone contact with clients. Eighty percent of the sales are by telephone. Service requests are handled via a process the company calls *telediagnostics*. The company's telephone work is highly centralized, and employees in this unit have expertise in products, networking, operating systems, and applications software.

Like many new firms, Dell Computer was founded with no seed or venture capital. Its growth pattern of full integration, rapid change in size, and expansion by adding products and entering new territories is characteristic of a successful bear. Dell had 39 employees at the end of 1984, its first year. In 1985, it introduced two products, the PC Limited turbo and the PC Limited 286-8, and grew to 133 employees. In 1986, it introduced two more products and grew to 280 employees.

The next three years were focused on entering new markets by tapping new kinds of customers and expanding geographically. In 1987, the company went international, opening an office in the United Kingdom, and began offering on-site, next-day service, targeting commercial accounts. It grew to 500 employees. In 1988, the same year Dell Computer went public, it opened subsidiaries in Canada and West Germany. Shortly after the Berlin wall came down, it offered its services in East Germany from its West German office. Company employment reached 1,000.

By 1990, Dell had opened subsidiaries in France, Italy, and Sweden and made another big expansion in product lines as ten new PCs were announced. The company employed 1,700 people, of which only 150 were in manufacturing. Indeed, manufacturing represented less than one-tenth of one percent of the total cost of the machines, a figure that has helped explode the myth that innovation in the computer industry is dependent on innovation in technology and manufacturing.

Michael Dell behaved like a traditional bear-model entrepreneur in the way he started his company and launched its early growth. However, he also established collaborative agreements that facilitated early international expansion, arranging key partnerships with Xerox and, in Europe, Bell Atlantic. In the future, Dell plans to announce an additional key relationship with EDS.

These partnerships show Dell's willingness to use external strategies to achieve rapid growth, but networking is not the core strategy for Dell. Instead, these partnerships are a means to an end: becoming a large, fully integrated major corporation. Large corporations may find that partnering with bears like Dell often serves the same purposes as partnering with other large companies, enabling them to complete the value chain but not necessarily access entrepreneurial resources.

Small-company entrepreneurs with large corporate visions should consider strategic partnerships as one tool in their rapid expansion. They most likely will not be looking for long-term equity investments but for more transactional exchanges. Once their adolescent growth spurt levels off, they will also face the large-corporation problems of maintaining speed and flexibility in getting new products to market. They will need to meet the innovation imperative facing all large corporations when they have become the next IBM.

Dell Computer, for example, relies on close personal contact and direct service for its success, and these elements are more characteristic of small companies than large. When asked how he will preserve this level of contact as the company grows, Dell responded: "The way we do that is to set up direct client teams of five to seven people. We keep the teams small so they can exercise their own entrepreneurial spirit."[3] Clearly, what Dell has in mind is an intrapreneurial strategy. Other baby bears should think ahead about how they will keep their entrepreneurial edge after they weather the growing pains of adolescence.

EXTERNAL SPECIALISTS: GROWTH BY NETWORK AND ALLIANCE

Small companies who specialize at one point on the value chain—custom R&D firms, for example—know that they cannot grow unless they link with large corporations. Like the clever, quick-moving, and sociable monkey, they use networks, develop linkages, and complete the value chain by forming alliances with other corporations. Since they rely on speed and innovation for their success, growing too large may undermine the qualities they rely on to stay profitable and competitive.

Companies with "hard" products like computers may decide to focus on development and manufacturing but rely on others for market access. Like bears, their goal is to grow quickly, but instead of covering all the bases, they plan to develop a large market share by relying on partners to help them complete the value chain from idea to final sale. We think of these companies as kangaroos, able to travel by leaps and bounds over large territories and stages of development through their alliances with large corporations and other small companies.

A bear-model company may expand territory internationally by developing a foreign sales staff and setting up outlets in new countries. A kangaroo-model company is more apt to access a new market in one bound, by linking with another company that has distribution networks already in place.

Entrepreneurial partnership, an external growth strategy typical of the monkey and kangaroo models, is the core business of the first and the core growth strategy of the second.

Monkeys: Growth by Network and Linkage

While beaver companies often sell to a niche market defined either by a narrow band of customers or a small regional territory, monkey-model companies have a different kind of niche—they specialize at one or two points along the value chain and market their services or product to large companies that need help with that link. A small company with a proprietary technology, such as Gateway Technologies, can form alliances with large corporate partners to manufacture, market, and sell products made by incorporating the new technology. The entrepreneurs at Gateway have consciously chosen not to develop a full-service company but to specialize in the linkage between Phases I and II on the value chain. Gateway executives don't want to head up a huge corporation; they do want their company to be very profitable. By brokering a promising technology with broad application, they plan to remain a small company while racking up big profits.

RELA, the Phase II specialist mentioned in Chapter 2, is a high-tech manufacturing company that designs and manufactures products under contract for other companies. RELA specializes in medical and automotive devices and hires mainly engineers and technicians. It does no research and does not market any of the products that it manufactures. Its marketing activities are focused on marketing its manufacturing services to large corporations. This company exists by virtue of its relation to others. Custom innovation in partnership with large companies is not just a way of bringing in some extra cash; it is the whole business of the firm. The monkey company's environment is not the self-contained ecosystem of the beaver pond but a network of relations in which it provides a key link from one phase to another.

Small import-export companies focus exclusively on the three stages of Phase III of the value chain—marketing, sales, and distribution. They have no R&D and no manufacturing capabilities, but they try to locate markets, distribution channels, and opportunities to sell products to new markets. Some companies might even focus on a single stage within Phase III. One very successful entrepreneur in Boston has developed an extremely profitable company whose only service is insuring the timely arrival of perishable vegetables from the West coast to the East.

Like monkeys, who are quick, smart, gregarious, active, and sociable, these small entrepreneurs depend for success on their inventiveness, their ability to move quickly and adapt, and their networking skills. Rather than trying to do it all, they market their distinctive capabilities in one phase of the value chain. They may not grow large in terms of employees or square feet of office space occupied, but they all expect to be very profitable. In fact, growing too large in the first sense may actually shrink what matters most in the long run—the size of their profits.

Dan Bricklin, creator of Visicalc and founder of Software Garden, which developed and marketed the demo program, planned from the start to make his second company a monkey. He told *Inc.* magazine that he wanted to keep the Software Garden as lean as possible and saw many benefits to this strategy—flexibility, adaptability, and a closer connection to the market. With a "lean and mean" company structure, says Bricklin, "I make midcourse corrections all the time. I've had my heart set on certain things about a product and then done total about-faces based on arguments from three or four test sites." Midcourse corrections are difficult for a large corporation that moves with all the weight and momentum of a grizzly bear, but Bricklin notes that "I've been able to turn the whole organization around because we were just two or three people. I don't know how I'd do that in a bigger company."[4]

For a monkey-model company, success isn't measured by size. It might instead be measured by Bricklin's ambition to see "how little I could get away with." Bricklin admired outfits like Funk Software in Cambridge, England. "I visited [Paul Funk's] place," says Bricklin, "and I was amazed. He had about six people at the time, and his company was doing a few million dollars in sales."

Another Cambridge-area company that has chosen a monkey strategy of growth is TTP, which developed the "clic" saber saw for Bosch. Gerald Avidson, president of TTP, describes the company as a collection of engineers who prefer "to work cooperatively, to stay relatively small and focused." The preference for staying small and networking mark TTP as a classic monkey-model company.

His peers call Avidson a "networking" entrepreneur. His style is to network to many others and give them credit for the work his company does. He likes to remain low-key and stay in the background: "Too much administration gets in the way of good technological research."

TTP works with large clients to perform contract R&D. Its engineers and other professionals have technical competencies in electrical, mechanical, chemical, and other fields, and they are skilled in strategy, innovation, creation, and automation. They perform custom innovation and can develop a range of products in many different fields.

Corporate executives who might otherwise set up a skunk works for custom innovation but are attracted to external strategies might consider using a partner like TTP as an "external skunk works." What TTP offers is the ability to innovate quickly and on demand, and thereby compress the value chain for its customers. It has no capability to manufacture and sell its own products, so it doesn't pose any threat as a competitor. It could be used as a partner in outmaneuvering competitors who are unwilling to employ an external strategy for innovation.

Kangaroos: Growing by Leaps and Bounds

The kangaroo model is appropriate for an entrepreneur who wants to start a baby company and grow it by leaps and bounds, but who doesn't want to develop all phases of the value chain. Such companies typically develop one or two phases of the value chain and link up with a large corporation—or several large corporations—to complete the value chain. Like the baby kangaroo who rides thousands of miles while maturing in its mother's pouch, these companies are on the move from the start, depending on others for their speed in covering lots of ground, fast.

Few entrepreneurs, and few companies, are good at everything; all have areas where they excel and areas where they need help. Rather than sweating through developing all stages of the value chain, some entrepreneurs focus their attention on the part they do best and "partner out" the aspects that interest them less. For example, a company involved in research, development, and manufacturing might form alliances with other companies to market and distribute a product. NeXT, which researched and manufactured its new computers, linked with Canon to provide markets in the Pacific Rim and with Businessland to gain access to more of the U.S. market. Another example is Hermann Hauser's Active Book Company (described in detail in Chapter 8), which has relied from the start on the large Italian firm Olivetti for seed capital, marketing, and distribution.

The former CEO of a small ceramics company, Ceramics Processing Systems, described how the firm assessed its options when planning its growth path.[5] First came a consideration of

94

the current situation in fine ceramics, where the market is dominated by large companies. In Japan, the packaging business was completely dominated by Kyocera Kyoto Ceramics, whose market share ranged from 90 to 95 percent in some segments to a low of 50 or 60 percent in others. MTK, a division of MTK Spark Plug, the world's largest spark plug manufacturer, ranked number two in electronic ceramics but probably first in engine components. The rest of the field was crowded with other big competitors.

As the CEO saw it,

> We had a choice. We could pick a couple of niches and become a $10–25 million company. Or we could try to leverage our technology on the backs of the big American and European and Japanese corporations who have an interest in particular markets . . . use their financial resources and market access to take the technology into many more markets than we would have the resources to do.

In our terms, what the company was considering was the choice between an internal beaver strategy (pick a couple of niches and become a $10–25 million company) and an external kangaroo strategy (leverage our technology). Kangaroos and monkeys both are in the leveraging business, leveraging their talents in some parts of the value chain in order to complete it profitably.

The kangaroo strategy, which employs entrepreneurial partnerships as the chief means of growth, was the one that Ceramics Processing chose. Once it had developed the capability to make and market substrates, the company negotiated partnerships with Alcoa, Celense, Cabot Corporation, and others. Again, the CEO:

> [With] each one of them, we've taken an equity investment from them and have reached agreements to use some of their money to help fund the application of our technology to specific end-use products. And then at the end of that, we'll establish joint ventures with them to take the technology into these industry applications. Then we use the equity that they give us to build our own businesses . . . this way, by leveraging our technology off of their financial

and market resources, we can play in a business that is really dominated by the giants.

In a business "dominated by giants," the kangaroo strategy makes a good deal more sense than trying to grow a baby bear from infancy.

In the computer industry, which has plenty of giants and small fry both, the kangaroo strategy makes sense for other reasons. Steve Jobs, founder of Apple and now NeXT, understands well how to leverage ideas into money in this field by using entrepreneurial partnerships. As *Fortune* writer Brenton Schlender sees it, "The tale of how Jobs joined forces with IBM, his old nemesis, provides a fascinating inside glimpse of how ... Steve Jobs is blending sharp technology and shrewd politicking to make his tiny startup company a well-financed force to be reckoned with."[6]

The tale provides a fascinating story of an infant kangaroo at work, setting up the multiple partnerships that will position the company to bound into the Inc. 500. The NeXT strategy is to leverage innovative technology to secure financing, distribution, and front-end software that will run on the new machines.

After leaving Apple in 1985, Jobs founded NeXT to develop a new computer that would be distinct from IBM and Macintosh models. He first planned to build "scholarly workstations" for universities, but the level of interest in the NeXT computer persuaded him to focus on developing a major general-purpose desktop computer aimed chiefly at the business market. Soon IBM became interested in the NeXT computer.

Lawyers for IBM and NeXT began negotiating in early 1988, more than nine months before Jobs's new machine was ready. In April, Jobs and IBM officials met in Dallas for a final bargaining session and closed the deal. IBM obtained the right to evaluate the software being developed to run on NeXT, and the partners agreed on royalty rates and contingency payments if IBM decided to offer the software on its workstations.

After hearing that IBM had licensed NeXTstep, the software layer that sits between the operating program and the applications programs, the CEO of Businessland, a computer distributor that serves large corporations, called Jobs and asked to become the exclusive U.S. distributor. This was the second partnership. Businessland agreed to sell $100 million of NeXT computers the first year of general distribution. Jobs next persuaded Japan's Canon, Inc., to handle distribution in Asia and to invest $100 million in the company.

The distribution and financing were now in place. NeXT could complete most aspects of Phases I and II of the value chain (developing and manufacturing the hardware in a new plant in Fremont, California), but it had linked up with Businessland and Canon for Phase III (marketing, sales, and distribution) within the United States and Asia.

However, the value chain for NeXT was not yet complete. Jobs had already learned that the success of any new computer is highly dependent on the amount of software available to run on it. So Jobs went to work coaxing and persuading at least 70 software companies to write software for NeXT, including such firms as Lotus and Informix. By developing the hardware and the operating system software, Jobs had completed much of the research, development, and design associated with Phase I on the value chain. Yet the NeXT computer could not be successful if software vendors did not write and introduce applications programs that would run on the NeXT computer—another piece of Phase I.

The arrangement with IBM was especially important for the software campaign because it "legitimized" the NeXT computer and its NeXTstep software. Although IBM had not promised to use NeXTstep, once IBM said it was "considering" offering the NeXTstep operating system on its new workstations, software companies became more willing to risk writing unique applications of software to interface with it. Since any software written for the IBM machines could also be used with the NeXT computer, companies buying NeXT hardware could be assured that there would be a number of software programs ready to run on that computer.

Entrepreneurs who plan a kangaroo growth strategy need to be well connected in the corporate world. Often the founders of these companies recently worked for large corporations and understand well the culture and needs of their large-company counterparts. Companies whose founding parents came instead out of academia might want to hire a well-connected top manager who can help set up the critical partnerships. Many young biotechnology companies have done this, bringing in professional management to complement the research strengths of their scientist founders.

Large-company executives looking for partners will find kangaroo-model companies ideal, for their commitment to partnership is central to their entire business. If there are several prospects to choose from, a further level of analysis would be to ask whether the small company is fundamentally committed to an external strategy. A kangaroo growth strategy can also be a temporary tactic for entrepreneurs who would rather be fully integrated bears but are finding this route too difficult.

To illustrate the difference, we turn to the roundtable discussions published in Ernst & Young's *Biotechnology 91* report.[7] In biotechnology, external strategies are the norm, with small firms having an average of three partnerships. The commitment to external strategies for growth varies widely, however, as illustrated by the contrasting comments of two CEOs, both of whom head companies with multiple partnerships:

Henri Termeer, CEO, Genzyme Corporation:

> The vision, and the goal, is the creation of a major, vertically integrated, health-care products company. ... Companies like Genzyme will grow not only through internal development and acquiring other technology companies, but also by acquiring pieces of the large companies.

Edward Penhoet, CEO, Chiron Corporation:

Chiron is trying to maintain a group of corporate partnerships where both companies work as collaborators, with no reason to try to manage each other's business in any significant way. A lot of other companies' partnerships have come and gone, but almost all of ours have lasted and seem to be working. We probably are the company that has been most committed to corporate partnering as a fundamental commercial strategy.

It is clear that Genzyme's core preference is for internal strategies, with an emphasis on integration and acquisition. Chiron, by contrast, is a dyed-in-the-fur kangaroo. Penhoet is well aware of this distinction himself, as he reveals in comparing Chiron with other biotechnology companies: "Many companies view corporate partnerships as a necessary evil to bridge the gap from start-up to the time they are fully independent. From the beginning, we viewed corporate partnerships as a productive way of doing business."

If you are a corporate executive seeking long-term entrepreneurial partnerships, a company with Chiron's philosophy would be a better choice than a company like Genzyme, which seems to view alliances as a temporary tool.

CONCLUDING THOUGHTS

What we have demonstrated, in this chapter, is that the choices for entrepreneurs are more varied than the media hoopla might suggest. Much of the general public seems to believe that small companies must grow large in order to be considered successful and to enhance profitability. But a company that starts small and stays small is not necessarily a failure or stagnant. A monkey-sized bear is indeed a stunted animal. But a bear-sized monkey is equally ill-equipped for success. As Bricklin of Software Garden commented:

> You really have to decide why you're in business. . . . Are you there because you want to grow the company, because you like the

growth experience? Are you building a company because you want it to last forever? Are you there to make money? Or are you there to have a certain lifestyle and get the most out of your product? Those aren't necessarily the same things.[8]

An internally oriented company might be successful and profitable in its own right, like many family-owned and run businesses, without growing into a major player. Sweden has many examples of these profitable family-based businesses. As described in Chapter 9, it also has technology brokers who specialize in buying up beavers and transforming them into bears.

Another path for entrepreneurs who would like to maximize profits without getting overwhelmed with employees and corporate structures is the externally oriented monkey model. These entrepreneurs may limit the focus of their company to one phase or stage of the value chain. They will need to define their market niche and exploit it through alliances with large corporate partners.

Some entrepreneurs want to have it both ways. They may have a talent for starting fast-growth companies but dislike large company settings. When the company gets big, they get restless or bored. For them, the real fun is in starting baby bear or kangaroo companies, getting them to a certain stage, then selling them to someone else to grow them into their full size. If that is the case, the best approach may be to delay financial gratification and manage the company so that its products and financial condition will be attractive to large corporations that are looking to gain new products and/or market share through an acquisitions strategy.

Large corporations intent on a merger and acquisition strategy will find it more satisfactory to acquire baby bear-type companies with aspirations, policies, and procedures that will facilitate their growing big quickly. Monkey-type companies are probably far less interested in being acquired, unless the acquiring company is explicitly committed to maintaining the integrity and autonomy of the small company. These companies rely on their networking skill for their success. A company's products and territories can be acquired, but networks—especially those that thrive on small-company agility and adaptability—are a more elusive quantity.

However, monkey and kangaroo-model companies are precisely the right partners for large corporations that are trying to speed innovation through entrepreneurial partnership. Because these externally oriented value chain specialists have built their companies through networking, they are also apt to be more sophisticated in partnering than beavers and bears.

Executives in companies both large and small who are committed to entrepreneurial partnerships need to be aware of the pitfalls of these alliances, and should follow good partnership principles to avoid some common disappointments. This kind of practical advice is the focus of Chapters 5 and 6.

NOTES

1. In 1990, during a speech given to the National Business Incubation Association, David Birch said that the data, when studied over time and by location, show that small business creates 40 to 100 percent of new jobs; firms with 20 or fewer employees add about two-thirds of the new jobs. Nor is this trend limited to the United States. Britain's treasury reports that between 1982 and 1984, the self-employed and firms employing fewer than 20 people created about 1 million new jobs, more than offsetting some 750,000 job losses in large firms.
2. G. Steven Burrill and Kenneth B. Lee, Jr., *Biotech 91: A Changing Environment* (San Francisco: Ernst & Young, 1990), p. 131.
3. Michael Dell, "Business Opportunities in Today's Eastern Europe" (Presentation delivered at the Fifth International Technical Innovation and Entrepreneurship Symposium: East-West Opportunities, Linz, Austria, 2–5 September 1990). Material also drawn from Michael Dell, personal interview, September 1990.
4. Bricklin, Dan, "My Company, My Self," *Inc.*, July 1990, pp. 35–44.

5. Clayton Christensen, personal interview, December 1986. Christensen is the former president of Ceramics Processing Systems, Inc.
6. Brenton R. Schlender, "How Steve Jobs Linked Up with IBM," *Fortune*, 9 Oct. 1989, pp. 48–61.
7. Burrill and Lee, pp. 115–18.
8. Bricklin, Dan, "My Company, My Self," p. 36.

PART TWO

Principles and Practices of Entrepreneurial Partnerships

CHAPTER FIVE

Making Partnerships Work: Principles and Practices for Success

By now you should have a good understanding of which types of companies, both large and small, are apt to make good partners. In this chapter we discuss 12 principles that can help a company find the right partners, create good contracts, and manage partnerships successfully. Our research suggests that the most successful large-small partnerships have, consciously or not, applied these principles. While the principles do not address every aspect of partnering and cannot guarantee success, companies that take them to heart will greatly improve the odds of establishing and maintaining mutually profitable satisfying partnerships.

The primary focus is on a long-term strategy of multiple partnerships, for example, the strategy being followed by large companies such as IBM or small ones like Gateway Technologies. Companies with a strong external orientation should have multiple partners and will likely be engaged in searching for partners and managing entrepreneurial partnerships on a continuous basis.

We also provide tips concerning short-term transactional arrangements such as those typified by the TTP-Bosch story.

The ways in which these guidelines are implemented often differ for large corporations and small entrepreneurial companies. Where this is so, we discuss the issues from these different perspectives, separately.

Large externally oriented corporations will already have some experience with partnerships, whether this has been gained through a history of spin-offs, joint ventures, or transactional arrangements with other large companies. Many of the guidelines here will be useful for all of these relationships. Companies whose experience is primarily with large-large ventures will find that partnering with small companies poses somewhat different challenges, and operating procedures that work well in dealing with large partners may well need some adjustment when working with small ones.

Small entrepreneurial companies ready for partnering will have completed the basic tasks of forming a viable start-up. They will have a well-conceived business plan, a functioning accounting system, and legal as well as business advisors. If not, they are probably not ready for partnership yet. As one banker told us: "The three most important things we consider when deciding whether to make a loan for real estate are location, location, location. The three most important things we look at when deciding whether to loan money to a start-up company are management, management, and management."

If start-ups don't have the management basics in place, they need to address this before approaching potential partners. An incubator may be a good place to access the resources they need. Other sources of assistance may be the local Chamber of Commerce or Small Business Development Center.

TWELVE PRINCIPLES

Ultimately, all companies enter partnerships in the hopes of direct or indirect financial benefits. The hope may be for a direct equity investment or increased market share from sales of more innovative products. Alternately, risk sharing may be seen as a way to improve the bottom line by cutting costs. Small companies may hope for management help to improve marketing and financial planning. All partners expect to profit from their alliances. How both sides can achieve these benefits is the story of successful partnering. Our 12 guidelines for action are basic principles that make partnerships work. They fall into three categories, and each category has four principles (see Table 5.1).

FINDING A PARTNER

While flying back from one of our research interviews, we had occasion to discuss this book with a fellow passenger. Having

---

TABLE 5.1: Twelve Principles

I. Finding a Partner
1. Follow a stage-by-stage partnering strategy.
2. Put a motivated "networker" in charge of the search.
3. Develop a profile of the partners you seek.
4. Contact multiple candidates.

II. Creating a Contract
5. Focus on mutual benefits.
6. Start simple.
7. Set benchmarks.
8. Involve the lawyers—later.

III. Managing the Partnership
9. Emphasize the partnership mentality.
10. Develop a team of champions.
11. Communicate frequently.
12. Think long term, but deliver short-term success.

---

had considerable experience in both small and large businesses, he grasped a key issue at once. "In order to locate a partner, you've got to kiss a lot of frogs!" He's right. You've got to do a lot of kissing before one of your candidates turns into a prince. The experience of both small and large companies suggests that for every hundred frogs on your list, you should expect no more than five royal candidates, and you may find only one.

Most small firms, and many large ones, are rather clumsy in their attempts to find partners. Blind dates are one option, though not too promising. Mixers, dancing, and dating services are others. Finding the right partner is at least half the challenge for most companies. The four principles of finding compatible mates are:

1. Follow a stage-by-stage partnering strategy.
2. Put a motivated "networker" in charge of the search.
3. Develop a profile of the partners you seek.
4. Contact multiple candidates.

1. Follow a Stage-by-Stage Partnering Strategy

Very few companies have thought through and articulated their strategy for strategic alliances in general, and entrepreneurial partnerships in particular. Corning has a long and successful history of joint ventures. But when it comes to working with small companies, one Corning executive admitted: "I never thought of partnering with the small guys. I assumed that all they wanted was money." Many entrepreneurs don't even consider partnering when developing their business plans, but focus instead on products or services, sales targets, and capital requirements.

Both small and large firms need to establish and follow a stage-by-stage partnering strategy that fits the larger goals and vision of the company. The strategy needs to be clearly understood and accepted by company employees, and the stages need to be established within a realistic time frame.

The Vision Statement. A good way to spread the word and get employees on board is to develop a vision statement that communicates how partnering fits the long-term plan for the company. Vision statements are important signals to employees who are trying to relate their career development to emerging challenges and opportunities. They alert managers and other employees to changes in the corporation's mission, goals, and strategies as well as probable changes in internal functions and organizational relationships. Current incentive and reward structures may also need to be reviewed and changed so that key managers will have clear incentives for making sure partnerships work. Announce incentives and rewards for employees who contribute to the success of the strategy, then work with senior managers and the human resources department to identify and remove institutional barriers to "extrapreneurial" relationships.

For a small company of five or ten employees, the function of the vision statement may be better served by a formal dialogue among staff. The discussion can help the company reach a consensus about partnering, and employees will begin to internalize the partnership strategy and its relation to the company's short- and long-term goals. If the company is somewhat larger, a clear written statement to all employees is one way to help prevent misconceptions.

One small software development and consulting company in Cambridge, Massachusetts, for example, had a track record of success. When it tried to expand its offerings to including desktop software decision tools, it found it needed more capital. The company hired software developers who were extremely good producers, but the owner and his two associates could not market the service fast enough. The incoming contracts could not cover the monthly "burn rate."

The president put together a list of options. Bank loans were out, wealthy individuals and venture capital seemed a possibility, but the most likely seemed to be a corporate partner—particularly a corporation who was already a satisfied client.

The first challenge the small company president had was to "manage the mood" of the current employees. Some sensed that the drive to raise capital meant something was wrong with the company; they wondered if they should dust off their résumés. Others, who saw it as an opportunity for growth, began to get unrealistic expectations. The vision statement and an explanation of the rationale for partnering can help prevent either misconception.

Timing. The business strategy that translates a partnership vision into action should explicitly address at least the three stages delineated here: finding a partner, creating a contract, and managing the partnership. The first stage should follow principles 2, 3, and 4 to ensure a well-targeted search. Focusing on the many steps involved helps those conducting the search to be realistic about the time involved in a long-term partnering strategy. In our private lives, different stages in a partnership or marriage occupy months, even years. It is not that different with business partnerships. One major lesson we've learned is that it takes longer than you think to find the right partner. Estimate how long you think it will take and then double it. If you think it will take you a year, think two. If you think it will be a few months, you're letting hope substitute for good management judgments.

Of course, the process can be greatly accelerated if a large company is looking for a monkey-type company that specializes in one phase of the value chain. Value chain specialists whose primary business is partnering actively advertise their services to potential customers and are typically skilled in establishing relationships. However, these types of partnerships tend to be more transactional than developmental. True entrepreneurial partnerships take time to develop.

The founder of the Cambridge software company skipped the vision statement and the partner profile, and saw no need to develop a long list of potential candidates. He already knew of an ideal corporate partner—ideal not because it fit the profile, but because he had a personal relationship with the large-company president. When he called the CEO, however, he got a quick lesson in timing.

The CEO's secretary answered the call. "Oh, Mr. Smith is on a business trip in Europe, which he is extending to a vacation. He won't be back for six weeks." Trying to get on a CEO's calendar when he's been out for six weeks is nearly impossible. Our small-company founder was crestfallen when he realized it would be months before he could even open the conversation to determine interest, much less sign contracts and secure financial assistance from a partner. He hadn't planned for a lengthy search and hadn't developed and screened a list of potential partners. Rather than moving on to the next phone call, he found himself almost back to ground zero.

2. Put a Motivated "Networker" in Charge of the Search

From a corporate perspective, the issue is whether to use your own employees to conduct the search or to contract with an outside individual or consulting firm. There are a variety of pros and cons to having insiders versus outsiders as your search specialists. Small firms face the same choice but are more constrained by cost and by the multiple roles already filled by key personnel such as the founder and vice presidents. Hence they face a somewhat different set of problems.

Corporate Perspective

Insiders as Search Specialists. Some of the corporations we interviewed have given a manager in the R&D lab or the director of the university relations program the responsibility of searching for and identifying sources of new technologies. If the corporation is looking for innovations in several technology areas, it may be expensive and time-consuming to develop an internal scanning mechanism. But an internal approach may be the appropriate way to go if the firm has a very well defined technology focus. If this route is chosen, corporations should put a senior manager in charge of the scanning process. One senior executive at Monsanto described some of the requirements of the job: "We need to be more like the Japanese: to travel more and visit companies in the United States and other countries. We need to keep our eyes open, ask questions, and learn from others rather than think we know it all."

In order for this process to be productive, the person who is looking, visiting, listening, and learning must be privy to the corporate strategy in order to know what technology and innovations will really fit corporate needs. Sometimes that person is the director of R&D. More often, it is someone else in the corporation with an even broader strategic perspective.

R&D directors, while very knowledgeable about the company's technology, can be problematic search specialists because of the motivation factor. Top management may assume that the director of R&D will be receptive to innovations developed outside the company, but that is often not the case. The comments of two former R&D directors, now retired, are typical.

> The CEO of our company [pharmaceuticals] sometimes asked me to look and see if some small companies wouldn't be good partners. If we had a real specific need and a small firm could fill it quicker than I could, I'd cut a deal. But as soon as we could catch up and do it in-house, I'd find a way to break the partnership because I wanted all the resources available to be used for our in-house research.

A retired R&D director of an American telecommunications company said the same thing in a different way.

It's unrealistic to think an R&D director will be interested in innovations developed outside the company. While I funded some R&D at selected universities, my job was to fight for resources, build and manage the research and development capability of the company, that is, develop and protect the company's corporate technology resource, not look for innovation outside the company.

As the person responsible for research and development, the director of R&D is naturally inclined to protect his or her turf and develop the corporation's internal R&D resource. The position is almost, by definition, internally oriented, so asking that person to pursue an external strategy is inherently contradictory.

For this reason, many companies with a long-term partnering strategy have created a new position, usually called director of business opportunities or director of strategic development, to support the strategy. This person searches for relevant technology and innovations developed outside the company, and may also look for entrepreneurs to develop shelf technology. Appointments to state or regional high-tech councils and technology incubator boards can provide excellent vantage points for spotting emerging technology in the local area.

Outsiders as Search Specialists. Instead of doing the scanning themselves, many firms have contracted with an external technology broker to keep them abreast of developments in their field, help locate technology and innovation that might be of interest, and find entrepreneurs interested in developing the company's shelf technology.

When choosing the technology broker, the corporation must locate a consulting firm with the specific expertise required. The firm should specialize in joint ventures or strategic partnerships, and its staff should have the skills and network of contacts needed to develop a strong list of candidate companies and/or technologies.

We know of one technology broker who signs up companies with similar or compatible technologies on a yearly basis, for a fixed fee. The principals in the firm spend two days per quarter at each company, reviewing the technology the company has developed as well as learning what new technology the company needs. The broker then serves as matchmaker and introduces companies with specified technologies to those that are looking for those technologies. The cost savings the companies experience in finding the developed technology is usually well worth the fee the broker charges.

A medical products manufacturer employed a consulting firm to query university researchers and practitioners in an effort to find new concepts, preferably products, that could be developed and marketed in the following year. In another case, a technology brokering firm was asked to find a buyer for some on-the-shelf technology the corporation had decided not to develop itself. In a third situation, a broker was asked to find a small company that had developed the specific technology needed by the major corporation to complete a technical process. The broker was to ascertain the terms and conditions under which the technology (and perhaps the company) could be acquired. In a fourth situation, a broker was asked to explore, with several companies, the possibility of developing a specific technology through a joint venture or some other type of alliance.

A company needs to decide whether it will be more advantageous to use its own management to do the search or to contract that activity to a third party.

Entrepreneurial Perspective

One issue that typically comes up in small companies is whether or not the company founder should head the search process for the corporate partner.

Externally oriented entrepreneurs must remember that finding the first set of partners is a critical move—much more crucial to the small company's success than it is for a large corporation. The collaboration a small company forms can make or break its business, so it is important to choose prospective partners carefully, wisely, and quickly, before the company runs out of capital. This puts pressure on the founder to be the one to conduct the search.

Small companies with scarce resources usually try to minimize outside consulting expenses. Fortunately, it is much easier to identify large corporations by using public information sources than it is for them to find small companies. Therefore, though it may be time-consuming to compile and then screen the list of suitable corporate partners, the biggest challenge is finding the right person to contact in those companies for a fair hearing, then tailoring the approach to match the corporate culture of each firm. This puts further pressure on the founder to be the one to conduct the search.

However, the founder may not be the best person to conduct a search. Often founders have too much at stake. They are motivated searchers without a doubt; the trouble is, they may be *too* motivated and end up conveying desperation rather than enthusiasm. One large-company executive told us: "I don't like dealing with small companies. I get the impression they're just looking for money." A more neutral go-between puts the search on a more objective basis.

Further, the founder may not have the time to conduct a search. His or her time may be better spent selling the company's product and employing someone else to conduct the search. There is a real opportunity cost if the founder spends time searching for and negotiating with partners rather than selling products or managing the company.

One solution is to form a board of advisors and ask them to help with the search and negotiation process. A retired executive or business school professor can be very useful and is sometimes willing to undertake this task and defer compensation. When an advisor makes initial contacts, the impression created by an objective third party is often more positive than the one created by a do-or-die founder.

Ideally, the search specialist should be someone with experience in both large and small business, someone who is familiar with large corporate culture and also understands the very different set of needs and pressures that plague small start-ups. If an outsider is used, take the time to educate that person thoroughly about the company's long-term goals, partnering strategy, and resources. The person needs to have a very solid understanding of how the company operates in order to determine which prospective partners will make a good match.

3. Develop a Profile of the Partners You Seek

If you are a small company seeking corporate partners, you may be prone to panic as you find yourself running out of capital and time. In your eagerness to stay afloat and close a deal, you may rush to sign a contract with any suitor who expresses interest, whether or not it fits your partner profile. Don't do it. If you haven't done your homework and checked out your options carefully, partnering with the wrong company could be more than a misstep; it could be a disaster. Your new "partner" might be eager for all the wrong reasons. One small company signed away marketing rights to a corporation that just sat on an innovative product. The company eventually realized that what its "partner" had really bought was exclusive rights to mothball products it saw as competition with its current business line.

Large companies can get taken, too. Investing in small companies that seem to have great ideas for new products but lack the "management, management, management" that bankers prize so highly can be a costly mistake. A start-up whose only proven talent is burning cash can burn its partner, too.

The partner profile helps ensure that you don't find yourself married to a suitor that wiser heads would have sent packing. The truly princely candidate will be a good match because its needs and yours will mesh in a win-win combination. Being willing isn't enough: A partner has to fit your strategy for innovation or growth. A value chain diagnosis can pinpoint weaknesses where you need some outside help; it can also highlight your company's competitive advantages, which can be used to your advantage during the negotiation process.

Corporate Perspective

Large firms that are losing ground or just barely keeping up with the pace of global innovation should look carefully at each link in their value chain for gaps and bottlenecks. Where is your corporation losing ground to the competition? Which of the three phases is weakest or strongest? Are the problems primarily in developing new products, in manufacturing new lines or products, or in selling and servicing existing products effectively? Any weaknesses are possible areas to consider for collaboration.

Many large companies find they have strengths in all three major phases, but that moving a product from one phase to another takes too long. They find it difficult to transfer technology internally. Sometimes it is difficult to get manufacturing, marketing, and other units to buy into a new concept from R&D. A key question is *why* manufacturing and marketing are balking. Perhaps the new product would require a major change in manufacturing procedures. Perhaps the market is too small or can't be reached with the company's existing distribution networks.

The "prince" to save the day might be a small company that specializes in custom manufacturing, like RELA. Or perhaps it is a company that reaches a niche market too small for the large company to serve cost-effectively. As the diagnosis proceeds, it will become clear what types of partners are needed, and a series of different partner profiles may emerge. Make note on each profile whether the relationship sought is short-term or long-term, and note any restrictions in terms of location or nationality of potential partners.

The IBM-NeXT arrangement could be a long-term partnership that could strengthen IBM's product line. IBM fits NeXT's need for a partner that would use NeXTstep software, hence create a market for software that would be written for NeXTstep. The Bosch-TTP deal was a transactional alliance that broke through a bottleneck at Bosch. Bosch needed a monkey-model partner with custom design and engineering skills, the time frame was short, and the need was urgent.

One medical products corporation needed at least two new products before the end of the year, since senior management had determined "we are not going to be able to produce anything that is marketable by the end of the year." Through a consulting firm that specializes in technology identification and assessment, the company was able to identify a class of products in which it was interested. In this case, the profile was focused on the kind of products needed—innovative, yet closely matched to existing business lines and able to be produced quickly.

A corporation that is looking for new ventures in which to invest takes a somewhat different approach. A senior executive from a large chemical company had experience in starting and operating chemical production plants. He borrowed a budgeting analogy from this previous activity to describe how he would evaluate the partnership profile. The analogy identified three types of projects: clearly profitable, highly desirable, and valuable to maintain operations.

Prospective partnerships were all measured against this grid. As the executive put it: "Show me the payout in hard numbers, and I'll fund it. Convince me it's highly desirable, though risky and intangible, and I'll consider it. Tell me it's valuable to maintain our operations, and I'll go to sleep." He felt that most entrepreneurial partnership proposals were in the second category—highly desirable—but to justify an investment, he had to find projects in the first category, clearly profitable, or transform second-category prospects to fit the bill.

An assessment of your corporate strengths will help you determine what your company has to offer. Are equity investments an option? Would the company be willing to guide another company's product through the regulatory maze and/or provide market access? Is promising technology sitting useless on the shelf? What partnership arrangements would be clearly profitable or at least highly desirable?

Entrepreneurial Perspective

Small firms need to focus on what kind of assistance they need. Where in the value chain does your start-up need the most help? Typically, small companies need help in marketing. They've got a good idea, perhaps a prototype, but don't know how to sell it. Small firms should also sketch out clearly what they have to offer a corporate partner, and brainstorm about what kinds of companies would be interested in them, their product, or their technology.

When developing the partner profile for Gateway Technologies, Ed Payne and his colleagues decided their technology should be of interest to companies that manufactured man-made fibers, textile fabrics, and developed consumer products. Armed with these three profiles, they used information in the local university's business school library to develop a list of 200 corporations that might be interested in thermally enhanced fibers: from large chemical companies to sportswear manufacturers and distributors, and everything in between. Each of the firms they selected had strengths in marketing. They didn't specify "external, autonomous" as the main criteria for a good partner, but that would be one way to describe their partner profile more precisely.

One way to conduct a background check is to skim recent articles about a company you are considering and make notes about the company's actions as well as the published remarks of top management. A business student at a local college or university could be used to collect relevant material about companies of interest. Alternately, some libraries will do custom research, for a fee. If you have a good network of contacts in the corporate world, you may be able to collect the same information through a series of phone calls.

What you are looking for is the orientation and direction of the company. The trajectory plotted by Kodak's recent history, for example, shows the company moving away from autonomy toward integration; IBM's actions, on the other hand, show sustained movement in the opposite direction. In ten years, the two might reverse themselves once again. For the time being, however, Kodak does not appear to be a good candidate for partnering unless your goal is to be acquired *and* you have a product that directly fits their core business. Corning, on the other hand, has a long, consistent history of spin-offs and joint ventures—evidence of an external orientation. The same is true of Perstorp in Sweden, if you seek a European partner. In Japan, Toray and Kubota have external partnering strategies. Fuji Xerox, by contrast, is internally focused with its New Venture Challenge Program, so it is unlikely to be as interested in partnering.

If you can't discern a clear direction in the company's recent history, published interviews can often convey whether the company values internal over external resources, or whether it prefers or emphasizes autonomy over integration. As the Genzyme and Chiron comparison in Chapter 4 illustrates, just a sentence or two can be very revealing about corporate values and preferences.

The director of an incubator can be an excellent source of information. Bob Calcaterra, director of the Boulder Technology Incubator, believes an important part of his job is connecting entrepreneurs with large companies in order to find appropriate partners. Since Bob used to work for Amoco, Monsanto, and Coors, he knows what the corporate executive and the entrepreneur need to make a match possible.

Sometimes the most likely large partners are not even in your industry. Lotus and Microsoft *might* be good partners for a small software company, but companies such as Arthur Andersen or Ernst and Young might also be interested. One of the big airlines might seem like a logical choice for a new electronic device, but a public utility electrical power company or one of the regional telephone companies may be possible partners, too.

One entrepreneur formed an advisory board to help him develop a profile. He put a man with extensive business contacts in large firms at the head of the board. Together, they developed a profile of the types of firms and names of specific companies the entrepreneur should contact:

> For example, I first thought of a Corning because of their history of joint ventures. Then Ford, because of their experience in quality management. Then I thought of one of the accounting firms, like Arthur Andersen or Ernst and Young. They have great distribution systems for my product. My advisor made me realize that what I really needed was help with distribution. Hence, accounting firms became the number-one priority of companies to contact.

4. Contact Multiple Candidates

Throughout the preceding discussion, we have said *partners*, not *partner*, to stress the importance of developing partnership arrangements with multiple companies. We've used marriage as a metaphor, but polygamy and polyandry should be the model, not lifelong monogamy. Kangaroos and bears don't mate with only one partner, and they don't mate for life, either. Neither should you, unless you are convinced the partnership will generate lifelong benefits. Even then (as we discuss in the next section), an exit strategy is recommended.

IBM has hundreds of partners, and its appetite for networking seems unabated. Perstorp in Sweden has 40 entrepreneurial partnerships. Among midsized firms, the *Biotechnology 91* survey found that the top-tier biotechnology companies—those with over 300 employees—have an average of nine strategic alliances.[1] If you have a broad agenda for partnering, no single partner is likely to provide all the benefits you desire. Diversity also protects you if one partner turns out to be a nonperformer.

Corporate Perspective

Large corporations with extensive partnering experience know that they have to examine many—maybe hundreds—of small companies before they locate a few partners with reasonable chances of success. Kodak found that about 4 out of 100 proposals by its own employees were viable internal ventures. Fuji Xerox chose 2 ideas out of 180 submitted internally. For external searches, the "deal flow" necessary to yield similar results is about the same. Volvo examines over 1,000 business proposals a year and winnows the stack down to the single digits. The innovation imperative is to develop a steady stream of innovations, and it makes sense to have several springs feeding that stream. As one corporate executive commented:

> It's taken us 20 years to get a return on our hundreds of millions of dollars of investment in corporate R&D, but we finally got it. However, our corporate executives, boards of directors, stockholders—the world—are not as patient as they used to be. Everyone used to be satisfied if we had a big home run innovation every 10 years. But now we need to hit singles and doubles. We're expected to produce $10–$20 million dollar "hits" across the board, on a routine basis.

Incubators and Institutes: A Fertile Environment for Entrepreneurs. One way to narrow the initial search is to go to incubators or university research parks. The designated search specialist should visit and inventory companies in the 35 or so technology incubators and the 130 university-related research parks. It will also be important to inventory university research centers and research institutes in areas of interest to the corporation.

Participation in public-private university research centers is another cost-effective way to support a long-term partnering strategy. Colorado's Advanced Technology Institute (CATI), for example, funds industry university centers such as the Center for Optoelectronics (now an NSF center), the Colorado Institute for Research in Biotechnology, the Colorado Advanced Materials

Institute, and the Colorado Advanced Software Institute. CATI's seed funds are used to attract industry funds. Participating industries gain access to technology and to promising students and faculty consultants, and they are well positioned for partnerships with any start-ups that might emerge from this fertile environment.

Welcome Entrepreneurs. Another way to discover potential partners is to take a close look at who's knocking at your door. Innovators who could give your firm an edge in the industry may well be trying to contact you. If they receive a polite brush-off, or a brochure that says, in so many words, "So you think you have an idea that might interest us. Fat chance!" they are likely to beat a path to the doorstep of your competitors, both domestic and foreign. Entrepreneurs have their own information networks, and word gets around when they receive particularly cold rejections or particularly warm welcomes. If the word on your corporation is "don't even bother," the percentage of promising candidates contacting your New Business Development office may decline until the message that "no outside ideas are interesting" becomes a self-fulfilling prophecy.

If your company is in the process of switching from an internal to an external focus, everyone who works with outside companies needs to understand what this entails. As we discussed under principle number one, partnering requires a company-wide commitment, and a crucial element of the partnership strategy is to make sure all personnel understand the rationale for partnering and are rewarded for supporting the external approach.

Sponsor an Enterprise Forum. Another way to locate promising entrepreneurs is to sponsor an enterprise forum. Invite local entrepreneurs to present their business plans at a private or public forum to a panel of experts. The Boulder Chamber of Commerce sponsors an "Esprit Entrepreneur" day every year. More than 50 entrepreneurs talk about their companies and exhibit their products. At least one company presents its business plan at an MIT Enterprise Forum. This is an excellent way for big business to become aware of new commercializable ideas being developed by small companies in their immediate area.

Entrepreneurial Perspective

From an entrepreneur's perspective, the critical issue is not just contacting multiple candidates, but deciding *which* companies to contact and *who* to contact within those companies that fit the partner profile.

Small companies rarely have the resources, time, or capacity to approach a large number of big companies as potential partners. For example, Exabyte—whose fast sales growth made it larger than most small start-ups—approached only a limited number of potential partners. When American companies did not warm to the prospect of partnering with Exabyte, negotiations ceased and Exabyte began to consider Japanese overtures instead.

The founder of a small company in Boston described a similar experience:

> We just didn't have time to check all the possibilities and go down all the dead ends. We approached several American corporations, but they were cool to the idea of a partnership. Why are some executives so slow to accept the idea of partnering? When I had to choose between the Japanese who are lining up to play and the Americans who are still sitting in the dugout, I decided to go with those ready to play.

Another entrepreneur from New England made it more specific:

> Should I use a rifle shot approach and go for 1 of my 4 best prospects, or should I take a shotgun approach and go for 16 companies? I don't have time to research 16. I've got to sell product! Maybe I personally should concentrate on the 4 best ones, and engage an advisor or broker to look into the other 12.

Small-company executives must decide how many corporations to approach. Exabyte contacted just a few, while Gateway sent out letters to 200 prospects. Either approach can work, but we recommend starting with your partner profile and developing a long list of prospects, then prioritizing the list and concentrating on a manageable number of the most likely "princes." If you start with a short list and dive into a time-consuming flurry of visits and negotiations without further research, you may waste your time kissing frogs that have no prospect of turning into princes. The Boston entrepreneur complained that "we just didn't have time to check out all the possibilities and go down all the dead ends." Because he didn't take the time to check out enough good prospects, he came up empty-handed.

Similarly, Exabyte may well have reduced its chance of partnering with an American partner by contacting people in R&D rather than researching *who* would be the best person to approach within each company. As we discussed earlier, R&D department heads are naturally oriented to internal innovation strategies, and this is likely to be true, even in companies that are otherwise open to partnership.

Mail and Phone Approach.   After developing a list of 200 corporations that fit its profile of potential partners, Gateway then located the name and address of an appropriate contact person at each corporation: the VP of corporate development, the VP of marketing, and the CEO or president. Gateway decided against anyone in the R&D department on the theory that R&D people would dismiss its technology as "not invented here." What Gateway did not do, and what might have saved time and heartache, was to examine which of the 200 companies were likely to be willing and compatible partners—that is, which were committed to or moving toward an externally oriented strategy that respects autonomy.

If you choose a mail and phone approach, you might want to send out 10–20 letters per week and follow up with personal phone calls to see what kind of response you are getting. Gateway executives planned to wait ten days before making follow-up phone calls to the companies they had written, but on the seventh day the phones began ringing off the hook. Corporate executives of a major chemical company called on a Friday and said they'd be arriving the next Monday to begin discussions. Thus started a series of face-to-face meetings. To save the heartache of negotiations that go nowhere, companies that respond positively should be checked to be sure they are not M&A junkies, using the background check techniques described under principle 2. If only a short, prescreened list of companies is contacted, negotiations can begin immediately with all who express enthusiasm.

Personal Networking Approach.   The president of a small services company decided to take a more personal approach to finding a partner. He convened a group of seven colleagues with whom he had worked and who had broad networks of contacts. Together, they generated a list of corporations with which one or more members of the group had worked in the past. The president and his chairman then made personal visits to the most promising contacts.

First impression, trust, and reputation are very important when marketing a service. If a technology is promising, externally oriented corporations will be interested in talking with whoever owns the patent or has the exclusive license to market the technology. On the other hand, corporations are not interested in a service unless they know something about the people who will be delivering it. This commitment is conveyed far better in face-to-face meetings than in letters and phone calls.

Seminar Approach.   One consulting company uses an approach that is rather like the enterprise forum recommended as a strategy for large corporations. This small firm offers a day-long seminar, free of charge, to executives from selected companies. The seminar is called "Technology Partnering." Usually, executives will come from about 10 to 20 companies. The seminar provides an opportunity to test personal chemistry and common interests; companies with tepid interest select themselves out from the start by simply not attending the event. Where prospects look good, follow-up meetings between attendees and/or seminar presenters are scheduled to explore partnering activities of mutual interest.

Still, the number of corporate executives interested in partnering is not large. As the head of the consulting firm explained:

> Even if you have credibility, as we do, you have to invite about 100 companies to get 15 to a seminar. Maybe half of these will be interested in further discussions about partnerships. For reasons of scheduling and travel, only half of them will actually follow up. By the time you're finished, you're lucky if you've got one serious prospect out of the 100 you started with.

This one percent success ratio underscores the importance of starting with a long list.

In summary, start early, develop a long list of possible partners, prioritize the list, negotiate with all who fit the profile and demonstrate interest, and carry out several types of due diligence examinations before getting too far in the process. Talk to many different people in various corporations. Use all your contacts in your network of colleagues, clients, suppliers, and associates in your industry to develop leads. As you cross suitors off your list, keep adding other prospects. If you get hung up on a single prospect, you might be closing yourself off to other possible partners and additional applications of your invention, service, or technology. There is no one right partner, so don't conclude that you have failed after the first promising negotiations fall through. Also, don't commit yourself to an agreement that you won't partner with anyone else. Your large corporate partner wouldn't accept that limitation, so why should you?

CREATING A CONTRACT

When one or more potential partners has gotten through the "dating" phase and passed the background check, it is time to create a formal agreement on paper.[2] Here are four principles to employ when creating a contract.

    5. Focus on mutual benefits.
    6. Start simple.
    7. Set benchmarks.
    8. Involve the lawyers—later.

5. Focus on Mutual Benefits

The point of an entrepreneurial partnership is to benefit both parties, so agree only to terms that benefit both. Avoid stipulations that are injurious to the mission and goals of either partner. Naturally, each prospective partner must look out for its own interests, but both partners must also consider the other's needs. If a genuinely productive partnership is the goal, neither can afford to sabotage the interests of the other party. A clear understanding of the benefits each party is seeking via the partnership is the basis for negotiating acceptable trade-offs. One partner may give up a point that will provide significant advantage to the other partner, if the advantaged partner reciprocates on another issue. Don't give up important rights in one arena without getting back additional benefits of equivalent value in another.

If you have a broad patent on a particular technology, remember the principle of multiple relationships and don't sign away all rights to one particular company. We heard far too many stories of corporations buying the rights to a particular technology just to sit on it. For instance, two inventors in the Pacific Northwest developed an electronic device to resuscitate heart attack victims. Their technology was top-notch, but they had no marketing capability. They formed a partnership with a European company whose business was the worldwide sale of CPR dummies. They signed away exclusive worldwide marketing rights, keeping for themselves only the marketing rights in their home state. The larger company sat on the invention, marketing it only to the extent legally required by the partnership contract. For them, the partnership was a way to eliminate a competitor to their profitable CPR product.

Be sure to understand the benefits the other party expects to derive from the partnership as well as the benefits you are looking for. If the entrepreneurs in the saga described above had spent more time thinking about the benefits their "partner" hoped to receive, they might have recognized the trap in time to avoid it.

Spelling out mutual benefits can also help negotiators uncover unrealistic expectations. Many a marriage has faltered because the bride and groom assumed they were contracting for benefits that never materialized—in many cases, because the partner never realized what was expected. The process of discussing the issues and negotiating their resolution is exceedingly important because it allows the parties to get to know each other, clarify expected benefits, and identify shared goals. Common objectives that clearly benefit both parties are a stronger force than tit-for-tat arrangements.

The contract also creates the framework within which incentive systems can be developed and future issues can be resolved. For these reasons, negotiations should be undertaken by the managers in each company who will be responsible for the results of the partnership as well as by those who will be working on a day-to-day basis to implement the contract. As partners in the contract negotiations, these key personnel will feel more directly vested; they are likely to try harder to develop a successful relationship when they intimately understand the benefits each side hopes to achieve.

6. Start Simple

Based on her analysis of strategic alliances, Debra Amidon Rogers advises that "in initiating a venture, one should start with simple problems and build to more complex interconnections. Establish flexible structures and processes that allow for changing needs of business partners. Monitor the progress carefully."[3]

Simplicity in mission and goals is important for the initial partnership agreement. Rather than developing a complicated contract with multiple goals, it is better to start with a simple goal and clearly articulated outcomes and/or measures of achievement. If all goes well, the partnership can be expanded down the road. Simple, well-defined goals on both sides will make it easier to assess whether the partnership is achieving its intended purpose. Goals also provide focus.

An alternative is to develop a multiphase contract, with continuation to the next phase dependent on reaching specified milestones in the current phase. This provides the opportunity for partners to build confidence in one another before moving on to increasingly more ambitious tasks. It also provides for exit points if the alliance turns sour, or if needs that were once similar begin to diverge.

7. Set Benchmarks

Successful relationships require continual interaction and communication. Just as interpersonal relationships require care and attention, so entrepreneurial partnerships require good management and regular maintenance. Periodic reviews allow both parties to assess progress or the lack thereof. Reviews also help manage expectations, and they enable both partners to make any necessary adjustments early rather than wait until deviations become substantial and are cause for alarm. Hence, setting clear benchmarks enables both partners to measure progress, recognize achievements, and identify any deviations from plan.

Some partners build trust and move from simple to more complex interdependencies by setting out a series of milestones or stages. Developing a plan that passes muster with the corporate management committee might be a first milestone that the small company will complete within a specified number of months. Stage two could be defined as the time when the prototype meets certain technical or performance criteria: For example, the proposed computer program will fit within 1 Mb of memory and have no noticeable response time delays, or the service company will have 25 people operating on its network with at least one joint project. Stage three may be a certain test market response rate in a target market. And so on.

In accordance with the principle of starting simple, the first stage might specify goals that won't involve an overwhelming commitment on the part of either firm. For example, rather than assume there will be a one-time infusion of funds by the large partner, specify amounts that will be provided upon attaining specified milestones. The large corporation may provide $25,000 for developing a plan in stage one. Stage two may involve $100,000 to develop a prototype. Stage three could be an amount to be determined to do market testing. Stage four might be construction of a pilot manufacturing facility, and so on. Alternatively, a service company might begin with a base fee of $50,000. As new joint projects develop, partners choose whether or not to increase their investment to achieve specified results one project at a time.

Another type of benchmark concerns provisions for renewal and termination. Allow for the possibility that the partnership will outlive its usefulness for one or both partners. Sometimes a large corporation uses the partnership as a test of the capacity of a small company. Its attitude might be, "Let's see what they can do if we give them a $100,000 project grant." Zyx Software in Stockholm had such an arrangement with Apple. Zyx thought it was performing according to expectation, but Apple lost interest. What one thought was the beginning of a long-term partnership, the other treated as a short-term experiment.

One way to avoid dashed expectations is to spell out, in the contract, the terms and conditions for renewal or termination. One tactic is to put in writing the outcomes that must be achieved in order for the partnership to continue. Another tactic is to list things that can lead to the termination of the arrangement. A third is to specify a requirement that the principals meet at least every year, review progress, and agree upon future plans and goals for the collaboration—revising terms and conditions for renewal and termination as needed.

If there are phases or stages in the contract, the collaboration agreement needs to specify what they are. Progress to the next stage should be suspended and negotiations reopened if either party fails to deliver its share of the bargain at the end of each stage of the contract. Olle Larm, the Swedish inventor of a process to prevent blood coagulation, sold rights to his patent to Pharmacia, a large Swedish pharmaceutical company. Pharmacia just sat on the technology and didn't develop it. Fortunately, Larm's contract included a paragraph that allowed him to assign the technology to other companies if Pharmacia failed to produce a plan for commercialization within six months. This clause allowed Larm a graceful exit from a partnership that was not mutually beneficial.

Relationships can outlive their usefulness even when they have a mutually productive history. The direction of companies change, and new management may have a different vision for the corporation. The founder of the small company may decide it's time to cash in and head off for new adventures. A good relationship and a well-conceived contract makes provisions for these possibilities.

8. Involve the Lawyers—Later

Say the word contract and most corporate executives think lawyer. But calling in the corporate legal department is not the first step: It comes later. Most corporate legal departments perceive their mission in life as protecting their corporations from risk. Lawyers' roles and orientation require them to take a defensive, risk-averse posture, and that can derail the negotiations before they get underway.

The quickest way to kill an entrepreneur's enthusiasm is to call in the lawyers too soon. In one case, a corporation summoned a team of a dozen lawyers to contract with a small company that could afford only a single lawyer. The small-company founders felt so overwhelmed that relations soured before the new alliance could take shape.

In another case, the small company presented a draft contract to several people in the large corporation who played the role of champions. Part of the champions' task was to shield the negotiations from the company lawyers, who were known to focus much more on corporate risk than opportunity. Only after convincing the president and the CEO that a partnership with the small company was a good idea did the champions get the lawyers involved. The lawyers' role, then, was not to advise top management on whether or not to enter into an agreement; that decision had already been made. Instead, the lawyers' role was to draft an agreement that would enable the company to achieve the benefits top management had specified.

The lesson here is to seek the counsel of lawyers *after* both parties have agreed in principle on how they want the partnership to proceed. The lawyers' job is to draw up a sound document to protect both parties and give the partnership a solid foundation. If the lawyers raise problems and objections about specific aspects of the partnership arrangement, further negotiations to address these legal problems should not be difficult if mutual trust has been established. This is very different from the "us versus them" atmosphere that often develops when lawyers face off in the early, delicate stages of negotiation.

If the parties feel the need for a go-between, the process of reaching an agreement may be better facilitated by someone with the perspective of a mediator. If an outside search specialist has helped bring the partners together, that person might make an excellent third-party mediator, assuming he or she is committed to making the partnership work.

MANAGING THE PARTNERSHIP

Finding the right partner(s) and negotiating a contract are simply means to an end: a partnership. However, successful partnerships do not just happen. They need to be well managed in order to be successful. Hence, we have identified four guidelines important to the effective management of a partnership:

9. Emphasize the partnership mentality.
10. Develop a team of champions.
11. Communicate frequently.
12. Think long term, but deliver short-term success.

9. Emphasize the Partnership Mentality

There's a big difference between calling the arrangement a partnership and acting like partners. Many companies are accustomed to operating in a supplier-buyer or a transactional mode: What did we contract for you to deliver to us, and are you delivering it? This is quite different from the partnership mode we have been discussing: What have we agreed to do for each other? A commitment to think and act as true partners is an important aspect of a partnership relationship.

Another important aspect is trust. It's people that make partnerships work. People in both companies should get to know their opposite numbers at upper- and middle-management levels. Friends can weather more storms and take longer to fall out. Trust in one another's ability to deliver is a key factor. Many of the best partnerships have started with managers and technical people working together on projects of common interest and concern.

Closely linked to commitment and trust is whether the partnership is equitably balanced. The term equity recognizes that the partnership is not necessarily equally balanced in terms of size or power, but it is balanced fairly in terms of attitude and respect. Only if IBM and NeXT continue to believe that each will be better off cooperating than competing will that relationship last. Only if partners respect each other's contributions, work to make the partnership a real collaboration, and periodically affirm the worth of the partnership will it last.

The CEO of Chiron, when asked what makes the company's partnerships work well, explained: "As much as anything, it's an attitude. . . . First, we get as close to equal participation in the relationship as we can, so that both parties have real standing. Second, we work at developing a positive understanding in both companies about the relationship."[4]

A senior executive of a large oil company, one of the Seven Sisters, was new to the partnership concept. He had recently been transferred and found himself responsible for a partner relationship initiated by the division's former director. His first reaction was: "What are we getting for our investment? Are these guys meeting our needs?" He called the entrepreneurs in for a "check in or ship out" meeting.

He began by demanding that the entrepreneur do more to meet his needs. During the conversation, however, he began to realize that the supplier-buyer mode in which he was operating didn't quite fit the relationship; it did not take into account the entrepreneur's needs and perspectives. By the end of the meeting, he had shifted to the partnership mode. He began to understand that he was equally responsible for making their joint effort work. While vastly different in size, the oil company executive and the entrepreneur were coming to see each other as equals in a shared relationship.

10. Develop a Team of Champions

Most people know the benefits of having a well-positioned champion in a large organization. A champion is someone who believes in your idea and works to get it accepted, then implemented by the rest of the organization. Entrepreneurs, whether inside a large firm or external to it, need champions who can steer the partnership project through the bureaucracy of the corporation and who will be credible when defending its worth.

What many entrepreneurs fail to plan for is the frequency with which corporate champions move on. Rising stars, who often play a champion role, frequently rise right out of the picture and beyond their role as champion—sometimes out of the corporation. Sound advice to all entrepreneurs in a partnership is to multiply your network of corporate champions. Sound advice to corporate executives is to develop effective contacts with small-company partners beyond the founder and president. One reason we recommend involving a range of players in contract negotiations is to ensure that the lineup of champions will be several layers deep.

One of the Big Three automakers had a partnership with a small company to create and supply innovative computer software. While the official commitment was for one year, the intention was to have a multiyear partnership. This was well understood by the entrepreneur and by the senior manager and his staff in the corporation. One day, the entrepreneur got a call from his auto executive counterpart that caught his attention. The executive said: "Jack, we're going through another reorganization. The recession is really affecting our bottom line. However, I don't foresee any problems with our contract. Incidentally, my early retirement has been OK'd, and I think I might take it."

The small-company president got the message. He asked for a meeting to present his company's progress and plans to his counterpart's boss, the boss's boss, and the staff. He even asked for, and got, representation from another related division. Over the next six months, he invested many days in reselling the partnership to the auto company. He diversified his relationships and supporters so that when the reorganization took effect, his partnership contract remained intact.

For some entrepreneurs, this "reorg" and new boss problem is all too common, and painful. "Just when we think we've got a deal worked out, our champion gets promoted. Or he gets moved to another division with responsibilities that no longer relate to our joint project."

An alliance between two companies is cemented by multiple alliances among the people in each company. Multiple alliances ensure a sense of continuity even when one of the champions of the partnership is promoted to another position or retires. The more numerous and redundant the organizational ties, the more secure the sense of interdependence and commitment among the personnel of both firms.

Contacts should go beyond upper-level management to involve mid-level personnel, who may inherit direct responsibility for the partnership when top managers get reassigned or leave, and who often have day-to-day responsibility for carrying out the provisions of the contract. Chiron CEO Penhoet warns that "Partnerships are hardest to implement at the middle-management level; that's where parochial interests can sandbag your shared interests."[5] If appropriate incentive structures and diligent networking bring these middle managers on board, their energy will go into supporting, not subverting, the partnership.

If the commitment to partnership involves just a few upper-level managers, there may not be enough champions to ensure the partnership's future. In the space of 18 months, one small company dealing with a large telecommunications firm found that all three of the champions who had engineered a three-year partnership agreement had disappeared. One took early retirement for health reasons, one was transferred to a radically different assignment, and one was moved from the East Coast to the South. The people who replaced the three executives felt no sense of ownership of the joint venture. They had no personal commitment to the partnership. If anything, they wanted to distance themselves from it because progress had been slow, and they feared they might be tagged with performance levels below expectation at the end of the three years.

To make matters worse, the executive who was placed in charge of the partnership with the small company developed a personality conflict with the president of the entrepreneurial venture. "You never communicate with us," said the telecommunication executive. "We just get these 'lobs' of ideas that you throw into our laps."

"And you work for a communications company but you never return my phone calls," retorted the entrepreneur. "How do you expect me to communicate?"

The partnership was dissolved—officially at the end of the contract, but in fact months earlier. Had both parties worked in advance to garner support for partnership from the top down, this story may well have had a happier ending.

11. Communicate Frequently

A culture of NIH—Not Invented Here—is a powerful deterrent to the formation of partnerships. A culture of NRTC—Never Return Telephone Calls—can kill a partnership in its infancy. All alliances develop problems, and all relationships suffer hitches and mishaps. The cultural differences between small and large companies discussed in the following chapter can exacerbate these misunderstandings. However, the leading cause of death of small-large alliances is not nonperformance or missed deadlines. It's poor communication.

Both partners need to take responsibility for communicating often and initiating questions and reports on progress or lack of progress. Some entrepreneurs want to be left alone; if this means keeping quiet, we predict an early end to the alliance. Some large-company executives don't return phone calls; if they fail to respond to their small-company partner, we foresee a quick divorce ahead.

Percy Barnevik, the CEO of Asea, Brown Boveri (ABB) in Europe, addressed this issue by instituting a management policy that all communications receive a response within 24–48 hours—no matter where, no matter what. For the over 1,000 small companies that are part of the worldwide ABB group, adherence to this policy makes the difference between working with an active giant and a dead dinosaur.

True partners also learn to share impending problems as well as report on good news. An important symbolic and practical act of partnership is establishing an electronic mail or phone mail system for partners. If the large company already has one, it should make sure the small partner becomes a part of it. If none exists, both parties should think of establishing one, or set up regular, scheduled times for telephone calls for status reporting.

12. Think Long Term, But Deliver Short-Term Success

Because the work of creating a partnership can be so difficult, we sometimes forget that delivering on the agreement is when the really hard work begins. If the contract calls for development of a prototype, the company must get busy and develop one. If the service company promised training sessions with well-known experts, they need to get busy and set up the sessions. Trust doesn't appear out of nowhere; it is built on the tangible experience of shared, easy-to-identify results.

"All this long-term perspective stuff sounds great," said one senior executive we know. "But you get back to your office on Monday morning, and you make investment decisions based on this quarter's earnings." He was responsible for the success of a small joint venture with a team of entrepreneurs who were providing management development support to those reporting to him. The way he dealt with his own need to make the joint venture survive and thrive in the long run was to look for some simple short-run successes.

He told the entrepreneurs: "You guys are out trying to hit home runs for us. Just give me some singles, or even bunts. Just put a man on base so I can explain to my peers how you're helping us." So instead of creating a full-blown management development program, the entrepreneurial team focused on delivering an assessment of the differing methods and providers of management development services. The principle: Think long, deliver short. (Think years, deliver next week.)

A well-constructed contract, one that starts simple and establishes benchmarks, designs in these short-term successes. If a less ideal contract has already been signed, there's nothing to prevent the partners from working out some less formal benchmarks and short-term goals that will provide each with a satisfying sense of progress.

SUMMARY

In this chapter we have discussed 12 principles for successful partnerships. We spent more time on the principles associated with finding a partner than we did on negotiating the contract or managing the partnership because we have found that companies need more help in this area than the other two.

While a chief goal of entrepreneurial partnerships is to accelerate innovation, the process of successful innovation is a long and continuous road. One or two home runs are no longer enough; small companies and large ones need to put together teams that have strong, consistent hitters—teams that can adjust their strategies as the global game shifts. Because of the need for long-term perspectives, good project management, periodic reviews, and multiple champions are important elements of a good partnership.

A strong partnership can survive a bad game or two, if it looks like there'll be a winning season. It helps to know the kinds of problems that are likely to crop up, and the next chapter provides a sampling of problems to expect.

NOTES

1. G. Steven Burrill and Kenneth B. Lee, Jr., *Biotech 91: A Changing Environment* (San Francisco: Ernst & Young, 1990), p. 5.
2. There are many other books and legal sources that will specify what elements and clauses should be covered in such a contract. We urge the reader to consult appropriate references and lawyers when negotiating a contract with another company, large or small.
3. Debra Amidon Rogers, *Global Innovation Strategy* (Austin, Texas: IC2 Institute, University of Texas, 1990), p. 49.
4. Burrill and Lee, p. 118.
5. Ibid.

CHAPTER SIX

Potential Pitfalls:
What Can Go Wrong

Entrepreneurial partnerships are no panacea. They won't cure all the ills that plague large and small companies. But several problems that many large corporations are experiencing, for example, a slowed rate of innovation and difficulty in getting a new product to the consumer in time to hit the window of opportunity, may be solved by collaborative partnerships with small entrepreneurial firms. Partnering and networking are ideal strategies for entrepreneurs who want to grow their companies quickly. But not every partnership yields happy results; ill-conceived partnerships can leave your company in worse shape than before. Bad partnerships, like bad marriages, can drain resources, end up in costly litigation, and sour both partners on future relationships. However, many failures are foreseeable and preventable. This chapter, though it focuses on the bad news about partnering, is written with the positive goal of helping readers foresee and prevent an unhappy ending.

Some of the pitfalls can be traced to bad-faith behavior. Some people try to exploit a relationship rather than promote its well-being; they define success as getting something for nothing. But other problems with partnerships result from cultural differences between large and small companies that are not understood or acknowledged at the outset. All joint ventures present challenges, and some of the pitfalls we describe are typical of any kind of relationship. Others relate specifically to cultural differences that can put large and small companies on a crash course.

In large-small entrepreneurial partnerships, differences in perception and attitude are natural because both partners are inherently different. One executive put it this way: "If the entrepreneurs are birds and the executives are fish, where will they make their home if they mate?" A heightened awareness of these differences should help executives and entrepreneurs understand one another better, avoid the obvious pitfalls, and keep on the lucrative path of complementary advantage.

We have identified five issues that can become trouble spots when large and small businesses try to develop alliances. These relate to

1. Trust and liability
2. Control and failure
3. Perceptions of time
4. Value and compensation
5. Cross-national differences

TRUST AND LIABILITY

Caveat: A contract works on compliance; a partnership requires commitment. One executive we know has consummated several alliances with companies similar in size to his own, yet has never even considered looking for small-company partners. He says, "Entrepreneurs are mavericks. They don't belong in a stable corporate culture."

His counterpart—the small-business founder—was equally skeptical. "You think that I should consider a partnership with that behemoth company? The reason I left corporate life was to leave company politics behind me. Besides, they will probably try to steal my technology and/or take over my company."

The attitudes behind these two statements are common: skepticism about the aims of the other, fear of unequal treatment, and a lack of trust. A partnership founded on trust and mutual respect is far more likely to succeed than a marriage of convenience supported by legalistic contingencies. Choosing the right partner and having a psychological commitment to the relationship are more important than legal documents in determining whether or not the partnership will be successful.

Kubota, an old-line Japanese tractor company that is using partnering to diversify, has invested in a wide range of small American companies, including Exabyte, Rasna Corporation (software), and Ardent Computer Corporation—since renamed Stardent. The first two partners report no dissatisfaction with the Japanese corporation. According to Rasna president David Pidwell, "I don't think I could have picked a better partner." The head of Stardent, however, has called their relationship a win-lose proposition, with the U.S. side taking the losses. Allen Michels of Stardent, which develops high-powered graphics workstations, was at first delighted when Kubota invested $45 million in his company over a three-year period. Kubota manufactures the computers and sells them to the Asian market. In 1990, however, Michels sued Kubota, claiming that the Japanese firm was trying to siphon off Stardent technology and had treated him "viciously." Some people inside and outside the company dispute his version of events, but there seems little doubt that Michels, who entered the alliance with great hopes and enthusiasm for his Japanese partners, feels that his trust was betrayed. Kubota management believes that Michels is acting maliciously, stirring up anti-Japanese sentiment to cloak his own abuses of Kubota.[1]

Clearly, partnerships can run aground when the intent of either partner is to use or abuse the other. Cultural differences can lead partners to misconstrue one another's actions. Choosing the wrong kind of partner can also lead to difficulty. In the Stardent-Kubota case, a key issue in the dispute seems to be the inability of Michels to force Kubota to either buy out Stardent or sell it to another, larger, company. Michels might have been better off choosing an M&A–oriented partner rather than one committed to external strategies. His desire to sell out indicates that a better alternative would have been to look for an internally oriented company committed to M&A, which would have allowed him to cash in his equity down the road.

The case of Total Solutions, a Colorado-based software company, suggests the opposite mismatch. The small company agreed to a buyout by Pioneer Hi-Bred International because it needed capital for expansion; the large company saw diversification as a strategy to cope with a slump in its core agricultural genetics business. When the small company failed to meet sales targets, however, Iowa-based Pioneer trimmed staff drastically and moved the small firm and its founder to Cedar Rapids, where close proximity intensified the conflict. The eventual divorce proceeded with a breach of contract suit on both sides.

In this case, when the small company failed to reach a benchmark and the relationship became strained, Pioneer switched to an integration strategy and tried to merge the small company. The establishment of sales targets suggests that the relationship was established according to principle 7 (set benchmarks), but then the small partner failed to meet the goals. Because the large company was under financial pressure, delivering short-term successes (principle 12) should have been a top priority for the relationship. A careful partner profile (principle 2) might also have revealed Pioneer's proclivity toward integration, sending up a warning flag for the small company seeking capital but hoping to remain autonomous.

Surprisingly, the experience has not turned entrepreneur James Howell against small-large liaisons. Selling some or all of your company to a bigger company, he commented to the *Wall Street Journal*, "is a logical way to grow if you pick the right people."[2]

A similar sentiment is expressed by Barnet Feinblum, current president of the herb-tea company Celestial Seasonings, which Dart & Kraft bought, then put up for sale again three years later. Celestial Seasonings executives managed to rescue the company from an impending sale to Lipton via a leveraged buyout, and the company is once again thriving. Feinblum's postmortem assessment suggests that a more balanced partnership to begin with—one that involved a minority equity investment, for example—might have served the needs of both partners better. "It was a good relationship," commented Feinblum, "but a bad marriage."[3] Multiple partnering (principle 4) might also have afforded Celestial Seasonings more protection.

Caveat: Big companies, like bears, attract hunters; entrepreneurs, like beavers, can disappear underwater. Large companies can be vulnerable to the actions of small ones even when the entrepreneur's intentions are good. In a litigious society, lawsuits and court actions are a constant threat, and large companies with deep pockets are far more vulnerable than small companies to disgruntled customers or stockholders. Large companies that partner with small ones are prone to challenges in court by third parties seeking retribution and redress for real or imagined actions of the smaller partner.

The head of Kodak's Office of Innovation gained experience in defending Kodak from suits when one of the small companies in his portfolio drew fire from angry consumer groups. Had Kodak not been the parent, the groups probably would not have gone to court because the small company had few assets worth pursuing. But when the parent is a major corporation with financial reserves, its legal exposure is magnified. "Every one of our companies had the tag line 'A Kodak Company' after its name. In retrospect, the liability we incurred was probably not worth the credibility we provided by letting those companies use our name," remarked a rueful executive.

A giant financial services firm known for stability and solidity made an alliance with a small firm whose founder had "a strong appetite for speculative profits and bare-knuckles boardroom warfare." The founder misrepresented his connection to the financial services firm by identifying himself as part of the group rather than as an independent entity. He used the credibility and financial reserves of the large company to take over and destroy other small companies. Some of those companies are now up in arms and are suing the large one. One company owner "is convinced that he has been the victim of a brutal ruse, and that the [large company] bears much of the blame. . . . [I]t was [done] with the intention of finding the quickest way of exploiting the company and making the quickest buck."[4] The large corporation is suffering double losses: its partnership with the small firm did not work out, and its credibility has been damaged.

Executives who have little experience working with innovative firms may not foresee the legal liability that can be generated by small companies in the United States. However, we never heard anyone from Japan complain about lawsuits, except when they occurred in the United States, as in the Kubota-Stardent case.

Entrepreneurs are also prone to overlook issues of legal liability. They are typically suspicious of legal counsel (even when the counsel is offered for their own good) and inevitably find bills for legal work too high. To avoid this pitfall, the following steps are important:

1. Take time to develop a sense of trust regarding the other party.
2. Ensure that the other party has the capacity to follow through and deliver what has been promised.
3. Develop clearly worded legal agreements between the partners.
4. Establish appropriate organizational structures within which the partnership can function.

Before entering into a formal contract, both parties may decide that a useful first step would be to develop an informal working partnership. Or the parties may opt for a short-term transactional relationship, with a contract that specifies services or products to be delivered.

Both these alternatives, which follow principle 6, (start simple), will build trust, providing managers in the large and small company with a base of experience in working with their counterparts and enabling them to determine whether the other company can deliver what has been promised. In all cases, clear legal documents delineating the roles and responsibilities of each company, their relationship to each other, and their liability vis-à-vis each other are important if the pitfall of legal liability is to be avoided. Later, assuming things work out as well as anticipated, the two companies may want to begin discussing a longer-term, full-fledged partnership. They need to consider, early, the organizational structure within which the longer-term partnership might be managed. Some partnerships are managed by the founder/entrepreneur at the small company and one champion at the large corporation on a one-to-one basis. Others, following the multiple champions principle, are managed by teams of people at each company.

A third alternative is to establish a separate, independent corporation through which the partnership will be governed and managed. One small company, whose intent was to ally with large companies, made a point of creating a separate corporation and established a board of directors before it began searching for corporate partners. Representation on the board by all partners was not considered essential in this case. In the case of Cormetech, it was; increased risk and liability was a price all three partners were willing to pay.

If mutual respect and trust between the parties are strong, then creating advisory boards instead of boards of directors may be yet another way to avoid the pitfall of directors' liability. Here, the partnership "managers" have opportunities to discuss problems and solutions with advisors who then provide recommendations without the legal obligations or responsibilities they would incur if they were members of a board of directors.

CONTROL AND FAILURE

Caveat: Entrepreneurship is messy and unpredictable; managers prefer predictability and order. One large company we know has an urge to control everything. Control issues dominate its every move. Its top executives acquired a small firm whose technology and talents filled a hole in the corporation's value chain. They sidelined the founder in an obscure business unit. At the first opportunity, he bailed out, then stood by and watched his former company languish. Time passed, and the corporation created a strategic plan that took it in new directions. When his company was put up for sale, the original founder seized the opportunity and bought it back for half what he had sold it for two years earlier.

Stories of entrepreneurs buying back their old companies from control-dominated large buyers are legion. In Sweden, the founder of Infrasonics sold it to ASEA, then bought it back. Celestial Seasonings traveled the same route with Kraft.

The need for control underlies the strategy of integration and is often expressed through mergers and acquisitions. In the 1980s, however, companies were acquired and merged for reasons that seemed far distant from growth and integration, and closer to simple greed. Paper profits took precedence over improving products and services. Innovation in the financial sectors, leveraged buyouts, junk bonds, and insider trading came to dominate and sometimes even destroy innovations in technology and distribution services.

Of course, many founders plan to sell out to a large company eventually, and in some cases mergers make good business sense. Most founders, however, are attached to their creation and hope that it will continue to flourish long after they have cashed in their equity. These autonomy-minded entrepreneurs worry that to merge means to submerge.

The need to control can be a real pitfall in developing collaborative partnerships. In times of stress in a relationship, it can overwhelm the partnership mentality, causing large companies to treat their small partners as subordinates rather than equals. Sometimes what appears to be a need to control, however, is really a quest for orderliness and predictability. Entrepreneurship is neither orderly nor predictable; it is messy and opportunistic. A large corporation develops a strategic plan, heads down that track, and puts resources in place to carry out the plan. Entrepreneurs, on the other hand, foster innovations that can pop up in unusual places.

As part of its strategic plan, Kodak established the Office of Innovation, whose job was to ferret out entrepreneurial ideas and to take advantage of what popped up unexpectedly. But, "it was a little bit like trying to create a free enterprise system within a planned economy," noted one executive. External partnering, by respecting the independence of both partners, avoids this contradiction. A certain amount of distance keeps the creative entrepreneurial "mess" from disrupting the "planned economy." Attempts to pull the small company tighter into orbit, such as Pioneer's strategy of moving Total Solutions to Iowa, usually exacerbate this cultural conflict.

Clear benchmarks and a series of short-term successes (principles 7 and 12) address the larger company's need for order and predictability and give champions some concrete achievements to point to before launching a more ambitious project. They also help corporate champions manage their fears about another tricky cultural issue: failure.

Caveat: Entrepreneurial business is inherently risky; executives try to control and minimize risk. The differing attitudes toward failure between entrepreneurs and executives is a serious potential pitfall for partnerships. While controlling and minimizing risk are important to corporate executives, the fear of failing looms even larger. In the case of Pioneer–Total Solutions, the road to disaster began when the small company failed to meet the sales target the large company had expected. Because the large partner itself was having financial difficulty, the small company's relatively small shortfall assumed larger proportions than it might otherwise have. Its response precipitated even more problems, lawsuits, and huge legal fees. Exit clauses in the contract should have allowed both partners to disengage rather than become enmeshed even tighter in an unsatisfactory alliance.

Most entrepreneurial partnerships entail smaller commitments of money and time than an M&A, so it makes sense to discuss a failure and renegotiate the contract, if necessary, rather than canceling or breaching the contract. Good communication can help establish whether the failure is one of the inevitable glitches in a fundamentally sound project, or grounds for divorce.

In another partnership, between Phillips Petroleum and Wadley Biosciences, the large company decided to cut funding for an entrepreneurial joint venture when oil prices plunged, that is, because of a change in the circumstances surrounding the alliance. The relationship ended, and Wadley Biosciences is now in the market for a new partnership. This time entrepreneur Arthur Bollon plans to include an option in the contract to pull out if sales fall short.[5]

One can't discuss entrepreneurship without discussing failure. The head of strategic planning at Volvo told us: "Our president, Pehr Gyllenhammar, gets nearly 1,000 new venture proposals per year. He or his staff sees about 200 to 250 per year. Only about 1 out of 10 are realistic. Of these, only 2 out of 100 make sense for Volvo. Of these, only 20 have resulted in actual businesses, and from these 20 only 4 are real success stories." Given the slim odds of success, how can large companies reconcile the fact that failure is inherent to entrepreneurs and success is a prerequisite for managers?

Executives and corporations who cannot tolerate the risk of failure, or who cannot use failure as a positive learning mechanism, are probably not well suited to collaborations with entrepreneurs. At the same time, collaborative arrangements have to build in mechanisms to winnow out business ideas that cannot succeed even with support from a large, established corporation. Starting simple, with a small level of investment and mutual interdependence, then escalating as short-term successes confirm that the concept is viable and the relationship is working, is a good way to manage risk. Should the alliance prove unproductive—for reasons that can range from malice to an infeasible idea to a poor partnership match to a sudden drop in oil prices—neither partner will sustain crippling losses.

One other way to reduce the risk is to look for multiple partners. Gateway Technologies is planning to license acrylic fiber rights to one company and polyester fiber to another, but Gateway is not planning to license the rights to all fibers to any single company. Hermann Hauser's marketing plan for the Active Book Company (described in Chapter 8) is to sign distribution agreements with three separate firms on three continents: Europe, North America, and Asia. A small company is especially vulnerable if a partnership fails, but a large company that is counting on the small company to develop innovations or provide manufacturing support also suffers a loss if a partnership fails. By diversifying their portfolio of partners, both companies can minimize risk.

PERCEPTIONS OF TIME

Caveat: New businesses take a long time to mature; large companies want quarterly results. "I've got a return-on-investment target to meet by the end of the year," said one senior executive. "But this portfolio of small companies I'm responsible for is still in the red."

"Why are you upset?" asked the president of one of those small companies. "We're right on target according to our business plan."

This exchange typifies the basic difference between executives who need results next quarter and entrepreneurs who are executing a multiyear business plan. Most entrepreneurs and executives have perceptions of time that are perpetually out of sync. Most small companies do not break even until somewhere in the three- to five-year time frame, but managers need positive quarterly results in order to receive positive performance reviews and salary increases.

One Corning executive told us: "If Amory Houghton hadn't taken the long-term view on fiber optics, we would have discarded the technology that is now one of our core businesses." The Houghton family has significant ownership in Corning; consequently, Corning was better able to withstand the pressures of developing a new business that for years showed no return. Perhaps this experience enables Corning managers to take a long-term view even now: Cormetech, started by Corning and two Mitsubishi companies in 1989, is not expected to have a major market until 1995.

The Japanese company Fuji Xerox gives its new ventures a four-year grace period before they have to show profits. Perstorp, a large Swedish chemical company, expects most of its companies to generate a positive cash flow within five years. Although Percell Biolytica, a small Swedish biotech firm and Perstorp partner, was making money in its second year, most biotech firms need a longer time frame to start showing sales, let alone profits. The Japanese and European corporations we interviewed seemed to have a more realistic understanding of the time it would take a small partner, and a partnership, to be successful. The CEO of biotech pesticide company Mycogen remarked that the "long-term perspective" of Kubota, Japan Tobacco, and Royal Dutch Shell was a positive factor in its partnerships with these companies.[6]

Many American executives dream of finding and nurturing the next Apple Computer. They forget that it took five years before Apple was profitable. One of the potential pitfalls is expecting too much too soon, and not allowing the small company time to mature. Large corporations should not expect that the small company with which they partner will perform like Dell Computer or Compaq. Time horizons with regard to performance, growth, and delivery should be realistic for both companies.

Entrepreneurs, who are typically overly optimistic in setting goals for their own companies, may magnify the problem by unwittingly promising more than they can deliver. A good rule of thumb is that any demand for immediate financial results is unreasonable, and the time span for reaching goals should be realistic. The contract benchmarks that set up some short-term successes should focus on tasks accomplished and stages of development completed, not quick financial rewards. Entrepreneurs whose products have a long developmental time frame should look hard at partnering with European and Japanese companies, which are under much less pressure to produce quarterly results than American companies are.

Another potential conflict concerns the amount of time a corporate executive may have to spend tending the partnership, especially in the early days, versus the return that the small company will initially provide. "I couldn't justify it," said one senior manager. "I had to spend 25 percent of my time on results that contributed less than 1 percent to my budgeted revenue." But partnerships do require management time, and managers in both large and small companies must view the time spent as an investment in the future. While it is useful to specify short-term, medium-term, and long-term benefits and results whenever possible, months of work must often be invested up front with no return on the investment for months, even years. When the lawyer asks: "How can I justify taking ten percent of the legal department's resources to work on a partnership that generates less than one hundred-thousandth percent of sales?" the champion-manager within the company must remind her that this is but one of a series of long-term investments the corporation is making in its future.

Caveat: Employees of large companies make a clear distinction between work and personal time; entrepreneurs often merge their business and personal time.   Another place where the time dimension creates conflict is the simple daily schedule. Most entrepreneurs work any and all hours. The intrapreneur/inventor in a large company who tries to work in his laboratory at 2 A.M. will usually find it locked. Entrepreneurs, on the other hand, can and do work long and odd hours. Many value weekends not as a break from work but as uninterrupted work time.

Japanese executives and entrepreneurs tend to work on the same schedule: Both are workaholics. An executive from Kao Corporation, a leading cosmetics manufacturer in Tokyo, said "We try to leave the offices open all the time at corporate headquarters. You never know when someone will get a good idea." Of course many American executives work long hours, too. But on the whole, they are more influenced by the hours and pace of a mature organization than the frenzy of a start-up. Most executives are told, for example, how much vacation time they are entitled to take each year. Some entrepreneurs don't know what a vacation is; others take off time whenever they like, not when the company tells them they can.

One West Coast entrepreneur was shocked when a partnering executive from a Fortune 100 company on the East Coast declined to attend a Monday meeting. When questioned, the executive said: "I don't like Monday meetings out of town. It means I have to fly on Sunday, and I jealously reserve weekends for my family." The entrepreneur, on the other hand, was used to spending the weekend at work and hadn't thought much about the impact that might be having on his family.

VALUE AND COMPENSATION

Caveat: Bosses crave large numbers of employees—it increases their power; entrepreneurs shun large numbers of employees—it increases their overhead. Some people maintain that entrepreneurs play a money game and executives play a power game. However, entrepreneurs tend to measure themselves on results, not inputs. They want to know how much they sold, not how large a sales force they manage. Their interest is in maximizing their output and minimizing the input.

Many mid-level executives have a somewhat different perspective. Of course they, too, are concerned with results. But they are also concerned with the size of their budgets. They frequently measure their own worth by the size of the budget they manage and the numbers of people reporting to them. This is a measure of their political power. The greater the resources at their disposal, the more power they wield.

People with a management power orientation are unlikely to find satisfaction in partnering with a small company. It takes a disproportionate amount of time but adds little—at least initially—to a manager's power base. Only after the little company grows and the partnership flourishes does it begin to add to the balance sheet of power. Of course, if partnering is a core strategy for the company rather than a short-term tactic, involvement in multiple partnerships can be a prestigious assignment for management-level personnel.

Many entrepreneurs loathe company politics. The desire to avoid company politics, and the inability to play them successfully, are two reasons why entrepreneurs start their own companies. A third reason is simply to be the boss, not report to one.

Restructuring incentives and rewards for partnering—part of the stage-by-stage partnering strategy identified as principle number one—is one way for large firms to counter the misperception that bigger budgets and more employees are ends rather than means to an end. Entrepreneurial founders who hate playing politics should assign a more diplomatically inclined colleague to handle the day-to-day business of networking with corporate counterparts. This delegation of responsibility can start with principle number three, by assigning a better "networker" to the task of seeking out corporate partners.

Caveat: Executives earn consistent monthly salaries; entrepreneurs share in unpredictable cash results. One fledgling software company in the late 1960s—a two-man operation—struck an alliance with a large computer service bureau. The two entrepreneurs provided the innovative software, and the large company sold their packages along with an array of other profitable services. The innovative packages were the draw or door-opener that lured customers to the larger firm. Trouble was, royalties on the innovative packages gave the developers an annual income double that of the large company's president. Year after year, the entrepreneurs pulled down whopping incomes. Year after year, the service bureau president reopened the partnership agreement negotiations around the compensation issue. The president simply could not accept that these (young and inexperienced) entrepreneurs were making more money than he was.

Hermann Hauser, an Austrian entrepreneur who founded Acorn Computer Company and the Active Book Company in England, recalled one financial meeting around corporate venturing where the European finance director said: "Why should we give these guys (the entrepreneurs) funding that will make them rich when we only get paid $X?" It's important to recognize that personal worth (as manifested in compensation), like beauty, may be in the eye of the beholder. The finance director and service bureau president failed to recall how many risks the entrepreneurs had taken and how many years they had had little or no income. To avoid this pitfall, separate out issues of ego and personal gain from the partnership whenever possible, and concentrate on the value that each company is bringing to the other. This follows the principle of focusing on mutual benefits.

The underlying issue, though, is often how much one individual, not a company, is benefitting. Corporate executives who are envious of entrepreneurs might consider whether their unhappiness stems from their own unrealized entrepreneurial ambitions. Perhaps the real cure for this pitfall is for these executives to start new companies themselves and experience the upside and downside of risk. CEOs who are open to a mix of external strategies might consider combining partnering with spin-offs. They could then encourage employees with an entrepreneurial bent to take the plunge themselves. This would be one way to channel these entrepreneurial energies productively, rather than having envious executives undermine the partnerships.

CULTURAL DIFFERENCES

Caveat: The definition of success differs by nationality. American entrepreneurs want a breakthrough; Swedish entrepreneurs want to break away; Japanese entrepreneurs don't want to break anything, including tradition. Not all entrepreneurs value the same things, and not all large-company executives look for the same results from small companies. American entrepreneurs and their corporate partners tend to look for breakthroughs. "We want to identify the next Apple computer," said one of the senior partners from a major accounting firm. The most admired entrepreneurs are those who create something fundamentally new. Apple Computer, Genentech, Federal Express, and Dell Computer fall into this category, and *Inc.* magazine annually selects as "Entrepreneur of the Year" someone who typifies this model.

To Americans with a breakthrough mentality, the idea of honoring someone who has developed incremental improvements on an existing product sounds preposterous. Yet there are many international examples where the basic premises, attitudes, and perceptions of what an entrepreneur is vary dramatically from the U.S. model. In Japan, the entrepreneur of the year might be someone (or more likely some group of people) many Americans wouldn't even recognize as entrepreneurial.

In other countries, what we have described as typical cultural attributes of large versus small companies are reversed. As the next chapter illustrates, the Japanese environment is less conducive to radical change. Japanese see *large* companies as hardworking and innovative, while Americans see *small* companies as plucky and adventurous. Some Swedish small firms appear timid, but Perstorp's portfolio is filled with many that are bold. In the United States, large companies typically buy out small ones. In Hungary, a small firm acquired and resuscitated a large one. In England, large companies seem aloof; in Sweden, many small ones are, too.

For Americans, the lesson is that when looking abroad for partners, it's important to do your homework before proceeding on assumptions that may be valid in the United States but don't hold water abroad. Don't fall into the trap of expecting entrepreneurs—or large companies—in other countries to behave according to the patterns we've come to expect in the United States. If your desired partner is Japanese or European, the partner profile should include a good briefing or background reading on the different business norms in the target country. Numerous consultants in the business of cross-cultural communication can help in this education and may be a valuable resource in the initial matchmaking process.

COMPLEMENTARY VS. CONTRADICTORY DIFFERENCES

Caveat: Too much similarity can be dysfunctional; the most successful collaborations are among partners that have complementary dissimilarities.[7]   As this chapter illustrates, much can go wrong with entrepreneurial partnerships. The potential pitfalls provide good reasons for corporate managers to be skeptical of entrepreneurial partnership. Yet the very attributes that make partners different also make them valuable to one another. Opposites can clash, but it helps to remind yourself that it is those very opposites that attracted each partner to begin with.

Entrepreneurial partnerships are founded on one company's strengths being able to compensate for the other company's weaknesses. A group of European executives recently studied alliances and concluded that complementary dissimilarities are an important characteristic of successful partnerships. Large companies are stable and predictable; small ones move quickly and change rapidly. Large companies develop; small companies innovate. The differences that create the pitfalls also create the opportunity to compress the value chain and enable each to become more competitive. Anticipating, managing, and valuing such dissimilarities is an important element in achieving the advantages of entrepreneurial partnerships.

NOTES

1. Andrew Pollack, "Ardent Boss Sues Partner Kubota as the Respect Turns to Rancor," *International Herald Tribune,* 21–22 July 1990.
2. Hal Lancaster and Marj Charlier, "Bigger Partners Can Cause Problems for Small Firms," *Wall Street Journal,* 4 March 1991.
3. Ibid.
4. *New York Times,* Business Section, 27 January 1991.
5. Lancaster and Charlier.
6. G. Steven Burrill and Kenneth B. Lee, Jr., *Biotech 91: A Changing Environment* (San Francisco: Ernst & Young, 1990), p. 64.
7. Quote from a director of Calor Emag, a small German company in the giant Asea, Brown Boveri group.

PART THREE

Global Opportunities for Entrepreneurial Partnerships

Every year, a group of executives gather at the lakeside center of Tallberg, in northern Sweden, to discuss current problems and future prospects of global business. Participants come from Western Europe, from the United States, and, increasingly, from Japan. In 1991, under the theme of "Leadership in Times of Real Change," participant Michael Maccoby summarized the major differences in perspectives among these three world regions:

> The American image of the leader is an entrepreneur and a performer. He or she is usually a single individual, a hero who has courage, vision, and drive. The Swedish model of a leader is an expert and an ombudsman. Swedish and other Western European leaders are usually individuals, worldly, cultured, and stand on principles. The Japanese version of a leader is a teacher and a shogun. Japanese distinguish between the function of leadership (held to be important) and the individual as a leader (held to be unimportant).

What are the implications of these different perspectives for partnerships? How do the principles of entrepreneurial partnership apply to such different cultural backgrounds? What opportunities or problems are American executives and entrepreneurs likely to encounter as they form more international partnerships? This final set of chapters explores these questions.

We look first at Japan and then at two Western European countries: the United Kingdom and Sweden. Japan is America's biggest trading partner and strongest competitor. Its *kaizen* and *keiretsu* traditions suggest that Japan will be a formidable adversary when it comes to entrepreneurship in general and entrepreneurial partnerships in particular. The United Kingdom is a Western European example of a traditional economy where the concept of large-small alliances has been slow to take hold. Sweden is a changing economy where this growth strategy is an opportunity waiting to happen.

We round out our international exploration by looking at Hungary, a country in the fastest-changing region of all, Eastern Europe. Hungary is the furthest along toward a free market economy of any country in the former Communist bloc, and it illustrates the opportunities and pitfalls of international partnering.

Our purpose is not to make judgments about which system or model is best. Too many books have already extolled the virtues or vices of Japanese management compared to management in the United States and Europe, and vice versa. Rather, we seek to explore how entrepreneurial partnering fits or clashes with other economic traditions, and to elucidate the international opportunities and obstacles it presents to American executives and entrepreneurs.

CHAPTER SEVEN

Japanese Entrepreneurship: The Power of *Kaizen* and *Keiretsu*

As Japanese business has flourished and made dramatic inroads on the American marketplace, American executives have paid more and more attention to the competitive strength of Japanese companies. Many, however, have reassured themselves that although the Japanese obviously have a knack for improving on existing technology, the United States has a resource that Japan simply lacks: a talent for innovation and a rich supply of entrepreneurs. The Japanese—so the stereotype goes—are clever imitators, not innovators, because of a culture that emphasizes group conformity rather than individual achievement.

Acting in concert with the group is indeed an important value in Japanese history and culture, and the Japanese educational system does not train students to challenge the group. Japanese university students are told, "If the head of a nail sticks out, it is hammered down," meaning they should conform to the group and not stick out by being creative. Employers generally prefer people who will fit into a system. Masaki Togai, a Japanese who founded a company in California, says that he could never have started the company in Japan. Says Togai, "The U. S. culture makes this kind of thing happen."

There's a problem with this picture, however. If the Japanese are neither creative nor entrepreneurial, then where did all the successful Japanese companies come from? Didn't they have founders? Of course they did. Soichiro Honda started in motorcycles and moved on to create Honda automobiles; Akio Morita cofounded Sony; Osaka entrepreneur Konosuke Matsushita founded what is now one of the world's largest electronics companies.

One reason Americans overlook Japanese entrepreneurs is that the Japanese approach to entrepreneurship often doesn't fit the American ideal of the entrepreneur. A Japanese entrepreneur is not necessarily an individual who starts a new company single-handedly, based on a radically new idea. As we have seen in previous chapters, not all American entrepreneurs fit that model either. Large Japanese companies tend to emphasize the *kaizen* approach of step-by-step, continuous improvements rather than major breakthroughs. But some Japanese companies do produce breakthroughs, and Japanese entrepreneurs do strike out on their own to create new companies.

Japanese *keiretsu*, the grouping of Japanese companies into a megasystem of support, also has a profound effect on partnering. *Keiretsu* tend to give Japanese executives and entrepreneurs a head start in forming entrepreneurial partnerships.

Japanese experience with the internal and external strategies we detailed in Chapter 3 is instructive. Large Japanese companies have been more satisfied than American companies with the results of internal venturing. They have also been practicing entrepreneurial partnership by partnering with small American and

European companies. And some small entrepreneurial companies in Japan have formed productive partnerships with large U.S. firms.

Executives from both large and small firms in the United States may find Japan a more promising source of potential partners than prevailing stereotypes might suggest. We present evidence for this growing opportunity and also discuss obstacles to Japanese entrepreneurship and pitfalls in international partnering.

TWO DIFFERENT MODES OF ENTREPRENEURSHIP

Before analyzing how the Japanese speed innovation on the value chain, we need to understand the concepts of *kaizen* and *keiretsu* and how they support and enhance the concept of entrepreneurial partnership. As background, Table 7.1 illustrates some of the more important differences between the Japanese and Western modes of innovation and entrepreneurship.[1]

American executives who are contemplating a U.S.–Japanese partnership need to understand these cultural differences. The mode of entrepreneurship is different, yet Japan has lots of entrepreneurs, both inside and outside its large companies.

The Tradition of *Kaizen* Entrepreneurship

The tradition of extensive *kaizen* entrepreneurship is rooted in Japanese business history dating back many centuries. Just as the United States has a tradition of garage shop entrepreneurship (for example, Hewlett and Packard), the Japanese have their own entrepreneurial legends. The earliest recorded story dates from the seventeenth century, when the Nikko Toshogu Shrine, some 50 miles from modern-day Tokyo, was constructed.

TABLE 7.1: Two Different Modes of Entrepreneurship

Japanese Mode	*Western Mode*
Kaizen (incremental)	Breakthrough
Keiretsu (business alliance)	Competition (individual business)
Innovation	Invention
Holism	Individualism
Big Companies	Small Companies
Long Range	Short Term
Civilian-oriented	Military-related
Low Risk	High Risk
Group Wealth Creation	High Individual Profit
Big companies are effective innovators (they rely on small companies to help).	Big companies are bureaucratic and muscle bound.
Small companies are the most likely to be hurt in a shakeout.	Small companies are the most resilient.
Tinkerers will come out ahead in the 1990s.	Dreamers will come out ahead in the 1990s.

At that time, Iwatsuki was a castle outpost on the Nikko Road, over which pilgrims and construction workers regularly traveled. In 1697, a Buddhist priest settled in Iwatsuki to recover from a sickness contracted during repair work on the shrine. During his recuperation, he mixed glue and paste with the paulownia wood sawdust left over from the shrine construction to form doll heads. These proved very popular with pilgrims, and the priest's roadside stand along Nikko Road became Japan's version of the garage shop.

Nearly 120 years later, another doll artisan took the priest's technique and founded the Iwatsuki doll industry. The product evolved from dolls' heads to complete figures, and more than 20 doll-making houses were formed to commercialize the new product. As late as the 1960s, Iwatsuki had a near monopoly on these dolls, which were sold all over the country.

Japanese refer to the priest and the artisan as the "two pioneers." One was the inventor, and one the organizer. Their names are not recorded. Their innovations did not involve breakthrough technology but the use of a new material to make an old product, and later, the evolution of the old product into a new one that was marketed throughout Japan. The same person did not invent the new technique and grow it into a huge industry. Instead, this happened step by step, with each of the pioneers contributing a different kind of innovation. This step-by-step, gradual evolution is the form that *kaizen* entrepreneurship still takes in Japan today, especially in the small-large subcontractor relationships typical of the Japanese industrial giants. The innovators often remain anonymous, and the person with the new idea or technique is not necessarily the one who commercializes it.

The Reality of *Keiretsu*

Keiretsu is the Japanese term for families of companies that support one another. The original monopolistic groupings (*zaibatsu*) were supposedly broken up after World War II; today they persist in the *keiretsu*. Some of the more prominent *keiretsu* are Mitsubishi, Mitsui, Sumitomo, and Fuyo. Each has members that span many industries. NEC, for example, is the computer-electronics member of the Sumitomo *keiretsu*. Toshiba is in the Mitsui group, and Fujitsu is in the *keiretsu* led by the Dai-Ichi Kangyo Bank. Toray is the fibers and textile company in Mitsui; Kubota is an industrial equipment company in the Fuyo group.

Companies in a *keiretsu* partner among themselves. A *keiretsu* is the ultimate business strategic alliance. When Japanese automotive companies set up factories in the United States, they try to bring with them their own suppliers who are in the *keiretsu*, thus shifting business from American suppliers to Japanese *keiretsu* suppliers. Because of this exclusionary nature, *keiretsu* are viewed with great suspicion by American antitrust authorities.

Keiretsu and *kaizen* work hand-in-hand to make entrepreneurial partnering easy. Finding a partner is simplified because the search is narrowed to *keiretsu* members. Creating a contract is easier because Japan puts little value in corporate lawyers. Managing the partnership is streamlined because *kaizen* leads to short-term successes, while Japanese executives are renowned for thinking long term.

Table 7.2 shows how the 12 principles of entrepreneurial partnership look from a Japanese perspective.

ENTREPRENEURSHIP JAPANESE STYLE: THREE APPROACHES

Large Japanese firms, like their U.S. counterparts, have tried to compress the value chain by internal venturing. In contrast to the generally disappointing American experience with internal venturing, the Japanese have been more successful. This is largely due to a difference in focus. Japanese companies have used a rifle shot approach—generating new companies within their core business—while Americans have tended to use a shotgun approach—supporting whichever ideas seemed most profitable. Cultural differences have led to alternative management practices in Japan that American executives could possibly adapt.

Secondly, the strategy of international partnering, which Japanese firms have used to tap into Western entrepreneurship, has yielded many successes. With some exceptions, large Japanese firms make good partners. American entrepreneurs who have

TABLE 7.2: The Twelve Principles from a Japanese Perspective

Principle	*Japanese Perspective*	*Reasons*
1. Follow a stage-by-stage partnering strategy.	Easy	Uses a *kaizen* process.
2. Develop a profile of the partners you seek.	Easy	Choose among *keiretsu* companies.
3. Put a motivated "networker" in charge of the search.	Easy	The representative at *keiretsu* meeting conducts search.
4. Contact multiple candidates.	Unnecessary	Not feasible to go outside the *keiretsu*.
5. Focus on mutual benefits.	Same	Same in Japan as in the United States.
6. Start simple.	Easy	Good tenet of *kaizen*.
7. Set benchmarks.	Same	Same in Japan as in the United States.
8. Involve the lawyers—later.	Easy	Lawyers not involved; very few lawyers.
9. Emphasize the partnership mentality.	Difficult	Japanese tend to think of supplier relationships, hierarchical reporting.
10. Develop a team of champions.	Unnecessary	Focus is on the position responsible, not the individual decision maker.
11. Communicate constantly.	Easy	Customary to communicate all the time to achieve consensus.
12. Think long term, but develop short-term successes.	Easy	*Kaizen* works well in short term; Japanese think well long term.

difficulty attracting the attention of large U.S. companies would do well to understand the Japanese goals and strategies for global partnering. The terminology Japanese use is confusing: they call the strategy international M&A (international merger and acquisition). These partnerships are international, but they rarely involve mergers and they may or may not involve acquisition. A more accurate term would be international entrepreneurial partnership.

The third form of entrepreneurship is the start-up companies founded by Japanese "nails" that stick out and were never hammered down. These men and women are more numerous in Japan than most Americans realize. Because they tend to apply the *kaizen* model of continual improvement and a step-by-step approach, new Japanese companies are seldom based on what we would call breakthrough ideas. Instead, they rely on better marketing of an existing product or a better process for making a product. "Japanese know how to make better things better" is the saying in Japan, meaning not only can they make better things but they can make them in better ways. *Kaizen* entrepreneurship means that a new Japanese company is more likely to resemble Dell Computer, with its marketing innovation, than NeXT, with its breakthrough technology.

Internal Venturing in Large Japanese Firms

The cultural preference for *kaizen* methods also applies to internal venturing. The ideas large Japanese companies select and support are seldom breakthrough ideas (which Japanese executives would assign to an R&D lab), but rather incremental ideas that are apt to succeed with less risk.

In the early 1980s, business leaders and government spokesmen from agencies such as MITI (the Ministry of International Trade and Industry) began to speak about the need to increase creativity and entrepreneurship in Japan. "The needs of the Japanese economy have outgrown Japan" was one way the new situation was described. Japan had reached a point where importing technology and new ideas from abroad (mostly North America) was no longer sufficient. There needed to be a way to actively support innovation and new-idea generation within Japan, rather than leaving the process to hit-or-miss market forces. Japanese view the U.S. approach, which results in an estimated 80 percent failure rate for start-ups, as an inefficient, wasteful system.

MITI articulated a national strategy called "creating creativity" in the early 1980s, promoting the importance of increased creativity in Japan. As is typical of such MITI statements, the national strategy did not specify how creativity was to be created. However (and this is also typical), nearly every executive, manager, and worker was aware of the MITI statements. Visiting Japanese companies in the 1980s was like listening to a tape: If you asked about creativity in Japan, every senior executive would tell you, "Creating creativity is our most important task."

From a Japanese perspective, creating creativity means compressing the value chain. The Japanese are already skilled at Phases II and III of the value chain—quality manufacturing and innovative marketing. Their relative weakness has been in Phase I—research, development, and design. Executives of large Japanese firms have tried many ways to implement creativity. Many created R&D labs based on American models.[2] Many, such as NTT (Nippon Telephone and Telegraph, the world's largest company), also started programs to encourage intrapreneuring. Others tried internal venturing, skunk works, and spin-off strategies.

One of the most popular strategies to create creativity has been internal venturing. Large Japanese firms studied American and European corporate models, took the best of these experiences, and then made incremental improvements. The result is a system that works. The rifle shot approach typical in Japan may be an option for U.S. companies committed to internal strategies but disappointed with shotgun results. Two good examples of Japanese programs are the Fuji Xerox Venture Business Challenge Program and NEC Corporation's research ventures.

Fuji Xerox: The Venture Business Challenge Program. Fuji Xerox, a partnership between the Fuji Photo Film Company in Japan and Rank Xerox in the United Kingdom, has been a leader in internal venturing, which is coordinated by the new business development department. Here's how it works, according to Shintaro Sakakibara, department manager and new business manager of the program:

The Venture Business Challenge Program, which Sakakibara implemented in January 1988, was designed to promote new business development within the company and to step up the pace of innovation. The first step was to solicit Fuji Xerox's 12,000 employees for new business suggestions. Within a month, 186 suggestions were submitted. In April 1988, a new business development committee selected 14 of the proposed ideas—none of which involved breakthrough technology—and asked their authors to create a business proposal. Two of the fourteen proposals were then chosen for development into full-fledged businesses within Fuji Xerox.

One became the Fuji System Brain Company, which provides comprehensive hardware and software services to meet the needs of small businesses who suffer from shortages of information-processing engineers. The other became PROTEX Company, which manufactures prototype components for office equipment and electronic devices. The total process, from the call for suggestions to start of the operations, took a year. Compared to what typical U.S. intrapreneurs or entrepreneurs usually require, these operations were quick and inexpensive. No lawyers were involved. No team of champions was necessary.

The authors and developers of the proposals became presidents of the two companies. Each put up 10 percent of the ¥10 to ¥20 million start-up capital; Fuji Xerox supplied the balance.

If the ventures fail, the presidents can come back to their old jobs within Fuji Xerox. Thus a safety net is built into the system, in contrast to most American venture programs.

To be considered successful, the companies have to make a profit by the fourth year, a crucial benchmark. If they don't, they have to "restudy the situation," which means the company will probably be discontinued. The time frame within which companies must prove their worth is clear. The exit strategy is also clear, and softened by the guarantee that "failed" entrepreneurs can return to their old jobs.

At Fuji Xerox, the whole process of internal venturing is closely tied to an overall strategic plan. The company's long-range corporate policy statement identifies business areas in which Fuji Xerox wants to be active within the next five years. These are artificial intelligence, software, new media, electronic devices, home automation, medical equipment, and information services. To be chosen for development, internal venture proposals must fit one of these areas. Fuji System Brain Company fits information services; PROTEX fits electronic devices.

Shintaro Sakakibara built his program on a simple and familiar assumption: "Everybody has a dream." Internal venturing at Fuji Xerox has helped make that dream a reality for well-focused ideas consistent with company strategy.

NEC: Internal Ventures and Spin-Offs. NEC Corporation, one of Japan's leading electronics firms, is clearly committed to autonomy as a strategy for entrepreneurship. Like Fuji Xerox, NEC supports internal venturing. In addition, many of the companies started through internal venturing at NEC have eventually been spun off—an evolutionary process comparable to the Kodak internal venture–spin-off process. The director of R&D at NEC, Dr. Michiyuki Uenohara, described five spin-off companies: one is a computerized fingerprinting security system; the others are based on biochips, computer vision, electronic biosensors for bloodless blood tests, and the use of sludge as a raw material for tiles.

Uenohara's strategy is as follows: First, he identifies a research scientist who has developed a good commercializable idea in the R&D labs. Together, they identify an entrepreneurial partner, an employee who would be interested in and capable of starting a new, independent company. NEC gives marketing and distribution help, especially when the end customer is a big one or where the new company needs someone to guarantee their credibility, which NEC can do. The resulting company is then spun off to operate on its own. Such was the case with NEC Security Systems.

The product of NEC Security Systems is computerized fingerprint identification; its initial target market was Japanese police authorities, who approached NEC because their old computer system took forever to search through fingerprint files. NEC employees were able to develop a super-fast way of scanning huge files of fingerprints and matching them against new prints. The key problem was the intransigence of most police officers, who opposed using computerized searches because it replaced their expertise. The new NEC system, however, maintains a role for fingerprint experts. This system was the basis for NEC Security Systems, which was spun off as a separate company. The NEC name was maintained to give credibility. As in the Fuji Xerox case, the employee who was the developer of the security system was made president of the new NEC security company. If the new spin-off company fails, he can return to his old job.

The city of Chicago is one satisfied client of the new company. During a test run, the new Automated Fingerprint Identification System identified a criminal who had been on the "Most Wanted" list in the city for the past 15 years—in 20 minutes.

Cultural Differences. Fuji Xerox, NEC Corporation, and other Japanese companies have taken practices initiated in the United States—internal venturing and spin-offs—and made them work in Japan. Some of the reasons they work are cultural. The nationwide consensus on creating creativity was certainly a strong inspiration to launch innovative programs, attract would-be entrepreneurs, and establish new companies. Internal venturing is also well suited to the *kaizen* mode of entrepreneurship. No one expects breakthrough results, and incremental improvements are deemed a success.

One weakness of U.S. internal venturing is the exposure of the mother company to lawsuits related to a new company's performance. Since Japan has no tradition of going to court to settle business disputes, this pitfall does not exist. This litigation-free environment is a great boon to new Japanese ventures and spin-offs, because agreements can be reached more quickly than in the United States.

INTERNATIONAL M&A PARTNERING

The American-European practice of merger and acquisition is not practiced in Japan for reasons that are inherently cultural. The business organization is considered a family, and no one should sell or buy someone else's family. The American raider T. Boone Pickens tried once to engineer a hostile takeover of a Japanese company. When he appeared at the board of directors meeting, he was sharply and publicly criticized. Hostile takeovers just don't occur in Japan.

Koji Kobayashi, the chairman of NEC, related a conversation he had with then–British Prime Minister Margaret Thatcher:

> The British have caught the merger and acquisition disease. They talk only about making money. I went to see the senior managers of General Electric Company about a joint venture. They assembled 15 presidents. Their only interest was how a joint venture with NEC Corporation would affect their merger and acquisition strategy. So I went to see Prime Minister Thatcher. I said, "We want a joint venture but can't find an industrial partner." She said, "Do

it alone." So NEC Corporation built a plant in Scotland. All the employees are Scots. Now the NEC plant in Scotland exports to the continent. Then a British MP came to me and said that he wanted NEC to start another plant in his district. Again I went to see Thatcher. Again she said, "Do it alone."[3]

Despite their disdain for M&A fever, Japanese companies have had no compunction about buying American families, including parts of Rockefeller Center, MCA (Music Corporation of America, bought by Mitsubishi in 1990), the Seven-Eleven retail chain, and others. However, when Japanese firms acquire companies, they usually don't merge them. Instead, they leave their partner with substantial if not complete autonomy. Normally, they do not attempt to change the name of the company. They do, however, institute procedures for the systematic transfer of the company's technology. Usually they provide ample financing. When the goal is to access U.S. entrepreneurial resources, most Japanese companies take care not to kill the goose that lays the golden eggs. Sometimes they insist on procedural changes and improvements. When NEC acquired a computer-chip facility in Silicon Valley, Kobayashi insisted that the employees wash more frequently because their clean room was too dirty.

The strong emphasis on autonomy makes Japanese companies good potential partners for U.S. entrepreneurs looking for large-company support and access to export markets. This sponsorship can be particularly welcome if large American companies show little or no interest in your idea or technology. We spoke recently to an MIT professor who had developed a new ceramics process. He took his idea to several U.S. companies but was unable to interest them in his work because it was still at a development stage, and they wanted to see prototypes. In exasperation, he turned to Japanese sponsors, who agreed to partner with him to develop the product. Exabyte and Gateway Technologies had the same problem. They wanted to partner with American companies but found Japanese firms much more responsive and eager to do business.

Some of the Japanese companies that practice international M&A are well known and sophisticated. Others are just getting started on this path. One of these, Toray Industries, has some interesting practices and provides some possible opportunities for American entrepreneurs—particularly those who have products that might do well in the Japanese and Far Eastern marketplace.

Toray Industries

One of Japan's largest textile companies, Toray Industries was founded in 1926 to produce rayon. More recently, Toray has transformed itself into a significant high-technology chemical and materials company, with 1987 revenues of $4 billion (135 yen to the dollar) and 10,000 employees. It has similarities to Perstorp in Sweden (described in Chapter 9) and competes with Du Pont. Its present corporate philosophy is "Creating new values through innovative concepts and technologies." The corporate slogan is "Better living through innovation." How Toray put this slogan into practice is largely a story of international partnering; the first chapter, however, is intrapreneurial.

As early as the 1950s, Toray Industries executives foresaw the saturation of the textile market and the need to develop new core products. Indeed, the 1960s were not profitable years for Toray Industries. In response to the downturn, the board of executives established a basic research center in Kamakura to develop new businesses not related to the company's main textile business, which was increasingly vulnerable to other Asian competitors. In contrast to Fuji Xerox and NEC, the new business thrust at Toray was not to improve core products (a *kaizen* goal) but to develop new core products (a breakthrough goal).

The major new directions set by the corporation were to develop technology in electronics, advanced composite materials, life science and biotechnology, and specialty polymers.

The research itself was very successful, contradicting the notion that Japanese companies are unable to come up with new technologies. Where Toray ran into trouble was in moving from Phase I (R&D) to the implementation stage, that is, in moving down the value chain to market. By the early 1980s, the company decided it had done enough research and that it was time to commercialize and turn the research into profit. As the senior manager of the new products planning department put it: "We became frustrated. .... It takes a long time to get results. We thought it was time to use Japanese technology ideas to make profits."[4]

To make this happen, top management announced a new policy. The new products department was instructed to "make global mergers and acquisitions." This came as a shock to department personnel. "We never thought of M&A because this is unthinkable in Japan. It's a 'sin' to sell one's own company. You cannot sell people to other people, just like you cannot sell family members."

Nonetheless, they proceeded to implement what Toray termed international M&A. In 1987, the company bought Trea Industries, a Rhode Island–based manufacturer of high-performance polypropylene films. Trea is now using Toray technology to produce films of even higher quality. To shorten product development and profit cycle time, Toray Industries' entrepreneurial strategy is quite simple: "Take over U.S. small venture businesses that have new technologies and new products in fields that we have identified as strategic."

In another field, a joint venture set up by Toray and a French company called Soficar is manufacturing advanced carbon fibers pioneered by Toray. The Toray story shows that Japanese companies can be strong in front-end R&D. However, like many large U.S. companies have discovered, the intrapreneurial strategy proved too sluggish in commercializing new technology. For this, Toray turned to small companies abroad, which it supplied with Toray shelf technology developed by R&D. The small companies applied the technology to improve and expand their product lines and are handling the manufacturing end. An important lesson for small companies is that Japanese corporations are not necessarily looking to acquire new American technology; instead, they may be looking for American companies to apply Japanese technology and complete Phase II of the value chain for them.

STRATEGIC ISSUES

When Toray buys foreign companies, it leaves the companies on their own for two reasons:

1. Because of distance and culture, it is impractical to integrate them into the Japanese home company.
2. Preserving their autonomy preserves their innovative qualities as well.

What the Toray case illustrates is important for both American entrepreneurs and U.S. companies. The misnamed international M&A is actually international partnering, a form of win-win entrepreneurial partnership. American entrepreneurs who want to link to large-company sponsors should take a hard look at companies like these. They offer good opportunities for growth.

Large U.S. corporations could follow Toray's example and play the same strategy in reverse: use the international partnering concept to make linkages with small-company entrepreneurs in Japan. This can be an excellent way of entering the Japanese market and tapping into a system of gradual improvement that might benefit some products originally developed in the United States. In the next section, we'll look at some Japanese entrepreneurs who might welcome partnership overtures from U.S. companies.

INDEPENDENT JAPANESE ENTREPRENEURS

Nikkei Award for Creative Excellence

Every year since 1982, Japan's leading economic newspaper (*Nihon Keizai Shimbun*) has presented the Nikkei Award for creative excellence for the best Japanese innovations. Periodically, the paper issues a summary of the awards, who received them, and for which innovation. The book is reminiscent of a similar landmark issued in Sweden: *The Top 100 Swedish Technical Innovations.* Both books make good reading, and the Japanese one especially gives a good perspective on the creativity widespread in the world's second-largest economy.

Some of the awards are for innovations well known to Americans. Nintendo, winner of the 1985 award, was developed by the small company that produces *famikon*: a family home game computer that hooks to your television set. In typical Japanese style, the company's small R&D department started by analyzing the products of two American companies, Coleco and Atari. "We learned what we could about every aspect of the software, from handling noise to calculating circuitry," says Masayuki Uemura, manager of R&D. From these examples, they made an "incremental improvement" that later took over 90 percent of the game market.

Other computer innovations are less well known. Heartner, a miniature electrocardiograph device that allows patients to take their own EKGs, was developed by Toshiharu Katahira, president of a Tokyo-based firm that imports and sells medical equipment. The idea came to him when he watched his wife press her hand over her heart one day. He discussed the idea with the head of his company's research department, and by the end of 1985 he had developed the world's first hand-held heart monitor.

Most of the Nikkei Awards go to companies, many of them large ones. Toshiba won several of the 1986 awards for development of "Spot," the personal portable fax machine, and NEC received a Nikkei for the first 32-byte microprocessor marketed in Japan.

Breakaway Entrepreneurs

Individual entrepreneurship is countercultural in Japan. In explaining the role of entrepreneurship, some people liken the Japanese economy to a wheel. In the center, conformist group behavior is strong. Out toward the rim, individual or small-group activity plays a larger role. Because of the strong emphasis on education in the "right" university as a prerequisite for advancement in large corporations, it is often the non-university educated who find themselves at the rim. With the emphasis on "hammering down the nail" at the universities, perhaps it's no coincidence that the Japanese men and women who didn't go to universities are more entrepreneurial than those who did.

In its annual report on small and medium-size business in Japan, MITI shows that as a percent of the economy, small business accounts for a portion of economic activity equal to or greater than that in the United States.[5] Much of this small-business activity comes from the extensive subcontracting system, whereby a small entrepreneur produces parts for a single large company. The best known are the auto parts suppliers, who are part of a system that is reminiscent of the many small shops in the Midwest that supply the Big Three automakers in America.

As Kuniyasu Sakai explains, this strategy of extensive large-small relationships is standard procedure in Japan, though the system has remained largely invisible to Western observers.[6] These large-small partnerships do not fit our concept of entrepreneurial partnership because the large Japanese corporation does not typically respect the independence of small subcontractors and innovators, exerting instead a dictatorial control. They do point out the two faces of Japanese large companies. One side shows great respect for the autonomy of foreign partners. The other shows a rigid need to control Japanese suppliers, who are not treated at all like equal partners.

Even in the highly controlled Japanese auto world, individual entrepreneurship can be found. An example is Shinji Masuda.[7] Like the legendary Soichiro Honda (who founded the Honda car company), Masuda never went to college. He liked tinkering with cars. In 1982, he left his job at Honda and launched his own company, developing car parts in the typical subcontractor role. His big break came when he responded to a request from the Tokyo branch of Domino's Pizza to develop a new delivery truck. His creation of the MRD Community Vehicle propelled his start-up to a company with annual sales of over $2 million.

This case highlights a potentially enormous opportunity for large U.S. companies: form partnerships with small innovative Japanese subcontractors who are fed up with feudal relationships. Just as Masuda broke from Honda with an offer from Domino's Pizza, many other subcontractors would be willing to slip through the cracks in the walls of the *keiretsu*. What U.S. companies have to gain by partnering with a small Japanese company is access to the Japanese marketplace, plus the speedy innovation that is a chief attraction of entrepreneurial partnership.

"The critical process today is not producing the product," says Masuda, "but originating the idea and executing it more quickly than a big company can." The success of small companies like Masuda's in meeting this imperative is borne out by a 1988 Japanese government survey showing that roughly 30 percent of small manufacturers moved products from R&D to commercialization in under a year.[8] Fewer than 5 percent of large businesses could match this record.

Another independent Japanese entrepreneur is Tamotsu Suzuki, founder of the Suzuki Sogyo Company, a technology firm located in the Shizuoka area between Osaka and Tokyo.[9] By the 1980s, when the firm was taken over by Suzuki's son, it had become a collection of small dedicated units, each concentrating on promising new technologies. Instead of competing with larger companies at manufacturing, Suzuki developed unique products, secured patent protection, and then approached larger companies to strike a deal. Suzuki Sogyo is clearly a monkey-model company, specializing in Phase I. As the founder explains, "We take advantage of the big companies, instead of their using us. We can use their money while we offer them the technology we already have." While the tone is somewhat adversarial, the elements being bartered are quite familiar: This is a classic entrepreneurial partnership.

OBSTACLES TO JAPANESE ENTREPRENEURSHIP

Growing numbers of breakaway Japanese innovators may be interested in partnering with large American firms, which are not bound by the social pressures and practices that keep some Japanese entrepreneurs "at the rim." When Analog Devices in Norwood, Massachusetts, wanted to open an office in Japan, it made an arrangement with Kozo Imai, whose career aspirations were frustrated in large Japanese electronics companies. The problem? Imai had not gone to one of the recognized universities. Working with an American company, he became president of Analog Japan KK. Kozo got a position commensurate with his entrepreneurial talents; Analog got access to the Japanese market.

Other aspects of Japanese social and economic life that constrain would-be entrepreneurs are lifetime employment, which results in a social stigma for those who leave large, established firms, and the lack of traditional venture capital.

LIFETIME EMPLOYMENT AND SOCIAL STIGMA

Lifetime employment is not an incentive for starting new ventures. According to NEC chairman Koji Kobayashi, lifetime employment in Japan did not exist before World War II. After the war, industry was destroyed, and strong labor unions flourished in the 1950s. They created the lifetime employment system which, according to Kobayashi, "restricts both the companies and the employees. Cross-fertilization from company to company is now of paramount importance."

The lifetime employment system can prove particularly vexing to foreign companies trying to establish new operations in Japan. How can they find employees with the experience and drive they need? When BMW came to Japan in the early 1980s, it had to find entrepreneurs to run its new dealerships.[10] Each dealership had to be exclusive. The problem was that even entrepreneurial employees of established Japanese auto companies would not leave their old jobs. Lüder Paysen, the Bavarian-born president of BMW-Japan, reported: "I tried to get a guy to leave Nissan. He agreed. But he eventually had to back down. His managers from Nissan called his parents. The whole family got so upset about his leaving Nissan that they obliged him to call it off."[11]

Where can a foreign company find employees, especially entrepreneurial types who would manage their own auto agencies? Well-established employees of Japanese companies are not a good bet. Instead, the three sources are (1) people like Kozo Imai, who are frustrated in their big-company jobs; (2) independent entrepreneurs like Tamotsu Suzuki, who are outside the big-company system; (3) breakaway subcontractors like Shinji Masuda.

People in the first category, despite their frustration, are still hard to lure away because of the pressures the BMW story illustrates. Leaving an established Japanese firm without a blessing carries a strong social stigma. The same stigma can be found in Europe and in many company towns (especially small ones) in the United States, but the disincentive to leave is enhanced in Japan by the lifetime employment system and the Japanese emphasis on the group. Independent entrepreneurial men and women on the "rim" are immune from these pressures, since they have no large-company security net to leave.

Employees of the numerous subcontractor firms, though affected by these traditions, do not have a lifetime guarantee of security. Although loyalty to the big company is presumed and also enforced, the subcontractors are not always treated well, and those who have experienced hard times when the large company unilaterally cuts prices, for example, might have less of an attachment to the big firm. Employees of the large firm might have secure jobs, but the subcontractors may go bankrupt during an economic downturn. And since the subcontractors are financially separate from the larger corporation, the attraction of breaking away from total dependence on one Japanese firm may be enough to overcome the fear of social stigma.

LACK OF TRADITIONAL VENTURE CAPITAL

The venture capital industry has been slow to develop in Japan. Large companies and banks provided much of the funding at low cost, so that venture capital was considered a second-best resource by many Japanese. As the cost of capital has risen in Japan, venture capital has begun to grow.

Dominique Turpin, a French economics researcher working in Tokyo, has studied the emerging venture capital industry in Japan. She notes two significant differences with its counterpart in America: It is young, and it is dominated by the big four Japanese banking groups rather than wealthy individual investors. While Turpin cautions about making direct comparisons because of these cultural differences, the conclusions she draws are interesting:

> Considering the scale of the Japanese economy to the American one (about 1:2) and the number of newly started companies in Japan versus the United States (about 1:12), the number of venture capital firms currently operating in Japan (55) appears adequate. However ... there is excessive competition when Japanese venture capital firms try to convince entrepreneurs to open the capital of their companies to outside investors.[12]

In other words, Japanese entrepreneurs are reluctant to accept the terms of venture capitalists. Other cultural reasons for weaknesses in Japanese venture capital are (1) many venture capitalists are ordinary bankers with no particular experience in venture capital or small business (a weakness we'll see echoed in Sweden and Britain); (2) few venture capital firms employ engineers able to evaluate the technologies of small high-tech start-ups; (3) Japanese venture capital does not always meet Japanese entrepreneurs' needs.

Financing from large U.S. corporations may be able to fill this gap. Subcontractors in particular may be open to U.S. capital infusions. However, in order for such "venture-like" capital to work in Japan, it needs to overcome two obstacles. First, it needs to be long term, and second, it needs to have *kaizen* expectations.

Paul Hsu of Hambrecht and Quist, the U.S. venture capital firm based in San Francisco, has noted that venture capital investments in Western Europe and Asia (including Japan) are rising. Cumulative investment in North America was $5 billion in 1988, compared to $1.7 billion in Asia. The figure for Western Europe had grown in the late eighties to slightly more than the American figure.[13] As we'll see in Chapter 9, this may be due to investments from nontraditional large-company sources such as the EuroVentures Fund, which pools large corporate contributions for longer-term development. Again, U.S. companies, singly or in partnership, have an opportunity to make investments in Japan in small entrepreneurial firms.

Japanese consider the U.S. model of entrepreneurship too focused on breakthroughs and too risky. They are not surprised by the high failure rate of small U.S. firms and would not tolerate this much failure in Japan. The fault, they find, is in the short-term perspective—particularly of venture capitalists who want to cash out after only three to five years. In order for venture capital to work in Japan, it will have to adapt to the Japanese *kaizen* style of entrepreneurship, and to longer time horizons. Nonetheless, these requirements could be met by large American companies and even large U.S.-based venture capital funds.

CONCLUSIONS

The cases and discussions presented in this chapter have relevance for both large American corporations and entrepreneurs.

- o The practice of both *kaizen* and *keiretsu* smooths the path for partnerships between large and small companies. It is quicker and less costly to find a partner in Japan than elsewhere. Japanese can create a collaborative agreement with less hassle than Americans can, and they can manage an alliance with equal if not more ease once it has been formed.

- o Contrary to the common stereotypes, Japan has lots of entrepreneurs. Many of them would welcome relationships with large American or European companies to avoid becoming captives of large Japanese ones.

- o Most Japanese managers and entrepreneurs inside or outside of large corporations have been trained to look for incremental improvements. Do not look to them for technological breakthroughs. However, linking with a Japanese entrepreneur is one way to break the barriers to entry in the Japanese market, and the entrepreneurs are a source of ideas concerning product modifications that may be applicable worldwide.

- o Contrary to the recent experience of several large American corporations, large Japanese firms have been successful at making internal venturing work. The reason is focus: They use the rifle approach rather than the shotgun approach.

- o Large Japanese corporations, with some exceptions, may be good partners for some small American companies. What large Japanese companies call international M&A is really international partnering. Small companies having trouble getting attention from American firms should investigate Japanese ones.

o If you do partner or co-venture with a large Japanese corporation, understand that its reason is probably to get access to your technology and then to improve on it. In some cases, however, the Japanese corporation may want you to commercialize its shelf technology. You need to understand what the Japanese company expects to gain from the partnership and then negotiate a contract that protects your rights and provides equal benefits for you.

NOTES

1. We are indebted to Gene Gregory, professor of comparative business at Sophia University, for this comparison.
2. For an early description of these labs, see James Botkin, Dan Dimancescu, and Ray Stata, *Global Stakes: The Future of High Technology in America* (Cambridge, Massachusetts: Ballinger Publishing Co., 1982).
3. Koji Kobayashi, personal communication, February 1989.
4. The case material and quotes for the Toray case are taken from T. Ono, "R&D Project Management: Case History at Toray Industry" (white paper, 1983), and from Mr. Tadahisa Tamura (former general manager, New Projects Planning Division), personal interview, February 1989. Ono was the managing director for Toray's R&D division.
5. *Small Business in Japan, White Paper on Small and Medium Enterprises in Japan,* Small and Medium Enterprise Agency, Ministry of International Trade and Industry (MITI), 1988, Tokyo.
6. Kuniyasu Sakai, "The Feudal World of Japanese Manufacturing," *Harvard Business Review,* November/December 1990, pp. 38–49.
7. The case information and quotes for the Masuda case come from Joel Kotkin, "Creators of the New Japan," *Inc.,* October 1990, pp. 96–110.
8. Kotkin, p. 97.
9. The case information and quotes for the Suzuki case come from Kotkin, p. 103.

10. BMW was one of the first non-Japanese car companies to make inroads into Japan. Jaguar and Mercedes were the two others. All had problems establishing dealerships and competing in the Japanese marketplace, partly due to the inaccessibility of people to run dealerships. BMW persisted. As of 1988, there were 108 BMW dealers in Japan.
11. Personal remarks, IMD Seminar, Tokyo, 1989.
12. Dominique V. Turpin, "Japan's Small High-Tech Enterprises and Venture Capital," *Sophia University Business Series* 106, Tokyo, 1986.
13. Paul Hsu, of Hambrecht and Quist, "Venture Capital in Asia, North America, and Europe" (Paper delivered at the Third International Technology Innovation and Entrepreneurship Symposium, Gold Coast, Queensland, Australia, 1989).

CHAPTER EIGHT

Entrepreneurial Nonpartners in the United Kingdom: The Case of the Missing Middle

THE ECONOMY OF THE UNITED KINGDOM

The value of studying the United Kingdom economy is to learn what happens when an important part is missing. Historically and presently, Britain has a wealth of new ideas—scientific and technological breakthroughs that have contributed to the invention of the computer and several new fields of biotechnology, to name but two. A growing number of small companies have been launched to commercialize these discoveries. These start-ups tend to be externally oriented networkers, making them ideal small partners for large corporations that are similarly inclined.

Britain is also home to many well-known large firms. Shell Petroleum, which has dual nationality with Royal Dutch Shell and a quasi-independent operation in Houston, has located its highly successful and innovative headquarters staff in London. Bass Industries is one of Europe's largest brewers, and Rolls Royce and Jaguar are world-renowned automakers. Barclay's Bank, known internationally for its travelers checks, is a symbol of London's stature as a global financial center.

In Great Britain, the worlds of these two groups are distant indeed. Small and large British companies are not linked by partnerships, for large British firms have a case of NIH (Not Invented Here) that makes the "don't bother us" brochures of 3M and GE look like warm invitations to partnering. The worlds of large and small are also not linked by a middle group of midsize, fast-growth firms on their way to becoming large companies, for example, firms such as Apple and Dell in computers or Federal Express and Microsoft in services and software. Such companies are the darlings of the American stock market because of their rapid increase in sales and profits.

In the United Kingdom, however, small companies tend to stay small, rather than moving into the fast lane. The complete disinterest of large corporations in partnering with them is an important factor in explaining what one British commission study has termed the "missing middle."[1] The absence of entrepreneurial partnerships—with no likelihood that they will blossom any time soon in Britain—presents a problem to the national economy and an opportunity to international companies.

ENTREPRENEURSHIP IN THE UNITED KINGDOM: TWO APPROACHES

Matthew Bullock, in a treatise well known in British innovation research, proposed that there are two types of entrepreneurship, one "soft" and another "hard."[2] Soft start-ups involve far less risk than hard ones. Soft companies can be categorized as consulting firms, contract research and development firms, and subcontract suppliers. Such soft companies often have multiple products and services, are flexible in responding to changes in the marketplace, require relatively little start-up capital, and have founders who are networkers rather than autocrats.

Using the terminology of Chapter 4, these externally oriented small companies, which rely heavily on relationships and networking, are monkeys instead of beavers. Many are also value chain specialists, with an emphasis on Phase I. The idea that these "soft" companies are more flexible and less risky suggests that an external orientation is a more reliable strategy for small firms in the 1990s than the "full-service" approach of trying to cover all phases of the value chain.

Hard entrepreneurship seems to be far more risky. Hard start-ups are most typically companies that have invented a single new technological product with little assurance that there is a lasting market for it. They often start in niches and try to expand to mass markets. Usually, they have a single product, have difficulty when the marketplace changes, require on average seven times more seed capital than soft start-ups,[3] and often have founders who were inventors, visionaries, or loners.

This meshes with our description of internally oriented start-ups. Like beavers and bears, companies that put a high value on self-reliance and do everything themselves require substantial inputs of resources and lots of hard work to get off the ground. The growth pattern shows a continuous enlargement of territory, not the quick leaps of monkeys or kangaroos.

Commensurate with the greater risks of hard entrepreneurship, Bullock suggests the rewards for success are far higher than for soft companies. What he probably had in mind were what we call the bears—companies that grow continuously at a very fast rate, like the bear cub who weighs less than a pound at birth but within a few years exceeds half a ton. In comparing British and American start-ups, Bullock found that the British tended to favor the soft model while the American economy had comparatively more examples of hard entrepreneurship.

Historically, some of the world's best-known inventions were developed first in the United Kingdom and then commercialized on a mass scale elsewhere (mostly North America, and increasingly, Japan). For example, television was first tried in England. The computer's basic concepts were invented in England (Charles Babbage in the 1860s). The discovery of the structure of DNA and the production of monoclonal antibodies were both pioneered in the United Kingdom. Unfortunately for the growth of the British economy, the big profits from these products are going largely to the foreigners who commercialized them.

The British tradition of invention and of soft entrepreneurship continues. We can witness the ongoing top-level scientific research and the proliferation of soft start-ups by visiting Cambridge, England, and observing "the Cambridge Phenomenon."

THE CAMBRIDGE PHENOMENON: MODERN-DAY SOFT ENTREPRENEURSHIP

A Japanese director of R&D for a large electronics company told us that when he went on a world fact-finding mission, the United Kingdom was his first stop—before Germany and the United States. The reason is the wealth of good ideas coming from British researchers, academics, and entrepreneurs. High on his trip agenda was a visit to Cambridge.

Cambridge was made famous to students of entrepreneurship by a seminal book entitled *The Cambridge Phenomenon*,[4] which traces the founding and growth of many small companies (mostly started since 1960) within a radius of 20 miles of the university. *The Cambridge Phenomenon* was itself researched and written by the founders of a highly respected small consulting company located not far from the university campus. The study reveals a wealth of small companies that have grown up in the environment which the University of Cambridge provides. There are presently over 600 new high-technology companies in Cambridge, and they continue to grow at the rate of two new ones per week. A company "family tree" from the book, reminiscent of the Silicon Valley family tree, tells a story of intensive innovation. The companies fit our "monkey" model of small firms that rely more on their ingenuity and quickness than on beaver-like industriousness.

The rate of small-company formation in Cambridge has been aided by the Science Park established there nearly a decade ago, as well as the St. John's Innovation Centre, which was filled with small-company tenants shortly after it was built in 1988.

Most of the Cambridge companies would be classified as the soft start-up that Bullock both identified and, as a financier for Barclay's Bank, helped support. Later in this chapter, we'll describe in detail an example of this form of entrepreneurship: TTP—The Technology Partnership—which provides contract research and other design services at the first phase of the value chain. Like Japanese subcontractors, British entrepreneurs tend to be relatively unknown outside of the local area. They normally don't make headlines. This can lead to the misperception by some American executives that entrepreneurship is neither plentiful nor successful in the United Kingdom.

While Cambridge is one of the United Kingdom's leading hotbeds of entrepreneurial activity, it is by no means the only one. Other reports show that new business start-ups are active in the general British economy and account for about the same percentage of employment and GNP as small companies in other countries in Europe. ACOST, the industrial and government Advisory Council on Science and Technology, commissioned a study of the role of small business in the United Kingdom.[5] What it found was that the British rate of start-ups compared favorably with the rate in other European countries, but that the further growth of these companies faced obstacles that needed to be overcome. This is the current problem for Britain: how to augment the excellence in scientific research and soft entrepreneurship with more commercialization and growth.

Cambridge is not only home to soft start-ups. It also has its share of hard companies and famous entrepreneurs. Clyde Sinclair, the founder and developer of the Sinclair computer, is one. Another is Hermann Hauser, the founder and developer of Acorn Computer, often called the Apple of Great Britain. His is the only British start-up to go from zero to £100 million in sales in its first five years. We'll take a look at Hauser's new company, the Active Book Company, which is inventing compact notebook computers and intends to mass market them in partnership with American, Japanese, and European large corporations; large United Kingdom–based firms are notably absent from this list of partners.

THE FUTURE OF BRITISH HARD ENTREPRENEURSHIP

Nick Segal, coauthor of *The Cambridge Phenomenon*, asks: "Will Cambridge continue to be concentrated on research, design, and development with only limited production?"[6] A point of debate among British economic thinkers is whether the national economy should remain specialized in scientific research and soft entrepreneurship—a sort of inventor to the world—or whether it can find a way to reap the rewards—in growth, profit, and job creation—that come with expansion in the hard entrepreneurship model.

From the perspective of soft British companies whose strengths are in invention and networking, there are two possibilities for the future. Both involve extensive partnering, and both can involve large companies from Europe, America, or Japan. The first possibility is for United Kingdom companies to play a role as inventor for the world, develop transactional relationships with international companies, transfer technology to them, and watch them reap the commercial rewards. The other is for British entrepreneurial companies to gain access to foreign markets and grow by leaps and bounds by partnering with large global corporations. This kangaroo approach could win British companies the rewards of mass marketing and global distribution.

From the perspective of large U.S. corporations, either scenario is one of opportunity. One possibility is to participate in harvesting the results of British science and technology research by linking with companies in British research parks. Another is to link up with soft entrepreneurs, infuse them with more capital, take their products into global channels, and to draw upon their excellent talents at the beginning of the value chain. There is considerable competition from other large companies—Italian, German, and Japanese—to do so, but there appears to be little competition from large British companies themselves.

LACK OF LARGE-COMPANY INTEREST

There is a story, probably apocryphal but readily believed in the United Kingdom, about a top British executive of one of England's large firms who had no use for small business. He summed up his attitude by saying this about small companies: "When they grow bold, they fold." His company, like most large British firms, showed little interest in small firms and did not engage in corporate venturing. In fact, we were hard-pressed to find any examples of large British companies actively working in collaboration with British entrepreneurs.

Clyde Sinclair's new company, Anamartic, was unable to get financing from large British firms.[7] Eventually, Sinclair raised £10 million from Fujitsu in Tokyo and from Tandem Computer in Texas. Hermann Hauser's new company, Active Book, got 7 percent seed funding from an Italian firm, Olivetti. No British company or venture capitalist showed interest. One important reason given for this apparent aloofness on the part of large

British firms is the outlook of British executives and the corporate culture in which they work. "Usually," says Alan Hughes, recently appointed director of the Small Business Research Centre at the University of Cambridge, "large company executives are acquisition-minded. They want 100 percent of a successful small company or nothing."[8]

This view was confirmed by the director of the Corporate Venturing Group. His company, BASE International, recently took over a government-sponsored program set up by NEDO, the National Economic Development Office. The director's job was to assemble a register of small firms wanting relationships with large companies, and to get large companies to buy subscriptions to the register.

On the surface, this seemed like a perfectly rational way to find a partner. In fact, the lack of interest on the part of large companies frustrated the director's efforts. What he dreaded most about his job were the sales calls on British large-company executives. "It's a really difficult call," he lamented. He would visit CEOs, directors of business development, managers responsible for mergers and acquisitions, and finance directors. When they were interested at all, they were acquisition-minded, and this was precisely what small-company founders feared. The director felt that the next strategic move for his registry was to expand its scope beyond British executives and build contacts with large Japanese companies.

There are, of course, some exceptions to the disdain large British firms appear to have for their smaller colleagues. Shell in London, the twin of Royal Dutch Shell in the Netherlands, has made some investments in small companies. But most financing of small firms by large British companies has been more for public relations purposes than investment. The goal has been job creation for people displaced by technological developments. For example, British Steel, Pilkington, and British Petroleum have made efforts to create and support small businesses to stimulate job creation in particular localities. So far, none of these has resulted in substantial growth.

Some people cite an antigrowth atmosphere in Britain as a reason for the "missing middle"—the lack of growth firms in the small-business sector. Others refer to the traditional low status of industry in English culture, and to the remnants of class and social hierarchy. Hermann Hauser believes that it's easier for him, an Austrian transplanted to Cambridge (where he earned his doctorate), to break through social barriers that might hold back a native-born Briton. "I'm expected to violate class etiquette," he says. "I don't mind getting my hands dirty, going down on a production floor or R&D lab, rubbing shoulders with Scots and Irish. Their accents all sound alike to me."

A report by Bain & Company in London confirms the lack of interest large British firms have in small ones.[9] Less than 9 percent of innovations in large companies have their source in small ones. According to one large British company: "Technology in our business today is so sophisticated, it is unrealistic to expect that small companies or individual innovators will have much to offer." When the Japanese, Swedes, Germans, Italians, and Americans are eager to partner with and access innovative processes and technology from companies such as Anamartic, The Technology Partnership, and the Active Book Company, one wonders why the British are not. The National Economic Development Council identified the same problem that plagues many American companies: the NIH syndrome. "British firms are often reluctant to adopt technology that was not developed in-house, be it of British or foreign origin."[10]

It is often said that British entrepreneurs who want to grow are reluctant to enter into relationships with large companies for fear of losing their autonomy. Most would decline a financial infusion that would result in ownership of over 50 percent of the company. Some are leery if the offer gets to as much as 10 percent. Like their Swedish counterparts, whom we meet in the next chapter, they often prefer to remain small rather than be acquired and merged.

A BRITISH PROBLEM AND AN
INTERNATIONAL OPPORTUNITY

The absence of fast-growth high-tech companies in an area re-
plete with high-technology ideas and research has intrigued
many observers, who have offered various explanations for the
phenomenon. One is scale and market size. David Connell put
it this way:

> Take two entrepreneurs in the same field, one American and the
> other British. Both achieve a 10 percent market share after five
> years. For the American, this might mean sales of $50 million; for
> the Brit, it means sales of only $5 million. Who's in a better position
> to expand a product line and international sales reach? [11]

Nick Segal echoes this sentiment. He notes that the Cambridge
phenomenon is minuscule compared to Silicon Valley. It simply
does not have the size or sophistication of Silicon Valley or Route
128 in Boston.

This analysis is certainly valid for hard start-ups that grow
by extending their territory and gradually increasing their market
share. For companies following the internal model, the growth
process starts locally and expands regionally, nationally, and ultimately (for bear-sized companies like IBM) globally. As Bullock
noted, however, most British start-ups follow the soft, networking model instead. Unfortunately, most of these companies aren't
showing the characteristic leaping growth of monkey and kangaroo-type companies. The missing piece is the large companies
with whom they need to network.

The British government is concerned about the lack of
growth of small companies. In a recent study, the ACOST report
concluded:

> We find it disturbing that the number of enterprises employing
> between 50 and 500 employees has declined over the period 1963
> to 1985. This is precisely the group in which one would expect

companies with the best prospects for rapid growth to significant size.[12]

While Thatcher government policies stimulated an entrepreneurial economy with many small businesses in the 1- to 49-person range, the number of growth businesses (in the 50- to 500-person size) has declined. Among the reasons cited by the report is the shortage of financing on an appropriate scale, that is, lack of seed funds. There seems to be little venture capital, and while statistics show that venture capital in the United Kingdom and in Europe is now reaching a level of that in North America,[13] the British describe their venture capitalists as "accountants in disguise." In other words, the conservative venture capitalists are not seen as supporters of innovation.

For a time, Barclay's Bank played an active role in financing many of the small businesses that are part of the Cambridge phenomenon. Bullock was a well-known champion of small companies at Barclay's who did much to finance a large portfolio of Cambridge companies. According to local sources, a headquarters study was issued by the bank that found small business too risky. The source of funds dried up rapidly, and the wariness of entrepreneurs toward bankers playing venture capitalist increased further.

Compared to North America, the informal sources of capital in Britain are weak. The United Kingdom has too few rich uncles interested in fast-growth firms. Friends and relatives don't have a tradition of putting up money for small enterprise. Wealthy British individuals seldom step into the business world, especially the high-tech area. Entrepreneurs themselves find less support for mortgaging their houses and betting their futures on their companies. There is obvious investment opportunity here for international sources of capital. Many British entrepreneurs are wary of venture capital firms, but offered the right partnership terms and conditions, they might welcome financing from large U.S. companies.

TALES OF BRITISH ENTREPRENEURSHIP

It's useful to compare two British start-up companies in the high-tech area. Both are located near Cambridge. The Technology Partnership (TTP) can be characterized as a soft start-up. Its specialty is accelerating the process of development and proto-typing, much as RELA does in Colorado. We see it as a monkey that relies on agility and external relationships and will probably grow quickly to medium size and stay there, although the level of profits may continue to grow.

The other company is the Active Book Company, which Bullock would characterize as one of the exceptional hard entrepreneurial start-ups. Founded by Hermann Hauser, it has developed a state-of-the-art notebook computer and is looking for relationships with Italian, American, and Japanese companies to help it reach mass markets just as soon as possible, since it is competing with other firms in a global race to see who can capture this lucrative market first. Active Book is a kangaroo—an enterprise that has large-company aspirations and has relied from the start on external relationships for growth.

THE TECHNOLOGY PARTNERSHIP

Gerald Avidson, head of TTP, describes the company as a classic case of soft entrepreneurship. He says, "We are a collection of engineers who in other conditions might have individually founded our own companies. But we prefer to work coopera-tively, to stay relatively small and focused, and to have a certain amount of security." That is, they prefer to draw a steady salary rather than risk uneven and uncertain cash flow, but they want to work on problems with the autonomy afforded to a small-company entrepreneur. Measuring a company like this against the standards of a full-service hard model is simply inappropriate.

TTP started when a group of 26 British consultants/engineers walked out of a larger firm, PA Technologies, over issues of autonomy. "I guess you could term it a "hostile spin-off," said Gerald. One of the principles of the new firm was employee ownership. At the old firm, no employees had an ownership share. At TTP, all employees became shareholders. In fact, they had to purchase shares as part of their employment package. Shares were priced at around £20,000 each. This gave a sense of ownership, and it gave TTP its seed investment.

Scope of Work

TTP has four major thrusts: strategy, innovation, creation, and automation. It has many technical competencies—in electrical, mechanical, chemical, and other fields—and is organized by market segment. The firm is able to innovate for clients, and it can create new products in many different fields. By 1990, TTP revenue had grown to £8 million, and the company employed 80 professionals. Its chief competitor is another "Cambridge Phenomenon" company. Scientific Generic has carved out a similar niche, and is somewhat larger than TTP in what might be called the supercontractor R&D business.

TTP has strong international connections. The Swedish consulting firm Indevo is an investor. Ericsson has become a large-company partner. Clients include Bosch and Fujitsu. Companies in the United States and Japan account for 35 percent of TTP's sales. There certainly is further room for American companies to actively work with—and perhaps create spin-offs from—companies like The Technology Partnership, which would welcome more such relationships.

THE ACTIVE BOOK COMPANY

An example of hard entrepreneurship on a grow-fast-or-die mission is the Active Book Company, which seeks to compete in the highly competitive, fast-changing world of portable, note-book-size computers. Before starting the Active Book Company in 1988, Hermann Hauser had founded Acorn Computer in 1978 with £200, and grew it into a £100 million company before the Italian electronics firm Olivetti bought 80 percent of its shares in 1985. Thus started Hauser's relationship with the Italian firm. "I didn't walk out in a huff," he says. "I stayed on and became vice president of research and development for Olivetti." He moved to Olivetti headquarters in Ivrea, Italy, and was responsible for directing eight R&D labs for three years.

When it came time to launch a new company, Hauser was an experienced entrepreneur, well versed in risky ventures and in partnering with large companies. Like the Swedish company Perstorp, which we'll meet in the next chapter, Olivetti has a well-developed strategy of strategic partnerships with small firms, with which it has made over 250 agreements worldwide. "In this aspect, Olivetti is the best large company in Britain," says Hauser.

One reason Hauser abandoned his internal position as R&D director to go "outside" again is that in his three years of trying to spark innovation within Olivetti, he was unable to get the results that he could as an independent. In the internal role, Hauser saw heads of R&D, himself included, unwittingly acting as barriers to innovation. To illustrate, he related a case where a personal computer broke down. The researcher said: "It's not my problem. I shouldn't fix it, it's not a good use of my time. I do R&D, not fix computers. We do the things we're good at, like innovation." Hauser, on the other hand, did just what an entrepreneur would do: picked up a screwdriver and fixed the broken computer.

He noted further: "Directors of R&D labs, myself included, have a big NIH (Not Invented Here) syndrome. They want to do everything internally. But this may be a mistake. Rather than trying to set up ten development programs and watching nine of them fail, a more cost-effective strategy is to invest in ten start-up companies. Start-ups are also faster. They are good at short-circuiting departmental barriers."

Active Book Vision

Hauser's vision is the fourth wave of computing: a notebook revolution that is the fourth in the progression from mainframe, mini, through PC. He is enthusiastically developing a four-pound computer with pencil input, portable fax via cellular phone, dictaphone, and handwriting recognition that can be turned on or off. The machine will have a new display technology and objects that not only look like objects but behave like them, and it will allow the user to keep a diary.

The Active Book builds on everyone's familiarity with a book as an organizing schema. Says Hauser, "The diary is to Active Book computing what word processing is to personal computing." He tells with delight his battles in getting marketers to understand the importance of word processing on the Acorn. "When the correcting selectric typewriter came out, they said that word processing would never sell because they could not visualize the new capability that word processing provides! The same is true today of my diary concept."

This time around, Olivetti is putting in some initial seed capital. They have supplied 7 percent of the initial $5 million raised, which represents 25 percent of the company stock. Hauser sees in Olivetti a large-company partner that has moved beyond the usual problems that large companies have with entrepreneurs. These, according to him, are:

o Most big companies don't like revolutionary products. The sales force won't accept a new product until the market is proven. Then, when presented with evidence that the market exists, sales departments pull out long-forgotten memos asking the R&D department to produce just such a product—years ago!

o Most large-company executives get tied up in jealousy over pay scale discrepancies between themselves and entrepreneurs.

o Successful partnerships require big-company champions, and these champions change jobs (sometimes companies) quickly. An entrepreneur can be left without a champion, and support may turn to indifference. "You have two years to diversify your champions," says Hauser.

Points of Collaboration: Seed Investment and Marketing

Hauser notes that Olivetti's help was crucial in two ways. It provided initial financing, but more important, it gave help in marketing and distribution. Olivetti has a tradition of investing in small companies. It put some seed capital into Stratus Computer, an American company in Marlboro, Massachusetts. Olivetti, as well as IBM, agreed to market the resulting Stratus fault-tolerant computer.

In terms of marketing the Active Book, Hauser's goal is to have distribution agreements with three big companies: one in Europe, one in North America, and one in Japan. "The big payoff is to enlist the large company in helping you do distribution and selling."

CONCLUSIONS

The economy of the United Kingdom is behind in terms of partnering. Most large British companies are not interested in finding partners. This means that when British start-up firms develop a profile of possible partners, they are obliged to look internationally. Going abroad means that initiating contacts with multiple partners is more costly, and the process of finding a partner is likely to take longer than it does for an American or

Japanese counterpart. European integration should help small British firms in this regard.

Since large British corporations are not interested in partnering, there are opportunities for other companies to initiate large-small partnerships. There is certainly ample opportunity for U.S. firms to link up with, and in a sense harvest, some of the exceptional innovative ideas that seem to abound in the Cambridge University environment. And for companies that want to get some experience before entering into a longer-term collaboration, working under contract with a firm like The Technology Partnership is a realistic option.

Another opportunity may exist for selected U.S. companies to network with soft British entrepreneurs by supplying the financing and marketing clout needed to move good ideas into the global marketplace. Some companies, like TTP, may prefer to stay independent. But numerous would-be kangaroos like Active Book have remained small because they don't have the partners they need to take quantum leaps.

While British entrepreneurs are likely to welcome linkups with large American firms, there is competition from large Italian and German firms. Japanese companies such as Nissan have discovered the talent of British entrepreneurs, who they believe hold a greater promise of access to the European Community than their American or Japanese counterparts. On the other hand, Britain and the United States have always enjoyed a special relationship, and there will surely be ample room for collaborative ventures between small British firms and large forward-looking American corporations.

The reverse case is probably less true. While a few large British firms (for example, Thorn EMI) do invest in small high-tech firms in the United States, these are rare. We identified few opportunities for small American entrepreneurs to develop partnerships with large United Kingdom companies. U.S. companies that would prefer to partner with a British company because of history, language, and the special U.S.–United Kingdom relationship should think again. Small U.S. firms seeking to go abroad should consider going to the United Kingdom independently. If they want to partner with large firms, we suggest looking to Italy or Germany for access to the European Community marketplace.

Another alternative is to look carefully, and selectively, at the situation in Sweden. In many ways, Sweden resembles Britain in that it is nearly English-speaking (seldom will one meet a Swedish businessperson who does not speak English as well as or better than native speakers). It is filled with entrepreneurs skilled in high-tech research and development. Like British entrepreneurs, Swedes have trouble growing their start-up companies to significant size and would welcome relationships with large U.S. firms. Unlike the United Kingdom, Sweden does have some large companies that have both experience in and a strong commitment to entrepreneurial partnerships.

NOTES

1. ACOST, *The Enterprise Challenge: Overcoming Barriers to Growth in Small Firms (in the U.K.)* (London: Advisory Council on Science and Technology, 1990).
2. Matthew P. D. Bullock, *Academic Enterprise, Industrial Innovation, and the Development of High Technology Financing in the United States* (London: Brand Brothers, 1983).
3. D. Connell, *Starting a High Tech Company: Strategies for Success* (London: Barclays Bank, 1985). With Deloitte, Haskin, and Sells. Connell found that the soft British companies he studied had a peak financing requirement of £83,000 versus £615,000 for hard companies.
4. R. Quince, W. Wicksteed, and N. S. Segal, *The Cambridge Phenomenon*, 3d ed. (Cambridge: SQW, 1990, reprinted with foreword). Originally published in 1985.
5. ACOST.
6. Quince, Wicksteed, and Segal, p. 79.

7. Anamartic is likely to be the first company to successfully accomplish "wafer scale integration," a computer-on-a-chip technique that has been tried unsuccessfully by IBM and Gene Amdahl's company, Trilogy.
8. Alan Hughes, personal interview, October 1990.
9. "Innovation in Britain Today: How Major Companies Can Help Innovation—And Themselves" (Bain & Co., 1990).
10. "Industrial Innovation" (National Economic Development Council, 1989).
11. David Connell, personal interview, October 1990.
12. ACOST, p. 4.
13. Paul Hsu, of Hambrecht and Quist, "Venture Capital in Asia, North America, and Europe" (Paper delivered at the Third International Technical Innovation and Entrepreneurship Symposium, Gold Coast, Queensland, Australia, 1989).

CHAPTER NINE

Entrepreneurial Partnerships in Sweden: An Opportunity Waiting to Happen

SWEDEN AS A LABORATORY

Historically, Sweden is home to the world's oldest continually operating corporation—Stora Kopperberg, which was founded over 700 years ago. Like America, the country experienced a golden age of large-company development in the early 1900s, when Volvo, SKF, Electrolux, and Hasselblad cameras were formed. It seems to have lost the knack for growing large companies, however. Although Sweden has an abundance of inventors and entrepreneurs, contemporary Sweden resembles Britain in its missing middle ground and scarcity of rapid-growth companies.

Sweden is geographically about the same size as Japan or California. Like Japan, only 10 percent of its surface is cultivated. However, Sweden is not crowded with only 8.4 million people, compared to Japan's 125 million. Ninety percent of Swedes live in the south of the country.

One of the most highly developed countries of the world, Sweden has the highest number of robots and mobile telephones per capita, and virtually no unemployment (a mere 2 percent in 1987), though some of the population is either underemployed or busy in government retraining programs.[1] Nonetheless, the contrast to the rest of Europe is extraordinary—comparable unemployment figures in the U.K., Italy, and France were 12 percent. In the mid-1980s, Sweden's growth in industrial production was the best in Europe.[2] By the late 80s and early 90s, the economic climate had begun to turn down.

SWEDEN'S ECONOMY: TWO EXTREMES

Sweden has an unusual economy, with a concentration of industrial power unequalled in any other economy. Volvo, the largest Swedish company, represents 14 percent of Sweden's GNP. The ten largest companies account for nearly 50 percent of GNP and over 80 percent of industrial R&D. As Sweden's industrial growth record suggests, these companies are doing well. Their strategies for innovation run the gamut from *kaizen*-style intrapreneuring to multiple partnerships with large and small companies.

Sweden also has a large number of small companies with a rich tradition of invention and entrepreneurship. Some observers claim that Sweden has more inventors per capita than any other nation. However, these small companies seldom grow, leaving the economy with a "missing middle" comparable to the British situation.

The question for Sweden, as for much of Western Europe, is how to support its large enterprises while at the same time diversifying the economy with smaller, more entrepreneurial firms. These two extremes—lots of entrepreneurs on the one hand, and the world's greatest concentration of large companies on the other—represent a problem for Swedish policymakers: how to stimulate growth and fill the vacuum with fast-track, medium-sized companies. Sweden, with its now non-socialist government is better poised than most countries to generate new forms of entrepreneurial collaboration that hold lessons for us all.

In the pages that follow, we will first look at how two large corporations are meeting the challenge of constant innovation. Then we focus on small entrepreneurial companies that have tried, with mixed results, to find partners to assist them in achieving rapid growth and success. Finally, we look at some uniquely Swedish institutions that are helping small companies grow and fill in the middle ground. For American corporate executives and U.S. entrepreneurs, the current situation in Sweden offers opportunities to develop transnational entrepreneurial partnerships that can benefit both countries.

CONCENTRATION OF CORPORATE POWER

Sweden's wealth of large corporations includes Volvo and Saab, Electrolux, Asea (now Asea, Brown Boveri or ABB), Ericsson, SAS, and SKF (a roller bearing company). Recent studies of the Swedish economy show that the large companies are doing well and improving their position. A Brookings Institution study notes, "The Swedish economy has a group of large firms with great expertise, deep pockets, and a global perspective. . . . They are winners. . . . They have dramatically improved their market positions since 1982."[3]

A recent article in *Affärsvärlden* (Sweden's *Business Week*) indicates that the large Sweden-based multinationals are growing at over three times the rate of comparable companies in the United States, and faster than the large Japanese companies.[4] One reason for this strong growth is their success in stimulating innovation.

Using internal strategies, Volvo and SKF have made internal venturing and a Western version of *kaizen* entrepreneurship work. American executives from internally oriented companies may find these cases instructive. Other companies have chosen external approaches. Both SAS (Scandinavian Airlines System) and Perstorp (a medium-size chemical company) have developed a strategy of partnerships which includes alliances between two or more large companies as well as collaborations between large and small companies. Large and small U.S. companies may find them attractive partners. Entrepreneurs concerned with maintaining autonomy, however, should be wary of some other large Swedish firms that, like British companies, prefer the M&A model.

LARGE SWEDISH COMPANIES USING INTERNAL STRATEGIES

SKF: Swedish *Kaizen* and Intrapreneurship

SKF is the large Swedish rolling bearing manufacturing company headquartered in Gothenburg. Its founder was inventor Sven Wingquist, who started the company in 1907. In the 1930s, SKF spun off business it thought would never succeed in Sweden, an automobile company named Volvo, which is now five times the size of its former parent.

Traditionally, innovation at SKF has been done in microsteps. The company has followed a Swedish version of the Japanese *kaizen* tradition of constant, gradual improvement. Over the decades since its founding, the trend has been for rolling bearings to get lighter, smaller, and slimmer, to perform the same job but with higher efficiency and quality. SKF has had no radical changes in direction or new markets. SKF has preferred instead to focus on its core business.

One reason given for the lack of radical change is that SKF's customers are rather conservative. Volvo is a good example of an SKF conservative customer. Knowing that Volvo is reluctant to experiment with new bearing designs, SKF ships them only traditional roller bearings. While SKF does conduct experiments on its own—for example, on radically different ceramics-based roller bearing systems—it has not yet adopted them as part of its standard product line. The SKF product line includes nearly 20,000 different types of roller bearings, but less than 1 percent use promising new materials like ceramics.

SKF has never lost a bid to a competitor with a radically different or newer product. Competition centers, instead, on price and quality differences. This situation has taught SKF that *kaizen*, or gradual improvement, works better for the company than radical breakthroughs.

In some ways, SKF resembles 3M in Minnesota, although it has one product with 20,000 variations rather than 20,000 different products. The key ingredient seems to be a corporate culture that favors and supports incremental but continuous innovation. Mauritz Sahlin, the CEO of SKF, is trying to strengthen that culture by asking each manager to act like an entrepreneur. By this he means they should

o Be externally oriented
o Expect and like change
o Exploit new opportunities
o Be motivated by ideas, visions, and goals
o Be results oriented
o Be starters and moderate risk takers

The last point, being "moderate" risk takers, is an important tip-off. Within the company, it is generally acknowledged that in the past, SKF managers have not taken a sufficient amount of risk. On the other hand, several spin-off projects that have failed have made the company gun-shy. The issue for SKF is what constitutes an appropriate amount of risk for the company and how this should be defined and operationalized.

In 1987, the CEO set up the President's Fund to support entrepreneurial ideas. Senior managers of each line of business contribute to the fund in proportion to their sales and receive money back according to the source of innovation projects. This process has also cascaded downward to some extent; individual business units may also have their own innovation funds. This internal approach succeeds for many of the same reasons that the 3M intrapreneurial strategy is successful.

Volvo: Swedish Internal Venturing

Volvo has made concerted efforts to become more innovative and entrepreneurial, but the going has been neither easy nor dramatic. Like many large companies, Volvo has developed some unique and interesting ways to promote innovation and internal entrepreneurship, but it has yet to create a system commensurate with its size and power as Sweden's largest company. Most of Volvo's focus has been on internal venturing, and several techniques discussed below have helped make this strategy successful.

Volvo receives and studies about 1,000 new venture proposals per year. They originate both internally and externally. After the stack is winnowed out by the Strategic Planning Department, 200 to 250 are sent on to the office of president Pehr Gyllenhammar. About 1 out of 10 of these are feasible business ideas, but only 2 out of 100 are ideas that make sense for Volvo.

Another related technique comes from intercompany cooperation on financing. Volvo participates in Euroventures Nordica (EV), a European version of a venture capital fund whose parent organization, the Euroventures Fund, was an outcome of the European Roundtable, which Gyllenhammar founded. The group of companies in the regional Euroventures Nordica fund help nurture their ventures by providing support through the appropriate group member. Volvo may link up one of its smaller companies to customers who are fellow corporate partners in Euroventures Nordica. Unlike U.S. venture capital funds, EV has a ten-year time horizon for its investments in small companies.

A practice that aids Volvo's internal venturing is the "invisible contract," a safety net that guarantees individuals their jobs back if their new ventures fail. The Swedish system is slightly different from the Japanese approach: An employee holds two jobs at once—his or her old (visible) job and the new venture (invisible) job. The entrepreneur ends up working not double time but about 1.4 times normal, since some assistance is provided to free up time. This arrangement usually lasts for about six months. If, at the end of that period, the new idea is feasible, the person may go full-time with the new job and is usually offered a promotion for successfully handling the increased work load. If the new idea fails, the person simply goes back to the old job.

According to Rutger Friberg at Volvo's corporate planning headquarters:

> Having this six-month invisible try at an innovation is a good way to overcome a Swede's fear of trying new things. You'd think, with the strong social safety net in Sweden, people would be willing to take more risks because even if you fail, you can never be destitute. The opposite, however, is the case. The education and social system have made most Swedes very risk averse . . . it discourages entrepreneurship.[5]

LARGE SWEDISH COMPANIES USING EXTERNAL STRATEGIES

Scandinavian Airlines System: International Partnership Strategy

When Jan Carlzon became president of Scandinavian Airlines (SAS) in 1980, the company was headed for a $20 million loss and had a poor reputation among its current and potential customers. By 1983, the company was profitable and was named Airline of the Year by *Air Transport World*.[6] By 1986, it had won the top service quality awards among international airlines.

In 1986, the company embarked on a new strategy to transform a Scandinavian air travel business for Europeans to a European travel business for a global market. It chose to do this by focusing externally and forming partnerships with other airlines and travel-related businesses, like hotels. SAS scored a first with business travelers: If you stayed in an SAS hotel, you could check in your baggage for your onward flight at the hotel's front desk.

Partnerships were formed with Continental Holdings and Canadian Airlines in North America, ANA in Japan, British Midlands in the United Kingdom, Thai Airlines in Southeast Asia, LAN Chile in South America, Swiss Air, Austrian Airlines, and Finn Air in Europe. Other partnerships were formed with International Hotels, with travel services, and with airline supply organizations. The goal of these partnerships was twofold: to expand service globally and to expand services to business travelers beyond air travel, but related to it.

All of these partnerships were strategic alliances from one large company to another. SAS has made more extensive use of this large-large concept than most companies. What are less well known are the company's experiments with large-small relationships, such as that formed with SAS Intercultural Communication.

The SAS Intercultural Communication Experience

To the outside world, SAS Intercultural Communication looks like an innovative program set up by SAS to train its personnel in how to operate and manage in cross-cultural environments. But to founder Lena Ahlström and training director Anders Hovemyr, the story is different. Ahlström founded the service as an independent company in 1984. Rather than struggle on her own, she decided to find a partner, that is, to network in order to grow. Ahlström managed to interest Jan Carlzon in her idea of partnering, and now she has what she calls "a semi-independent business" operating within SAS.

Ahlström's business specializes in offering three-day courses to families who have been given international assignments, or two-day courses on the topic of international business. About half the courses are for SAS; the rest are for other companies, primarily Scandinavian. While her agreements with SAS carry some restrictions, Ahlström and Hovemyr certainly feel and act like entrepreneurs.

Her experience in building this partnership is instructive to other entrepreneurs: "The first middle-level SAS executives we initially approached tried to steal my idea. Then I wrote to the president, who agreed to a partnership. This taught me not to give up at the first sign of resistance."

It took eight months of negotiations to work out the terms of agreement, and there was a six-month trial period when she was an employee. It took five years before the operation became profitable. Thereafter, she became completely responsible for her own profit and loss.

SAS Intercultural Communication is housed on the ground floor of the all-glass SAS headquarters just north of Stockholm. The company pays rent for the offices, but SAS provides the phones. Ahlström receives a salary from SAS, and most of the profits go to SAS. "I'm glad to repay SAS to the best of my ability," she says. Her value to SAS became apparent in an unexpected way. The airline has begun offering her services to train other large-company executives whom the airline wants to lure as corporate clients. "We're a marketing device as well as a training group," says co-worker Hovemyr. "This becomes part of our competitive advantage."

SAS Intercultural Communication has some restrictions. It cannot solicit business from direct competitors of SAS, nor can it turn down requests for business from SAS. Sometimes situations arise where a totally independent company might have behaved differently. But Ahlström and Hovemyr made choices that are right for them. They have a virtual guarantee of 50 percent of their business from SAS in exchange for certain restrictions on growth. They get salaries in exchange for giving up rights to substantial shares of profit. They could sell out and leave SAS, but they have no intention of doing so. They have settled successfully into a niche and are behaving like a monkey-type company, with a network of instructors, subcontractors, and other partners totalling over 90 people, and SAS acting as parent partner.

Perstorp: A Strategy of Entrepreneurial Partnerships

Perstorp is another Swedish company that has an innovation strategy based on partnerships. In contrast to SAS, most of Perstorp's partners are small companies. It has been practicing entrepreneurial partnership for nearly 20 years.

A producer of specialty chemicals, Perstorp was founded more than 100 years ago. The company had 1987 sales of 4 billion Swedish crowns (Skr) and a 1988 return on assets of more than 21 percent.[7] The company incorporates innovation, entrepreneurship, and creativity into its strategy. Karl-Erik Sahlberg, former president and CEO, says, "Creative chemistry is the fundamental element in Perstorp's overall business concept." Some of the more visible elements of that strategy are:

o   A culture that supports creativity. Perstorp avoids rules and regulations. The only uniform rule it has is how to get reimbursed for travel.

o   Decentralized close-to-the-market R&D. Perstorp executives, fearing that central research was creating white elephants, closed the central R&D lab in 1971. "Scientists paid more attention to molecules than to markets," said one executive. Today, Perstorp spends only 3 percent of sales on R&D and gets a big bang for its investment. *Veckans Affärer* rated Perstorp number two in Sweden for R&D payoff (number one was Ericsson); in comparison, a drug company like Pharmacia spends 9 to 10 percent of sales on R&D.[8]

o   A long-term commitment to goals. Perstorp's decentralized strategy has been in place since 1970. Innovation and creativity are not a fad for Perstorp; they are a long-term commitment pursued via university links, an incubator, and funding of both internal ventures and external projects.

o   A university strategy. In 1982 Perstorp, along with Ericsson, became one of the pilot companies at the University of Lund incubator and research park called Ideon, which is located "a coffee break away" from the university.

o   Pernovo: a company for growing new companies. Pernovo, a corporate incubator for Perstorp, is located in the Ideon research park. It is a separate, arms-length company whose purpose is to look for businesses that will succeed in the next five to eight years. It provides marketing, patent know-how, and links to other companies in the Perstorp system and specializes in companies where both the technology and the market are new. Pernovo has supported 33 companies in three business areas, which account for 20 to 25 percent of Perstorp's sales.

o   The President's Fund. Up to Skr 100,000 can be granted on the strength of a phone call. Often the money is used to support feasibility studies, market tests, and prototypes. When asked whether this much-touted "grant by phone" was really true, Dr. Ulf Ljungberg, research coordinator, replied, "Yes, it happens all the time. Obviously, the head of the fund knows the person on the other end of the

line. But the main question he asks is whether the re-
quester believes in the project. If there is hesitancy, he
doesn't grant; otherwise, he does."

o   The Perstorp Research Foundation. The Research Foundation finances projects external to the company, often
in cooperation with universities and other research institutions. Funds come from corporate budgets and are
not charged to operating units. A hallmark of the foundation is its ability to react quickly to proposals, and with
a minimum of paperwork. Half the funds are spent outside Sweden.

One of the 33 small companies within Perstorp is Percell
Biolytica, founded by Kjell Nilsson. His saga reveals a lot about
how a good entrepreneurial partnership works.

Percell Biolytica: A Large-Small Partnership
that Works for Both Parties

Percell Biolytica is a biotechnology company founded by Swedish
inventor Kjell (pronounced *Shell*) Nilsson, who chose a Swedish
partner over American biotech firms that had also offered support.
Sten Nordberg, Perstorp's senior vice president for corporate development, believes that Percell Biolytica is a good example of
what the Perstorp approach to large-small alliances is capable of
producing.

In 1979, Nilsson was working on his doctorate in biochem-
istry at the University of Lund in southern Sweden. During the
course of his work, he invented and patented microcarrier animal
cells whose properties permitted monoclonal antibodies to stick
to their surface and reproduce. This was the beginning of an
important process technology that enabled genetically manipu-
lated material to be rapidly and inexpensively reproduced. Nilsson's early invention had flaws. The microcarrier had to be sus-

pended in a medium, and when the medium was stirred, the reproducing cells on the outside were damaged by the stirring blades. Nonetheless, the patent was purchased by Corning Glass.

Nilsson finished his doctorate in 1983 and solved his earlier problem. He discovered how to make a porous microcarrier with the desired cells growing on the inside, where they were protected from stirring blades. When he tried to commercialize his new finding, he had two offers. One was from an American biotech company, which offered more money; the other was from Perstorp, where friends were already working, and which offered more security. Nilsson chose the latter, saying:

> I'm scared of large American companies. They are far away, and they could cut me off so easily. It was not a question of moving to the United States; they were willing to build a plant in southern Sweden. But I knew that Perstorp had a long-term orientation. They could withstand losses my company might incur for a couple of years without getting upset. Also, I watched what happened in America to my patent with Corning. They had not pushed its development very hard, and transferred it to a subsidiary, KC Biologicals. Then it became caught up in the American M&A game. KCB was bought out by Hazelton. Later, Hazelton was bought out by Corning. So the finances went full circle, but the patent went undeveloped.

Nilsson and his former professor own 9 percent of Percell Biolytica's stock, and Perstorp owns 91 percent. In return, Percell Biolytica gets a five-year agreement with Perstorp. The first two years, Perstorp provides two million Swedish crowns (equal to about $350,000 in late 1990), which covers all development work including the founder's salary. In years three to five, the amount of continuing funding is negotiated annually. A kicker is that if Nilsson sells his shares of the stock in Percell Biolytica (which he must offer first to Perstorp or to his joint owner), he receives double its proportional value, which itself is determined by a formula based on profit performance.

When Nilsson signed the agreement in June 1987, he was spending 90 percent of his time on developing the technology.

By late 1989, he was spending 90 percent of his time developing the business, its strategy and markets. "I'm not your typical university researcher," he says. "I love the business side too."

From its base in Sweden and the solid partnership with Perstorp, Percell Biolytica has formed relationships with American companies SmithKline and French as well as Genentech. The company has also acquired a U.S. producer, HyClone Labs in Logan, Utah. Perstorp owns 51 percent of HyClone.

What was the advantage of linking to a large firm? Time and credibility. "First, I saved time," said Nilsson. "Perstorp provided not only funds, but office space, secretaries, telephones, and other equipment. Most importantly, it provided credibility. I could tell SmithKline, for example, that I really would be around for the long haul because Perstorp has been in business for over a century. If I were on my own, I couldn't say that with conviction."

What was the advantage of going with a large Swedish company rather than an American one? Time and trust. "What Perstorp did was support my work in the way I wanted to organize this business. The Americans are still too focused on financial arrangements—mergers and acquisitions. They risk losing the entrepreneurial spirit."

A CAVEAT: SOME LARGE SWEDISH FIRMS SWALLOW SMALL ONES

U.S. entrepreneurs seeking partners should keep in mind that not all Swedish corporations are as enlightened as Perstorp. While more open than their British counterparts, many Swedish executives are more interested in control and integration than in fostering entrepreneurship, and many large Swedish companies have the reputation of gobbling up small firms. For entrepreneurs who prize their autonomy, large firms such as these make poor partners. For those who want to sell their companies and be merged, most large Swedish firms will be only too glad to oblige.

There is a story, probably apocryphal, that during the 1950s and 1960s, large Swedish company groups refused to do business with small companies, saying they were unreliable and drained management talent from the large firms. While this story is strongly denied by responsible high-level corporate leaders, entrepreneurs and researchers believe it is probably true. Hence, some Swedes are very wary about the power of the large companies to harm as well as help small ones.

CONCENTRATION OF INVENTORS

Sweden has a rich tradition of invention that has concentrated a large number of inventors in this small country. The tradition is symbolized by the Gnosjö spirit, which refers to the southern province of Småland and its tradition of inventing by necessity. Småland is known for its hard life and autonomous spirit. Many inventors—including Kjell Nilsson—come from Småland, and the province and its values have come to represent the ideals of Swedish entrepreneurship.

In *Sweden: The Land of Today*, William Mead describes the tradition:

> The inventors include Gustaf de Laval, who produced the original cream separator and early versions of the milking machine; Alfred Nobel, inventor of the dynamite that was critical for mining and construction operations in the hard rocks of Sweden. L. M. Ericsson produced the telephone in Sweden at about the same time as Alexander Bell; Husqvarna conceived a sewing machine to rival Singer; Dalén invented automatic lighthouses. Sweden had an almost worldwide match monopoly before the crash of the Kreuger empire in the 1930s.[9]

One may add to this list Sven Wingquist, inventor of the self-aligning ball bearing and founder of the SKF company; Baltzar von Platen and Carl Munters, whose invention of a refrigerator with no moving parts led to the success of the Electrolux company; and Jonas Wenstrom, inventor of the three-phase electric motor that helped create the giant ASEA company, now merged with the Swiss Brown Boveri to form ABB.

Sweden has an extensive network of public support for inventors, including the Swedish Inventors Association, International Inventors Awards, and the Gold Medal awards from the Royal Swedish Academy of Engineering Sciences. Governmental organizations like STU (National Board for Technical Development) and SIND (National Industrial Board) are increasing their support for small companies and research parks at most major universities. When it comes to partnering with large companies, however, the record is definitely mixed, as the following case studies show.

TALES OF SWEDISH ENTREPRENEURS

Many Swedish entrepreneurs launch beaver-model companies. They start small, stick to building their own territory, and remain small. Many are family firms, founded by a gritty patriarch who wanted a small business to maintain his autonomy and control his cash flow (an important consideration in a country with the world's highest marginal tax rates).

Other Swedish entrepreneurs, like Lena Ahlström, behave more like gregarious monkeys, anxious to seek partnerships and to grow beyond the confines of a limited domestic economy. Below we profile four entrepreneurial companies. The first is Upnod, a data communications company in Uppsala (Sweden's Cambridge) that is ripe for a large-company partner. Second is Zyx, an upstart new software company with links to Apple and Hewlett-Packard in California. Zyx tried but failed to partner with Ericsson in Sweden. Third is ITERA, a company that tried to produce a new bicycle but failed for the want of a good partner.

And fourth is Medicarb, a medical process company that has gone through several partnerships and has yet to find success.

Upnod: Looking for a Partner

Upnod, a data communications company, was founded in 1979 by Norwegian Pål Kruger, who is married to a Swede. His wife said he was crazy when he left his post as a professor at the University of Uppsala to start manufacturing multiplexors and LAN equipment. "I said I would take a year off, and I could always go back." But he never did. Now his wife works in the company. By 1988, sales were about $5 million, with some 40 employees.

Much of Upnod's financing came from Euroventures Nordica, the venture capital firm described earlier. EV Nordica is one of several pan-European investment groups that gets its capital from large companies. "Euroventures Nordica has been a great help to us," says Kruger. "They give us the credibility we need."

Forming relations with large companies has not been so easy. Upnod found itself in competition with Nokia, a Finnish conglomerate, that was far more successful because of its size and reputation. As Kruger noted: "We found ourselves competing against Nokia for a Skr 1 million contract with a large Swedish company. We lost. The buyer said that the contract was too big for a small firm."

Kruger would like to expand, but he lacks the resources to do so. He would particularly like to generate international sales, first in the European Community (especially Germany) and then beyond Europe. Other than Ericsson, there are no Swedish large companies in his field with which to partner. He would look kindly to possible linkups with American firms or Japanese companies to help with the distribution and marketing ends of his value chain.

Zyx: Found American Partners

Zyx, a software company in Stockholm, was founded by 28-year-old Jan-Erik Gustavsson, who dropped out of the Royal Institute of Technology (Kungliga Tekniska Högskolan, or KTH) to found his company. "If I had gotten a diploma, it would be too great a safety net, I might go out and get a job," he says. "I felt like an 'average engineer' at KTH, and I didn't want to be average."

Zyx got its working capital from large companies, but they were all American ones. Sweden has no large computer hardware companies except Ericsson, which is in telecommunications. According to Gustavsson, "Ericsson Information Systems saw me as a small insect. They had a big-company mentality, so they turned me down. But at Apple and Hewlett-Packard, where they had an entrepreneurial mentality, we got contracts."

Zyx got $200,000 from Hewlett-Packard, and $100,000 from Apple, plus machinery. When that ran out, Zyx had to go to venture capital sources but could locate only two in Sweden. Now Gustavsson is trying to start a relationship with DEC or with Sun MicroSystems.

Zyx's strength is in Phase I research, development, and design, and in Phase II production. The company can produce software for another company under contract, or it can do R&D, designing products that can be marketed and distributed by large corporate partners.

Gustavsson noted the dangers of dependence on a single partner.

> When the recession hit the computer industry, HP shut down the activities in the organization with which we were working. Lots of products suffered, and our newly introduced HP Prolog II was one of them. Since our main channel to the market for the product disappeared, I am now forced to "sell out" to a larger company. So, this particular example did not turn out to be a winning combination in the long run, but I still believe in the idea and will try it again.[10]

ITERA: Needed a Partner

Like any country, Sweden has a high rate of entrepreneurial failure. Some of these failures are well known in the country.

Two former employees of Volvo had a great idea for a plastic bike that would not corrode in Sweden's damp, cold environment. Their company was called ITERA. After a previous failed attempt to produce a plastic car, Volvo spun off this initiative to let it sink or swim on its own. The cofounders constructed a modern bicycle factory in northern Sweden, which needed the employment for regional development.

ITERA was a huge flop, and the company went bankrupt. The concept was good, but the marketing was nonexistent. ITERA has come to be considered Sweden's Edsel. Undeterred by this nationally famous failure, a Småland inventor created a bicycle that required no chain. It, too, went nowhere. While the technical concept was intriguing, the notoriety of the ITERA case foreclosed further experiments with bikes.

What ITERA illustrates is the all-too-common case of a good technical idea—and the concomitant growth and employment—being lost due to lack of marketing and access to distribution channels. Had ITERA's developers secured large-company backing in consumer markets for bicycles, the company might have had a better chance of success.

Medicarb: The Hazards of Swedish Entrepreneuring

Olle Larm's saga tells a lot about the hazards of Swedish invention and entrepreneuring, and reminds us of the bittersweet safety match story. After graduating from Stockholm University in 1973, Larm took a post as assistant professor at the Swedish University for Agricultural Sciences in Uppsala, which had cutting-edge research in carbohydrate chemistry.

In 1981, Larm, together with scientists at the Karolinska Institute, perfected the process of preventing blood coagulation. They figured out how to mimic the interior of vascular walls, where blood passes but never clots. The process involved coating metallic or plastic surfaces with the high-molecular carbohydrate Heparin, which prevents blood clotting. This invention proved to be particularly useful for oxygen regenerators, which remove carbon dioxide for patients with lung damage. Previous machines were effective for only five minutes; this one could work for more than two hours.

The test case was a woman who had caught pneumonia and was at the verge of death. In desperation, the doctor used the new machine. In a dramatic turnaround, the woman's carbon dioxide blood-count returned to normal, and her life was saved. From this started a long process of commercialization, which has not yet been completed.

Rights to the 1981 patent were bought by Swedish pharmaceutical companies Pharmacia and IRD Biomaterial, which sat on the technology and did not develop it. Fortunately, Larm's contract included a paragraph that allowed him to assign the technology to other companies if Pharmacia or IRD did not produce a business plan to develop the technology in the area or market specified by Larm within a six-month period.

Larm next managed to interest Norway's largest company, Norsk Hydro, and the robot company ASEA (later ABB) in the technology. After long, complicated discussions, the invention ended up with Norsk Hydro's group, which proceeded to restructure the company and rename it CARMEDA. Larm retains a 5 percent share, and his original company, Medicarb, became the R&D company to CARMEDA. Larm heads Medicarb, and 80 percent of his business is from CARMEDA, which is headed by someone else who earns double Larm's income.

Larm also fell victim to the Swedish tax system. When he originally sold the license to Pharmacia, he and his wife were ecstatic. They received Skr 200,000 from Pharmacia. However, the ecstasy soon turned to dismay. First, Larm had to repay Skr 100,000 to the Swedish Board of Technical Development, which had supported his original research. Then he had to pay taxes on the entire Skr 200,000. The bottom line was that he lost Skr 60,000 on the sale of the license!

AVAILABILITY OF ENTREPRENEURIAL TALENT

What the tales of Swedish entrepreneurs tell us can be summarized by the following:

Swedish Inventiveness with Technology is Top Rate.   Upnod had data communications hardware that is technically among the best in Europe and beyond. Zyx developed software tools for creating expert systems so good that the Japanese chose to use this technology in their fifth-generation computer project. The failed no-rust, no-chain bicycles were clever innovations. Olle Larm, for all his difficulties, invented an important medical advance. There is no shortage of innovative ideas in Sweden.

Swedish Entrepreneurs Tend to Be Wary of Large-Company Relationships, Particularly with Large Swedish Firms.   The Zyx software company was turned down by Ericsson and preferred to take contracts with Apple and Hewlett-Packard in California.

In their classic study, *100 Important Swedish Technical Innovations from 1945 to 1980*, Torkel Wallmark and Douglas Mc-Queen confirm the widespread nature of Swedish inventiveness.[11] They note that 60 of the 100 innovations they identify were invented and absorbed into large companies. There are remarkably few spin-offs from Swedish corporations, which may help explain the dearth of fast-growth companies. One reason for this may be financial. With high taxes on wages, very few executives are able to accumulate the savings needed to finance an independent business spin-off.

The Wallmark-McQueen study identifies another important parameter: the role of Swedish universities in compressing the value chain. They found that 18 of the 100 most important innovations originated in the university environment. This phenomenon was especially strong in the pharmaceutical and medical industries. Three of the four entrepreneurs mentioned in this chapter, the founders of Zyx Software, Medicarb, and Upnod, had strong university affiliations.

Wallmark, a distinguished inventor himself, has been instrumental in founding a university-based incubator at Chalmers Technical University in Gothenburg. Over 160 companies have emanated from that program. The University of Lund's research park, Ideon, groups large and small companies together. There are over 85 companies now operating in the Lund research park.

What is notably absent from the Swedish scene are fast-growing companies like Apple, Compaq, and Federal Express.[12] Gambro, perhaps Sweden's second-fastest-growing company, took 24 years to grow to 3,700 people.[13] Started in 1965, the company makes medical disposables. Recent sales were Skr 2.6 billion (approximately a half billion U.S. dollars). In the late 1980s, Gambro was acquired by a larger firm and thus lost its visibility. What this suggests is a gold mine of innovations and opportunities for large American and other companies to partner with Swedish firms. Partnering could bring growth to Sweden's inventors and potential access for multinational partners to the European Community.

BROKERING SWEDISH ENTREPRENEURS: ADDRESSING THE MISSING MIDDLE

To find a partner, create a contract, and manage a partnership, Sweden has developed several unique companies that link entrepreneurs to growth strategies, either taking them public, providing more professional management, or linking them to large firms. Incentive and Hexagon are two examples; Innovation Institute is vying to become another.

Torbjörn Ek is vice chairman of Hexagon, a company that specializes in acquiring and growing small family businesses. Having worked with many conservative Swedes who founded and own family businesses, Ek observes:

> The mental mindset of Swedish entrepreneurs is a generation behind the times. The Swedish inventor does not want to share his invention. He will not accept professional help or outside capital. If it's a good idea, he wants 100 percent ownership. He'll accept venture capital only if it's a bad idea. He wants co-losers, but never co-winners. He's usually a technical person who won't accept marketing help. He is unwilling to yield to the notion that he needs commercial help.[14]

James Utterback and Goran Reitberger noted a similar tendency in their studies of Swedish entrepreneurs.[15] In only one case out of 60 they studied did the founding group move from a majority to a minority position as shareholders in order to finance growth. In comparison, U.S. entrepreneurs owned only 40 percent of their firms' stock after initial financing, and held only 30 percent five years later.

INCENTIVE, INC. AND HEXAGON, INC.

The main purpose of Incentive and Hexagon is to acquire small companies, usually family-owned businesses, and to grow them into significant size. We know of no equivalent to Incentive or Hexagon in the United States. Sten Gustafsson, the first director of Incentive in 1963 and still its chairman (as well as chairman of Saab), and Torbjörn Ek, a recent director of Hexagon, provided information about these companies, which have some very special characteristics:

o Like venture capital firms, they often provide equity financing, but they are not just venture capital operations.
o Like consulting companies, they provide management advice, but they are not just consulting companies.
o Like "headhunter" firms, they look for personnel to staff top management positions, but they are not executive search firms.
o Like marketing and public relations agencies, they are constantly building a network of sales and distribution channels relevant to their various businesses, but they are not marketing organizations, either.

Incentive was founded in 1963 at the inspiration of Marcus Wallenberg of Sweden's foremost industrial family. Before launching Incentive, Wallenberg and Gustafsson scoured the United States for ideas, but they found nothing like the "brokerage firm" concept they eventually developed. Hexagon was spun off from Incentive. Hexagon bought and transformed Fristad, a producer of workers' uniforms, and Infrasonics, which makes a device for chilling materials. They are interesting case studies.

Fristad: A Family Sells to Partners

Fristad produces uniforms and overalls for workers, in both winter and summer versions. The clothing has good pockets for tools.

The company was 80 years old when the family sold it to Hexagon in 1984. Pre-1984 profits never exceeded Skr 15 million, though the operation never lost money. By 1988, the profit level was Skr 44 million, and in 1989 it was expected to exceed 50 million. Presently the company does the bulk of its business in Germany; the textiles are still woven in southern Sweden.

Hexagon's role in this case was:

o To bring in professional management, especially a board

of directors. The owner wanted to retire, but he was persuaded to stay for another 18 months. Hexagon then accepted his recommendation for an internal man to be CEO, and the former owner was made chairman. Now the company has a balance between an elder, wise chairman and a younger, aggressive CEO.

o   To help formulate strategy by asking questions. Usually, Swedish small business is run by statements, not questions.

o   To help the company establish sales and distribution channels abroad. Now, Germany is its largest market.

o   To provide capital for expansion. Unlike typical American venture capital funding, which expects a three-to-five-year payback, Hexagon provides longer-term ownership financing.

Infrasonic: Founder Looks for a New Partner

Infrasonic AB was once owned by ASEA, but its founder bought the company back when he became dissatisfied with the partnership. Infrasonic makes an ultrasound device for quickly chilling products like steel in order to harden them. The product can also be used in the home-grill market to control heat in cooking.

The director of Hexagon had to negotiate with the owner for months to convince him to accept outside help. The owner wanted to hold on until the product was developed further, sales increased, and the product could be priced higher. Infrasonic had all the characteristics of a permanent start-up company.

Hexagon provided Infrasonic with the right marketing channels, better financing, a strategy to prioritize the many products and many markets, and a method for expanding abroad with a subsidiary.

Firms that manage entrepreneurship, like Hexagon and Incentive, speed up the process of growth. They take good ideas and grow them. They get small firms past the stage of start-up, often by helping them to expand abroad. They provided assistance in developing a second and third product, moving into the export market, developing sources of financing, and organizational growth.

Both Fristad and Infrasonics could benefit from further growth through partnerships with large, multinational corporations.

CONCLUSIONS

The principles of entrepreneurial partnership are working in Sweden. It is possible to find partners among some of the large Swedish concerns and among some of the more progressive entrepreneurs. Agreements have been successfully concluded, and partnerships have been reasonably well managed. Companies like Incentive, Hexagon, and Euroventures tend to have longer time frames for success than companies in the United States. However, champions and benchmarks play similar roles everywhere.

Some large Swedish companies are having success with a *kaizen* approach to innovation and with internal venturing. Companies like SKF have been able to develop a culture of constant innovation in a core business that has worked for them. Others, like Volvo, have made internal venturing quite successful by using techniques such as financing and safety nets (invisible contracts) that could possibly be adapted to large U.S. companies.

Other large Swedish companies, like SAS and Perstorp, have taken external approaches to increasing innovation. SAS has partnered with many other large firms and with some small ones. Perstorp has built a success story out of developing partnerships with small companies. Both can serve as models of success for large companies and their relationships with entrepreneurs. Entrepreneurs and executives in America and elsewhere can learn from their examples and may find specific opportunities to work with such firms.

Research conducted by Swedish-American teams like Wallmark-McQueen and Utterback-Reitberger confirm that there are many practical inventors in Sweden with breakthrough ideas. They have a tradition of technical excellence that is world-class. Sweden is fertile ground for large multinational corporations to explore partnership opportunities. American partners will be welcome to the extent they respect the desire of Swedish entrepreneurs to retain autonomy within a partnership. Swedish entrepreneurial brokers like Incentive and Hexagon can help arrange such relationships.

Sweden is a great test market for other countries in Europe, and it is a likely doorway to the European Community. It also had been a country with a strong socialist tradition, which made it an attractive model for the newly emerging economies of Eastern Europe. Next, we turn to entrepreneurship in Eastern Europe—particularly Hungary—in order to examine the opportunities and pitfalls of partnering there.

NOTES

1. Unemployment in Japan in 1987 was 3 percent.
2. Growth of industrial production from 1982 to 1987 was 16 percent in Sweden, 14 percent in the United Kingdom, 9 percent in West Germany, and 7 percent in France, according to Bo Ekman, *Sweden Works: Industry in Transition* (Gothenburg: Volvo Media, 1987).
3. Barry P. Bosworth and Alice M. Rivlin, eds., *The Swedish Economy* (Washington, DC: The Brookings Institution, 1987).
4. "Swedish Industrial Companies Grow More than the Giants," *Affärsvärlden* 14, 5 April 1989.
5. Personal communication, July, 1989.
6. Jan Carlzon, *Moments of Truth* (Cambridge, MA: Ballinger, 1987).
7. The exchange rate in early 1990 was about six Swedish crowns to the dollar. Some further Perstorp statistics: There are 7,000 employees at the town of Perstorp, with an additional 4,000 outside Sweden. Sixty percent of production and 80 percent of sales are outside of Sweden.

8. Data from a personal presentation by Ulf Lindberg in Lund, Sweden, July 1990.
9. William Mead, *Sweden: The Land of Today* (Guildford, UK: Colour Library Books, 1987).
10. Jan-Erik Gustavsson, personal correspondence, May 1991.
11. Torkel Wallmark and Douglas McQueen, *100 Important Swedish Technical Innovations from 1945 to 1980*, Studentlitteratur ed. (Lund: Chartwell-Bratt, 1988).
12. A possible exception is Inter Innovation, founded by super entrepreneur Leif Lundblad. Inter Innovation makes machines that count banknotes. They have orders from IBM, Olivetti, and Citibank; sales are about Skr 100 million. Now Lundblad has gone on to head a development company that makes health equipment.
13. Tetrapak, which started in 1940, was perhaps Sweden's most successful postwar start-up.
14. Personal communication, July, 1989.
15. James M. Utterback and Goran Reitberger, *Technology and Industrial Innovation in Sweden: A Study of New Technology-Based Firms* (Stockholm, Sweden, and Cambridge, MA: STU and MIT, Center for Policy Alternatives, 1982).

CHAPTER TEN

Central European Entrepreneurship: Spotlight on Hungary

One of the most dramatic events in recent history has been the collapse of Communism in much of Eastern Europe. When the Berlin Wall came down in November 1989, it marked the end of an era and the beginning of a new chapter in the history of Europe. The changes still underway are immense.

Enormous problems and huge opportunities appeared almost overnight as the physical Wall and the cold-war division it symbolized were dismantled by enthusiastic Germans. The political and economic turmoil created by the change continues to unfold as this book is written. Countries from the former Eastern bloc and the republics of the former Soviet Union are attempting to shift from centrally planned economies and rigid political systems to market economies and greater democratic representation. We draw first on some examples of the problems from former–East Germany, the country that has experienced the most dramatic shift in identity. It presents a stark juxtaposition between its

Communist heritage and the thriving economy of the Western world it has recently rejoined.

One of the most-talked-about issues in reorienting the Eastern economies has been the role of entrepreneurship. Although our initial examples are drawn from the newly reunited Germany, we focus the rest of the chapter on Hungary, a more typical example of a former Eastern bloc country that is feeling its way to a new economy. Hungary has led most of its Eastern European neighbors in the transition from a centrally planned to a free market economy, and in some ways is the most promising place to look for prospective entrepreneurial partners.

THE CURRENT HISTORICAL AND GEOGRAPHIC CONTEXT

The opening of the frontier between Eastern and Western Europe was an event of immense importance. Where border guards and barbed wire once stood, hikers now cross freely on warm summer days. As the borders have all but disappeared, so have the old meanings of East and West. To speak of Eastern Europe today is an anachronism.

First of all, the historic term for the region is Central Europe, or *Mitteleuropa* in German. The Danube water basin, which directly touches all the countries of the former Eastern bloc except Poland and Albania, was the focus of attention for more than a thousand years of history. Now this area is regaining its Central European identity and is reaching out to Western Europe. Within the next years, the Danube will be connected by canal to the Rhine and Main rivers, a dream that Europeans have had since the time of Charlemagne. Yet despite the opening of the frontier and the moves toward integration with the West, Central (Eastern) Europe is far from united. It is no longer a bloc. It is no longer a pact. Each country is as different from the others as the former Eastern bloc differed from the West.

Unfortunately, most Americans still think of these countries as a bloc. Businesspeople lump them all together, questioning which of them will provide best access to all the others. This is like thinking that investments in Korea will position a company for business in Japan. Hungary, Poland, and Czechoslovakia are quite advanced and are moving toward a market economy. Romania, Bulgaria, and Yugoslavia have not yet solved internal questions. The German Democratic Republic no longer exists.

The central question for the region is the future role of the Commonwealth of Independent States. As of this writing, all republics have declared autonomy. The largest is the Russian republic itself, with well over 100 million consumers and a stretch of land mass that, even separately from the other republics, makes it a country with the largest geographic area in the world.

The Ukraine declared its independence. At a recent workshop on economics and entrepreneurship, one panel of experts from the Russian republic gave their assessment of future economic reforms and invited Western business leaders to enter into future joint investments. At the end of their presentation, a man in the audience jumped up and got the attention of all when he shouted: "I am from the Ukraine Chamber. My business colleagues and I are here at the back of the room ready to discuss business with anyone from the West right now!"

Some of the issues behind the transformation underway in Eastern Europe can be best seen by looking at the former East Germany and the fate of some of its companies.[1]

LARGE-COMPANY OBSOLESCENCE: TRABI IN THE TRASH

One of the best-known companies in East Germany was the large government enterprise that produced the Trabant or "Trabi," as the ubiquitous and long-obsolete East German automobile was called. Six months before the Berlin Wall came down, the waiting time to purchase a Trabi was 14 years. An East German citizen who had ordered his car in 1976 could expect delivery in 1990. One month before the Wall came down, this waiting time had been reduced drastically. Citizens were faced with a wait of weeks instead of years as the factory finally became more responsive to consumer demands. During this period, production was ramped up as the ideas of a free market economy began to be discussed, and a small inventory of Trabants was established.

Then the Wall came down. Within days, the Trabi was unsalable. Even though few East Germans had the money to buy a Western car, they believed that could soon be a possibility. And patience was a quality that East German citizens had been obliged to learn. Within a week after the Wall was down, newspapers carried photos of the "Trabi in the Trash," with an unsalable new auto balancing precariously in a dumpster awaiting disposal.

The "Trabi in the Trash" story illustrates not only the need for innovation, but the fact that such innovation is not likely to be forthcoming from the large, formerly state-owned factories that had the power of monopolies. This story of overnight obsolescence is being repeated elsewhere. An example from the consumer electronics field underscores this point.

OVERNIGHT OBSOLESCENCE: EAST GERMAN RECORDERS

Until recently, a large factory in the Weissenberg District of East Berlin produced tape recorders rather like Dictaphones. It was an old technology, but nonetheless up to the standard of the time for the centrally planned German Democratic Republic. The tape recorder sold for 1,000 East German marks (*ostmarken*), and the factory was unable to keep up with the demand for the product from eager East Berliners. In October 1989, the factory doubled production to meet demand.

In November 1989, the Wall came down. East Berliners were free to cross into West Berlin to buy products. Many went to the *Kaufhaus des Westens* (Shopping Center of the West), where Sony tape recorders were selling for 126 West German marks. Even at the black market rate at that time (1 West mark for 3 East marks), the Sony cost only 378 East marks compared to 1,000 East marks for the technologically inferior model from East Germany.

Overnight, the East German model was obsolete. The factory that had doubled production a month before had a mountain of unsalable inventory, and within a week it shut its doors. The story illustrates the extreme case of large companies unable to anticipate or adapt to rapidly changing market conditions, in this case triggered by unprecedented political changes. It also illustrates the overwhelming need for innovation in Eastern Europe, and the significant pent-up demand for more technologically advanced products.

Other countries in Eastern Europe are similarly experiencing the danger of instant obsolescence and the need for instant innovation. The most likely impetus for innovative action will be entrepreneurs. Some of these will come from the West—and most Eastern countries are eagerly seeking Western technologies and the Western entrepreneurs that go with them. But entrepreneurs can also be developed internally in the East, and here large Western firms and governments can play a supportive role: for instance, sponsoring science parks and incubators in exchange for a stake in the results.

Thus, entrepreneurial partnerships may offer a promising mechanism for those companies wanting to take advantage of business opportunities in Eastern Europe. At the same time, they may provide a way to help modernize Eastern European economies and enterprises and make them more internationally competitive. Along the way, the risks and dangers will challenge both sides. In the pages that follow, we explore the opportunities in Hungary: economically troubled, yet still one of the most promising countries in Central Europe.

HUNGARY: THE WORLD'S BEST
ENGINEERING BARGAINS

Although their country's economy is in better shape than that of many neighbors, Hungarians are experiencing serious hardships, and the shift toward privatization is proving difficult. Recently released finance ministry figures indicate that the nation's GNP dropped 5 percent in 1990, while real wages fell by nearly 9 percent. Ninety thousand Hungarians have lost their jobs, and government officials predict that the ranks of Hungary's homeless, currently estimated at 50,000, will continue to grow.

Yet the news is not all bad. A closer look at the problems in the economy show that in Hungary, as in former–East Germany, the big companies have been hit hard while the smaller companies are showing remarkable resilience. While big industry has suffered, the output of small (under 50-employee) companies has increased nearly 200 percent, a good indicator that entrepreneurial activity is thriving.[2]

Hungary is probably the most Western of Eastern—or Central European—countries. For more than a century it was part of Austria. It has a Germanic tradition in education and engineering, and its corporate laws are based on familiar Austrian models. For business, one of the great attractions of Hungary today is the low wages its highly qualified engineers are paid. An electrical engineer who would earn an annual salary of $50,000 in the United States earns but one-tenth that amount in Hungary. This means that foreign companies can find brilliant brainpower at low wages and costs.

The possibility of combining high-powered, low-cost brainpower from Central Europe with the management and marketing power of the West makes the notion of collaboration very attractive to international business. What Central Europe lacks most is sales management in a market economy and after-sales service—precisely the elements that companies like DEC, IBM, and others in the more developed West have mastered. Even Dell

Computer, a small company by comparison, has built nearly its entire business on innovations in sales and service.

THE IMPORTANCE OF EQUALITY

The description of low Hungarian wages coupled with evidence of strong entrepreneurial activity may have already whetted the interest of large corporate executives. At this point, a word of caution is in order. Successful entrepreneurial partnerships must have as their basis a sense of equality between partners, at least in their attitudes toward one another. The recent radical change in Eastern Europe has generated attitude problems on both sides: problems that must be addressed if the goal is partnership and not the M&A model of absorb and integrate.

Some American businesspeople have a Klondike mentality. They think Eastern Europe, especially the more advanced countries like Hungary and Czechoslovakia, have "gold" waiting to be picked up, bargains with cheap exchange rates ready to be plundered. At the same time, they may feel a responsibility to help countries who suffered Communist oppression for four decades. Thus, to exaggerate for the sake of clarity, their attitude can be characterized as "help through plunder."

On the other side, many people in Eastern Europe feel they need to sell their assets at any price to Western collaborators. They believe that there is, or will shortly be, a competition among several Eastern European countries to attract Western know-how and capital. They think that whichever country runs the fastest and gets there first will benefit most from Western investments.

This rush to sell off assets is also based in part on political reasoning. Many of the former Eastern bloc countries believe that the former Communist elite oppose the sale of assets because they expect to return to power and regain control of those assets. From this perspective, relations with the West became an insurance policy against the resurgence of Communism.

No outsider is able to judge the validity of this reasoning. What we can note here is that for collaboration to be successful in the long run—a five- to ten-year time frame, which is the gestation period for most new ideas—the partnership has to be based on mutual respect and solid gains for both parties. Western partners operating from a Klondike mentality are not likely to persevere; Eastern partners who might later be seen as selling the country's soul are not likely to remain in the good graces of their countrymen and women.

A RELATIVELY TRADITIONAL JOINT VENTURE: GE-TUNGSRAM

The readiness to do business between the formerly divided halves of Europe was evident in the creation of 3,400 joint ventures in Hungary in 1989 and 1990.[3] The majority of the joint ventures were German, and many others were based in Austria. Other international ventures joined Central European companies with American or Japanese firms. *Joint venture* is the term used throughout Eastern Europe to designate most business relationships with Western firms. Like most Western strategic alliances, most joint ventures are between one large company and another.

One of the best-known examples is the joint venture between Tungsram and General Electric. Tungsram, a large lighting and electronics company of Hungary, had been founded in Budapest in the early 1900s. It produced quality light bulbs for sale in Western Europe. At the end of World War II, much of its production was diverted to the USSR, but it still retained significant markets in West Germany and the United States. Tungsram competed successfully with Sylvania and the German company Osram. After an infusion of capital from the Austrian National Bank in Vienna, GE purchased half the newly issued shares of Tungsram.

In many ways, the GE-Tungsram relationship illustrates a West-East pattern that is partway between a traditional merger and acquisition and a strategic alliance. This case is certainly not a merger: The complexities of Hungary assure that Tungsram will retain its own autonomy. Nor is it a case of two equal partners entering a strategic alliance: GE will clearly be the guiding force in modernizing Tungsram, and it has already appointed a new president who is a Hungarian-American.

The GE-Tungsram case also illustrates some of the important issues and surprises that the West-East joint venture can bring. One major surprise was the accounting systems, or lack thereof. Tungsram was the very first Eastern European enterprise to have a profit and loss statement and a balance sheet, which was created in 1989 with the help of Price Waterhouse, for the years 1986, 1987, and 1988.[4] The statements showed losses for all three years, except for a below-the-bottom-line subsidy from the state in 1987 equal to a full year's sales revenues.

PARTNERSHIP ISSUES WITH FORMERLY COMMUNIST COMPANIES

The difficulties in creating even a traditional partnership with companies in formerly Communist economies are numerous. A key issue for the future of such joint ventures concerns the fundamental question of ownership. Who owned Tungsram? Who will own any of the large state enterprises that were built over the past four decades? Who will own the cooperatives? Who can engage in entrepreneurial partnerships when private ownership, which lies at the heart of Western entrepreneurship, was outlawed for 40 years?

Privatization is the word used to describe the move away from state control of enterprises toward private ownership of companies. We have had some experience with privatization in the West. The breakup of AT&T in 1984 was a form of privatization, which was called divestiture. The process started with one set of private stockholders and ended with several sets of private stockholders who invested in AT&T as well as the regional Bell operating companies that were created.

Britain has taken state-owned companies like British Telecom and sold the government shares to the public. In contrast to countries like Hungary, British privatization has taken place with a citizenry that understands very well what stock ownership means. Hungary, which is ahead of the other Eastern countries in moving toward a market economy, only recently developed a stock market. The educational task ahead is enormous. As one Hungarian economist noted, "Margaret Thatcher in the United Kingdom has managed to privatize one major company or sector each year. We've got 10,000 per year to do!"

Currency convertibility has been another major issue that continues to stymie American thinking. "How do I get paid?" is a common question businesspeople ask, concerned that payments in Hungarian forints, Czech crowns, or Russian rubles will leave them with a pile of worthless paper. In the recent past, Western companies had to be creative to address currency inconvertibility. Coca-Cola, for example, took its profits in Russian vodka instead of rubles or forbidden dollars, and then sold the vodka. Other companies were paid in ships, or in furs. McDonald's was able to negotiate some hard currency profit repatriation, but it took more than half in goods for resale to the West. How can one think about entrepreneurial partnership in this context?

There are two responses to this question. One is that even in this transition period, many Eastern restrictions against convertibility are disappearing. Hungary has gone the furthest and guarantees that 100 percent of profits can be repatriated in dollars or marks. The black market exchange rate differs from the government-mandated rate by only a few percent between the Hungarian forint and the dollar. In contrast, the differential for the ruble is enormous. Eventually, all the currencies will become convertible. The question is not only, at what rate of exchange, but even what the new currencies will be.

The second response is that if anyone can figure out how to deal with the transitional problems of currency convertibility, it will be entrepreneurs. Entrepreneurial spirit and inventiveness thrive on overcoming obstacles, and in the new climate of Eastern European countries moving toward market economies, entrepreneurs will have myriad ways to deal with uncertain currencies. What is important to remember is that currency convertibility is not the driver of good economic health, but a consequence of it.

HUNGARIAN ENTREPRENEURS

Entrepreneurship has been repressed for 40 or more years in Eastern Europe, but executives of large corporations may wonder whether it is blossoming now, just like pent-up consumer demand. Where are the Eastern European entrepreneurs? Are partnerships between large Western companies and small Eastern entrepreneurs a plausible and productive way of participating in the future of Eastern Europe?

Nowhere is the contrast between East and West more pronounced than around this issue of entrepreneurship. Employment in countries like Hungary—and also in other relatively advanced countries like Poland and Czechoslovakia—shows a top-heavy pattern. Large state enterprises or collectives predominate. Until 1981, firms with less than 20 employees were forbidden in Hungary, so nearly all employed Hungarians worked for large or medium-sized enterprises. In the West the pattern is reversed.

But Hungarian entrepreneurs do exist, and their number is growing. Where they exist, and how they are likely to grow can be illustrated by looking at several entrepreneurial Hungarian companies.

SZKI Research, Inc.

SZKI (pronounced *Es-Sky*) is a Hungarian computer company that develops software for personal computers. It is located in a rather shabby industrial building on the outskirts of Budapest. Its engineers work on computer hardware from Germany or illegal clones of American systems. Yet their software was anything but shabby or cloned, as the following story illustrates.

An American writer went to Boston to visit MacWorld, the trade show held by Apple every year to demonstrate the latest Macintosh hardware and software. He was interested in software programs for optical character recognition, since writers have dreams of scanning journal articles and storing them for later use in quotations.

Popular scanning software packages from Silicon Valley firms cost about $800. They can scan articles at the rate of about one page per minute and recognize most words written in the familiar Latin script. Their accuracy is about 95 percent, depending on the quality of the text. These performance specifications paled in comparison to their Budapest counterparts. SZKI's software package costs about $100 (depending on the exchange rate), can scan eight pages per minute, and recognizes words in any of 10 different scripts, including Latin, Cyrillic, Greek, mathematical symbols, and Arabic. So why is it not challenging California competitors? The main reason is that the company lacks marketing, advertising, and packaging expertise. And, since the telephone system outside of Budapest is unreliable, it is difficult to get technical assistance more than a mile or two beyond the city.

SZKI's scanning software story underscores something we may have forgotten. Hungary, like many Eastern countries, is home to intellectual and cultural giants. In test scores that measure the output of educational systems, Hungary consistently ranks near or at the top of the list in mathematical and scientific achievement. One may recall, perhaps with mixed emotions, that the brains behind the development of the atomic bomb in the

1940s at Los Alamos Laboratories included recent Hungarian immigrants such as Szilard and Teller. Other examples of great inventors and modern entrepreneurs are waiting to be publicized.

Müzhertechnika: Hungary's Most Entrepreneurial Company

Müzhertechnika (MT), whose name means instruments, was started by Gabor Széles and a colleague in 1981, in typical garage-shop fashion in Budapest. In that year, a new law passed by the Communist regime permitted new-company start-ups and private ownership. Thus, Széles became one of the first of a new breed of entrepreneurs in Eastern Europe and was well positioned when more dramatic changes swept the Communist regime from power.

Since its founding, Müzhertechnika has grown to become the biggest private company in Hungary. Its growth story has been anything but traditional by Western standards. Along the way to success, it has made partnerships with no fewer than 13 large companies in seven different countries. It also acquired a moribund state-owned enterprise 10 times its size and successfully transformed the mind-set of its managers and workers to an entrepreneurial spirit. Bonuses that can double salaries, weekend work to win important contracts, and a union-free environment in a socialist state are some of the features of a company that has invented its way to entrepreneurship.

Müzhertechnika produces computer hardware and software (mostly personal computers and specialized software) and electronic display boards of the type used in sports stadiums. From a humble two-man beginning in 1981, it had achieved sales of $60 million in 1989, with 400 employees. As of 1990, it was Hungary's largest PC company, with a 30 percent market share.

Müzhertechnika Innovations. The company's primary innovation was not a new technology (it primarily assembles Western components), but a new way of doing business in a state where Communism was declining. Müzhertechnika entered into alliances with numerous Western companies, partnering with Siemens to sell Siemens equipment in Hungary, with ABB to sell MT software for power line control systems in the West, with Procomp's Taiwan branch to ensure an inexpensive source of components supply, and with Prognoinfo as a sales outlet in the Soviet Union. It also has strategic partnerships with AEG, Fujitsu, Novell, Seagate, Sony, WordPerfect, 3Com, 3M, and Chinon.

"Especially at the beginning, these companies played a critical role in our success," says Daniel Bardossy, MT's vice president for new ventures. The large partners provided seed capital, technical assistance, marketing and distribution, and contracts that enabled MT to act as a trading company in Hungary and the Soviet Union.

MT's acquisition of a far larger company that had been owned by the Communist state and then was privatized presented a new kind of challenge. All of the workers, and especially the managers, had to change their behaviors and attitudes. More precisely, those who had been part of a highly structured economy had to become more entrepreneurial. Instead of executing orders, they had to initiate new business. Instead of sullenly performing duties, they had to become customer focused. To achieve this end, MT applied its innovative resources to the task of reeducation.

When MT acquired it, the state-owned manufacturer of sports stadium lighting equipment had 800 employees. Most were let go, but MT judged that 100 were capable of being retrained. Three methods were used. One, the so-called "sandwich" technique, involved sandwiching the retrainee between a boss and a subordinate who were both highly entrepreneurial. The second was to split up those being retrained, preventing them from reinforcing one another in the old ways. The third was to introduce a bonus system.

Salaries in 1990 Hungary are low by world standards. An entering engineer earns 20,000 Hungarian forints, which is about

$300, or just under $4,000 per year. MT introduced bonuses based on the company's profit, the department's contribution, and the individual's performance. A bonus could be another $4,000 per year for an engineer, or as much as an additional $6,000 per year for a top salesperson.

In 1989, MT bid on a project to provide the scoreboards for the World Cup Soccer held in Italy in 1990. Workers and managers had to work Saturdays and Sundays to meet the contract deadlines. When it delivered scoreboards to Bari, Verona, and Rome, the company knew it had broken the old lethargy and won converts to the entrepreneurial economy.

Although the bonuses were important incentives, MT's Bardossy feels that "money was not the motivating force. Our people wanted to show they could compete with the West, that they could work just as hard as anyone else."

A Müzhertechnika First: The FBI and Sales Calls. Since computer equipment was classified by NATO as militarily restricted until 1989, MT had some special problems when it tried to do business in the United States. The FBI kept a close watch on the MT sales force as it tried to sell products and ideas to potential American clients. "The FBI couldn't believe we were selling. They assumed we were either buying or spying!"

MT went to the American embassy for help in stopping the FBI from interfering with its sales effort. After some discussions, the salespeople managed to make friends with the FBI. "We offered to share the rental car costs with the agents. They showed a lot of interest in cutting costs, and we gained their confidence. Pretty soon they left us alone."

Lessons from Hungary. The Müzhertechnika case suggests several lessons. One is that entrepreneurs are good at solving unconventional problems, such as dealing with problematic bureaucratic entities (including the American FBI) and motivating people with 40 years' experience in a system where motivation to improve productivity went unrewarded.

Another is that entrepreneurship is alive and well in Hungary, as it is in other parts of the former Eastern bloc. Alliances between entrepreneurs and large companies outside the country are a natural, almost necessary, way to start new companies. The benefits are clear, perhaps because they are so mutually reinforcing. MT gained access to world markets; its foreign partners gained access to the Hungarian market and even the Soviet one. Technology was transferred. MT received new 286/386/486 computer chips from the United States, and American and Western European companies got new, top-quality software at excellent prices.[5]

Hungarian economists see a future where small private companies like Müzhertechnika become more dominant in the national economy. Not only do they create jobs, they also help transform older, inefficient state-run enterprises. As of 1990, Müzhertechnika was the only start-up among the "Hungarian Fortune Top 100." Within two years, Hungarians hope there will be ten Müzhertechnikas among the Top 100.

ADVICE FOR WESTERN ENTREPRENEURS AND EXECUTIVES

From an Eastern European perspective, Western investments are highly attractive because they open the doors to Western technology and finance. Eastern European countries are competing among themselves to attract innovative entrepreneurs and large corporations from the West. Should an Entrepreneur of the Year like Michael Dell try to break into the Eastern European market? Dell Computers has gone beyond North America already, with operations in the United Kingdom, Germany, France, Italy, and Sweden. Its German plant sold computers in former–East Germany even before reunification. Should it move farther east? "It would be a real challenge," says Dell. "The shaky phone system would make it very difficult to provide after-sales service in the way which is our competitive advantage."

American entrepreneurs are understandably cautious. This helps explain why most of the joint ventures are done by other Europeans, not Americans or Japanese. The existing American joint ventures primarily involve large companies. From an entrepreneur's perspective, there are many reasons for caution.

o Eastern Europe wants to attract small U.S. entrepreneurs, but so do the Japanese and the Western Europeans. Why should American entrepreneurs venture into uncertain territory when more proven suitors exist?

o Entrepreneurs are very selective about the risks they are willing to incur. Many are very conservative when it comes to giving up control.

o Electronics, a mainstay field for American entrepreneurs, is one of the most difficult fields for joint ventures in Eastern Europe. There are several reasons: underdeveloped laws (or their irregular application) for software protection; a poor communications infrastructure; and the COCOM lists, which still allow the U.S. government to restrict activities in formerly Communist countries if it thinks a technology critical to U.S. security interests is involved.

However, if some entrepreneurs would like to try the waters, here are some questions to ask when considering a joint venture with a former Eastern European company:

1. How reliable is the Eastern European partner? Is it a large company whose assets are possibly obsolete? Does it have good access to the local markets? Can it be used as a basis for future business with the larger republics further to the East?

2. What is the quality of the company's human resources,

and can they be retrained to be entrepreneurial if necessary?

3. Is there internal, invisible inflation in the country? For example, in Czechoslovakia the official inflation rate was 1.7 percent in 1989. The actual rate was 10 percent, expressed not as a price rise but as a shortage of goods.

4. What is the degree of mutual dependence on the former CMEA countries and the now autonomous republics of the former USSR? If the Soviet economy collapses, will the economy of that country collapse as well? Recall that Vaclav Havel, the president of Czechoslovakia, asked the U.S. Congress for help not for his country, but for what was then called the Soviet Union.

Finally, corporate executives and entrepreneurs attracted by the idea of partnering with firms in Central and Western Europe, in Japan, or in any other part of the world should keep in mind that each country is distinct. None can be taken as representative when it comes to forming partnerships. What is true for Japan will not hold true for China or Korea any more than U.S. business practices will hold true for all of North America, from Canada to Mexico. It may be easier or more difficult to apply the 12 principles and practices of successful partnership, depending on the country and the culture of the individual firm.

We do encourage all corporate executives and entrepreneurs to consider foreign companies as well as other U.S. firms as partners. They may turn out not to fit your partner profile, or a background check of the country's economic structures may convince you the time is not yet right. On the other hand, you may find a perfect match in Sweden or Japan or Mexico to complement your U.S. partnerships. The business world is becoming increasingly international, and we foresee that the world of entrepreneurial partnership will follow a similar trend. Companies that ignore the emerging changes in the business world and try to meet tomorrow's challenges with yesterday's strategies are likely to falter and fail. Companies that meet the innovation imperative and adapt quickly to changing conditions will continue to grow and prosper through this century and the next.

NOTES

1. The illustrations are from Dr. Klaus E. Czempirek, an international economic advisor from Linz, Austria, with long experience in Eastern Europe.
2. Girard C. Steichen, "Lean Times Ahead in Hungary," *Christian Science Monitor*, 8 March 1991.
3. Ivçn Toldy-àsz, president, Joint Venture Club of the Hungarian Chamber of Commerce.
4. Even when standard accounting reports such as an annual report are produced, the extent to which they reflect reality are questionable. For instance, balance sheets need to be adjusted for the fact that no real estate assets are included because there is no private ownership. Also, depreciation rates are nearly always wrong because accurate ones would expose the terrible obsolescence of the equipment: for example, what value should be assigned to the Trabi automobile inventory? In addition, accounts receivable may need to be discounted or discarded altogether.
5. Hungarians are among the world's best software engineers. Their mathematical and technical training is regularly rated at the top of the international scale. Some 40 percent of all university graduates are engineers. As a popular example, the developer of the Rubik cube (Erno Rubik) is a Hungarian, but he made next to nothing from his invention since the then-Communist state kept all the proceeds.

AFTERWORD

In Chapter 2, we characterized entrepreneurial partnerships as the third "wave" of entrepreneurship. The first was garage-shop entrepreneuring, where the inventor tried to develop a start-up company in his garage, largely alone and working against great odds. The second was intrapreneuring, where large corporations tried to encourage employees to become more inventive and behave like entrepreneurs. Given the corporate culture of most large companies, which is often at variance with people who try to be entrepreneurial, those who attempted intrapreneuring found themselves also working against great odds. The third wave, entrepreneurial partnerships between large and small companies, might be categorized as *extrapreneuring*: Companies of all sizes link up with other large and small companies, as well as with universities, to find the innovations, manufacturing resources, or marketing and distribution networks that they need. We believe the odds of succeeding are greater using third-wave extrapreneurial strategies than they were for second-wave intrapreneurial methods. And while we hope that there will always be a continuous flow of garage-shop entrepreneurs, we suspect that they will face ever greater difficulties in launching fast-track, growth businesses. We predict that the most successful entrepreneurs of the 1990s will be those who forge creative links with forward-looking large corporations—and vice versa.

Even though this book promotes the concept of entrepreneurial partnerships between large and small companies, it is clear that these partnerships will not work for every company. That is why we have taken great pains to spell out the pitfalls, and to analyze why some companies will be no more successful with extrapreneuring than they were with intrapreneuring. Our experience suggests that partnerships work best for small companies that are monkey- or kangaroo-types, that is, companies that do not want to become full-service companies and complete all the phases of the value chain by themselves. Conversely, partnerships work best for large corporations that have identified a "hole," or missing link, in the value chain and realize that by the time they fix the problem, market opportunities will have passed them by.

A large company should not even consider entrepreneurial partnerships until it has completed a value chain assessment and has identified its strengths and weaknesses along the value chain. Likewise, a small company should have determined that it wants to be a monkey- or a kangaroo-type company. Only then is the large or small company in a position to begin determining what it needs and what it has to offer a partner. The next step is to identify potential partners, select a set of companies that appear to be optimal partners, and begin negotiations with them. The corporate managers who will be involved in managing the partnership should be the ones to negotiate the contract. The partnership must produce a win-win situation for both companies: that is, it should be clear how and why each company will benefit from the relationship. While lawyers will be necessary when the final contractual document is drafted, their role in the negotiation process should be minimized.

Once the contract has been signed and the partnership commences, managers on both sides need to pay considerable attention to the relationship. Specific milestones and deliverables, periodic meetings to review progress, frequent communications concerning what is going well and not so well are important elements of a successfully managed partnership.

Large companies may not warm to the idea of entrepreneurial partnerships because countless corporations suffer from the Not Invented Here syndrome: people in the R&D labs and top management of large corporations are often unwilling or unable to accept the fact that innovations and high-quality products appropriate for their corporation could be developed by anyone from outside. They refuse to believe there are holes in their value chain that are more easily plugged externally than internally. Entrepreneurs, especially those starting companies for the first time, likewise may not welcome the idea of partnering because they are concerned that large corporations will try to steal their technology or take over their companies. They think that keeping their distance from corporations will ensure that this will not happen. But a poster in the office of one of the corporate managers we interviewed says it all: "The tiger that does not prowl may end up as a rug." Companies—large or small—that do not look for new ways of meeting the innovation imperative may not be around ten years from now.

During the course of our research, we discovered that the principles and practices of entrepreneurial partnership apply to many situations that go beyond our original focus of large-to-small alliances. Take dealerships, for example. Scores of large companies rely on exclusive or independent dealers to complete Phase III of the value chain. Their relationships have tended to be transactional in nature and have been built around a customer-supplier model reminiscent of the Japanese "captive" automotive suppliers described in Chapter 7. Insurance companies like Allstate or State Farm, or real estate operations like those of Prudential-Bache or Coldwell Banker, also deliver their products and services through "captive" agents.

Saturn is one of the few auto companies trying to use the entrepreneurial partnership model in the establishment of its retail outlets. The office furniture company Herman Miller has been reviewing its relationship with its dealer network and is moving toward more of a partnership model. We believe that other forward-looking companies that seek to improve the effectiveness of their relations with dealers may likewise benefit from the principles and practices outlined in this book.

Another group of businesses that could benefit from the third wave of entrepreneurship are franchise operations. Examples include Holiday Inn, with over 1,000 independently operated hotels, car rental companies like Hertz and Avis, food chain companies like McDonald's, and so forth. At the time when such franchise operations were established, the goal was conformity with corporate norms, uniformity of operations, and predictable profits. Executives of franchiser and franchisee operations may want to compare the principles and practices of entrepreneurial partnerships with the principles underlying their traditional relationships and consider whether the whole concept of franchising might be improved by adopting some of the key concepts outlined in this book.

The forces of change described earlier in this book are driving every corporation to consider new strategies and new organizational forms to enable them to compete in time. Hence, there is a new willingness to consider and explore a concept such as entrepreneurial partnerships. Our research indicates that many of the new corporate models in the United States and other countries are predicated on the principles of partnership. Dynatech is a good case in point.

We discovered Dynatech Corporation just as we were finishing this book. Headquartered in Burlington, Massachusetts, Dynatech is a corporate partnership of some 45 small electronics firms. While each company is 100 percent owned by Dynatech, the corporate promise and strategy is to leave each entrepreneurial partner alone, that is, entrepreneurs are allowed to manage the companies as if they were their own, as long as agreed-upon levels of growth, profits, and other benchmarks are achieved. Directives from corporate headquarters are kept to a minimum. This strategy is reminiscent of the one utilized by Perstorp, the Swedish company described in Chapter 9. Even though the past few years have been difficult ones for electronics companies, Dynatech's diversity has enabled it to continue growing. By 1991, it was approaching the ranks of the Fortune 500.

Built primarily on the principles of entrepreneurial partnership, Dynatech's main challenge for future growth is what its president terms "organizational learning," that is, creating an environment that enhances shared learning, teamwork, and collective wisdom among the 45 small-company presidents. The challenge to Dynatech is to take greater advantage of the partnership side of the equation while still preserving the entrepreneurial factor. Given its increasingly competitive challenges, Dynatech's organizational learning strategy is the most promising way to achieve future success. The Dynatech and Perstorp models may well be useful ones for other companies to analyze and adapt depending on their own particular circumstances.

The future of entrepreneurial partnerships as a strategy for innovation will hinge largely on the acceptance or rejection of a new premise: cooperating in order to compete. Cooperation implies an equality to the relationship that has not been the usual modus operandi when large corporations and small companies get together. In order for these partnerships to work, both the large corporation and the small one must understand that they need each other and that together they are stronger than either one of them is separately. Entrepreneurial partnerships flourish best when large and small companies realize that cooperation makes good business sense—when they both understand that the partnership enables them to develop innovations that the market wants; manufacture new products more quickly; and market, sell, and distribute new products before competitors do. This book should provide many suggestions and insights for achieving that end.

INDEX

DATE DUE
